T0272702

THE GREAT RETREAT

THE GREAT RETREAT

HOW POLITICAL PARTIES SHOULD BEHAVE AND WHY THEY DON'T

DIDI KUO

OXFORD
UNIVERSITY PRESS

OXFORD
UNIVERSITY PRESS

Oxford University Press is a department of the University of Oxford.
It furthers the University's objective of excellence in research, scholarship,
and education by publishing worldwide. Oxford is a registered trade mark of
Oxford University Press in the UK and in certain other countries.

Published in the United States of America by Oxford University Press
198 Madison Avenue, New York, NY 10016, United States of America.

Library of Congress Cataloging-in-Publication Data
Names: Kuo, Didi, 1983- author.
Title: The great retreat : how political parties should behave and why they don't / Didi Kuo.
Description: New York : Oxford University Press, 2025. |
Includes bibliographical references and index. |
Identifiers: LCCN 2024041626 (print) | LCCN 2024041627 (ebook) |
ISBN 9780197664193 (hardback) | ISBN 9780197664216 (epub) |
ISBN 9780197664223 (ebook)
Subjects: LCSH: Political parties. | Political socialization.
Democracy—Social aspects. | Capitalism—Political aspects.
Classification: LCC JF2051 .K86 2025 (print) | LCC JF2051 (ebook) |
DDC 306.2—dc23/eng/20241030
LC record available at https://lccn.loc.gov/2024041626
LC ebook record available at https://lccn.loc.gov/2024041627

DOI: 10.1093/oso/9780197664193.001.0001

Printed by Sheridan Books, Inc., United States of America

To ABD

Contents

Preface and Acknowledgments

We seem to live in an era of crisis—of political crises and attacks on democracy; of economic crises and profound inequities; of transnational crises related to climate change, migration, and war. Many of us struggle to contextualize and understand these crises, and, more important, to envision a path to a better world.

While journalists may write the first draft of history, it is the job of scholars to go deeper—to provide a framing and analytic approach that might shed light on how we got here. There has been no shortage of books explaining why the United States is polarized, why authoritarianism is on the rise, why contemporary capitalism helps the rich and hurts the poor, or why people turn against democratic institutions in desperate times. All of these important contributions fill in our understanding of twenty-first-century political and economic dynamics.

This book goes into more detail about an institution central to democracy and critical to the relationship of democracy and capitalism. Political parties are the foremost intermediaries tasked with representing the interests of a diffuse citizenry, and also with carrying out a vision of society through a governing agenda that addresses these interests. A wealth of scholarship in the social sciences explains how parties shaped democracy itself; parties are crucial to democratic stability and success. But there is a pronounced antiparty sentiment in discussions of democracy today. This sentiment is pervasive and can be found in media coverage of politics, in the goals of political reformers and activists, and, of course, among antidemocratic candidates and demagogues. These attitudes stem from a sense that parties command massive power and resources over the democratic process but are deficient in their basic responsibilities to address the concerns of citizens or to govern effectively.

To understand what has gone wrong with democracy, we need to understand how parties have changed. There is no parsimonious explanation of why American democracy is at risk, or why citizens across the globe are so fed up with their governments. There are also limits to blaming problems on failures of democracy or capitalism writ large. These concepts are too macro; they contain many distinct moving parts. Lumping everything into "democracy" or "capitalism" also makes fixing problems difficult, since you cannot create better institutions or economies wholecloth.

If we disaggregate these concepts, we find that what really seems to be lacking across democratic capitalist countries is effective representation. Political parties, when working well, socialize citizens into politics and provide a consistent mechanism for citizens to have a voice in their government. Parties also institutionalize the diffuse power of "people" versus concentrated power (of, say, capital). But their ability to do these things well is not constant or consistent. While we know that young democracies need strong parties, we are also discovering that long-standing, wealthy democracies can be eroded from within when parties atrophy. This book takes a closer look at these dynamics. While it is mainly about the United States, it draws on lessons of party development in Europe and Latin America to show how American trends might play out.

* * *

Although this is a book about political parties, it will always be, for me, a pandemic book, one that I struggled mightily to finish. Writing a book during this time felt hard on the good days and, quite frankly, irresponsible on the bad days. That it exists at all is a testament to the support and patience of many friends and colleagues.

I am grateful first and foremost to my intellectual home, the Center on Democracy, Development, and the Rule of Law at Stanford University.

I began this project while overseeing the Program on American Democracy in Comparative Perspective. The program faculty—Stephen Stedman, Francis Fukuyama, Larry Diamond, Bruce Cain, and Nathaniel Persily—helped me to conceptualize and clarify the book's ideas. Daniel Stid, then at the Hewlett Foundation, offered intellectual and material support for this research. Thanks to Anna Grzymala-Busse for being a caring mentor and for leading the Project on Global Populisms, which shaped much of the thinking for this book. Kathryn Stoner, the Mosbacher Director of CDDRL, mentored me through the second book process, as well as the faculty promotion process—for which I am deeply and eternally grateful.

Other wonderful colleagues at Stanford, including Michael McFaul, Alberto Diaz-Cayeros, Beatriz Magaloni, Lisa Blaydes, and Hesham Sallem, were integral to this project's success. Thanks to the pre- and postdoctoral fellows at CDDRL with whom I workshopped various chapters of this book. And immense gratitude to the CDDRL team of Kristin Chandler, Audrey McGowan, Nora Sulots, and Amye Whalen, who made writing this book possible while I served as CDDRL's Associate Director for Research.

In 2018, a New America Fellowship provided a wonderful opportunity to learn and grow as a scholar. I am grateful to Awista Ayub and Peter Bergen, as well as the Political Reform team. Lee Drutman never hesitated to read drafts or offer advice. Mark Schmitt and Maresa Strano were helpful collaborators on many party-related projects. New America cohort-mates became superb colleagues, including Marcia Chatelain, Theodore Johnson, and Erin Snider. Christian Hosam has been an astute interlocutor and friend.

I am fortunate to be part of a community of scholars who have taught me about parties, democratization, and effective scholarly communication. Anna Grzymala-Busse, Nathan Grubman, Noam Lupu, Paul Pierson, and Daniel Ziblatt generously participated in a book workshop and offered trenchant, tractable feedback. Thanks to Tabatha Abu El-Haj, Abhay Aneja, Julia Azari, David Alexander Bateman, Sheri Berman, Thomas Carothers, Kathy Cramer, E. J. Dionne, Lily Geismer, Shelby

Grossman, Peter Hall, Alisha Holland, Ira Katznelson, Andrew Kelly, Noam Lupu, Julia Lynch, Dan Slater, Susan Stokes, Steven Teles, and Deborah Yashar for helpful conversations. I received excellent comments from conferences and talks at Columbia University, the Social Science Research Council, the University of Massachusetts–Amherst, the University of California–Berkeley, and Northern Arizona University.

I am grateful to my students in the Fisher Family Honors Program at CDDRL, and to many talented research assistants. Whitney McIntosh helped in the early stages of this book and made sense of freewheeling ideas. Hannah Kunzman, Sarah Lee, Andrew Gerges, and Caroline Zdanowski contributed enormously; Brandon Rupp was crucial in the final stages.

Thanks to Meg Rithmire and Kristen Looney (CGH) for our incredible multidecade friendship, and thanks to Kate Bersch for our magical accountability system. These amazing women got me over the finish line, and I get the honor of watching them each excel.

Thank you to Katherine Flynn, agent extraordinaire, who has taught me so much about writing, audience, and translation, and to David McBride, my editor at Oxford University Press. Their belief in this book, and their patience through the writing process, was crucial to its completion.

Thanks to my family: Chung and Josephine Kuo, Martha Bedell and David Dryer, David Dryer and Elizabeth Broadwin, Eliza Dryer, Lauren Scott, and Colleen Brouillette, for always listening and understanding. To my children, thank you for your effervescence, affection, and silliness.

This book is dedicated to Alexander Dryer, who has been patient, supportive, pragmatic, and contrarian (when necessary!). Z - Writing this book would have been impossible without you, and I am grateful for the wonderful life and home you've created for us.

CHAPTER 1

Introduction

If a political party does not have its foundation in the determination
to advance a cause that is right and that is moral, then it is not a
political party; it is merely a conspiracy to seize power.
> —President Dwight D. Eisenhower, remarks at Fourth Annual
> Republican Women's National Conference, 1956

Do political parties serve the interests of democracy today? Historically,
parties have performed many duties in representative democracies. They
organize factions in the legislature to fulfill policy goals; they cultivate
voters and supporters. Parties are sites of deliberation, responsible for
crafting policy agendas around how government might best solve public problems. Political parties are meant to embody values and priorities
that transcend the dictates or whims of any one leader, allowing people
to choose their governments and hold leaders accountable. Elections give
us, as citizens, the chance to see our preferences and interests enacted by
government—all through the work of political parties. They compete
with one another to secure majorities and, in theory, deliver on their
campaign promises once in office. Parties are integral to the functioning
of democracy, because they give meaning to participation, to political
conflict, and to the very purpose of government.

Yet citizens around the world have become cynical about the role
parties play in democratic governments. Parties are some of the most
unpopular institutions in democracies. In poll after poll, Americans
report trusting any number of institutions—including business leaders,

the police, and journalists — more than they trust elected officials or the parties.[1] Citizens believe that parties care only about short-term goals rather than the public good, catering only to special interests and economic elites. Many politicians are wealthier and better educated than the people they represent, and they spend their time currying favor with donors, lobbyists, and allies who help them maintain their hold on power.[2]

While historically parties have been integral to making democracy work, today they seem at best to slow democracy down—or worse yet, to undermine it completely. The number of self-proclaimed independents is rising; many of them are turned off by the party system entirely, even if they tend to vote for one of the main parties.[3] Even avowed partisans report feeling that parties serve special interests over the public interest. A deep suspicion of political parties reflects a broader erosion of faith in liberal democracy.

This is a global problem. Surveys show that citizens of Asia, Africa, and Europe feel less trusting of parties today than decades before. In Western Europe, for example, parties have been losing members, with fewer voters joining parties or participating in party activities.[4] In the long-standing democracies of North America and Western Europe, far-right and extremist politicians have capitalized on resentment toward the ruling elite to win popular support. This is a far cry from the exuberance for democracy at the end of the Cold War, when Western countries assisted democratic transitions around the world.

Most definitions of democracy look only to institutions and democratic processes to gauge whether or not a country is democratic. Free and fair elections, representative institutions, mechanisms of accountability, and the neutral administration of the law are critical to democracy. Parties provide the connective tissue between these institutions and the people they serve. They bring together like-minded politicians and candidates and organize them into coherence: parties are not just groups that seek elected office, but are also sets of ideas, values, and shared interests in the public as a whole. Parties are bottom-up, with ideas emerging from the citizenry, but they are also top-down and define the issues and divisions that become salient in politics. They determine how quotidian concerns can be translated into policies, and how the state can, and should, serve its citizens.

Without parties, there is no representation; without representation, no democracy. Why is it, then, that parties, which have long been critical intermediaries in modern democracies, are now the object of scorn? The answer lies in changes to party organization and political economy—the way economic concerns are reflected in politics. Rebuilding democracy today will require rethinking the purpose and structure of parties in a society undergoing rapid structural transformation. Shoring up democracy will require creating defenses, such as blocking antidemocratic candidates or fighting antidemocratic propaganda. But it will also require proactive strategies, like building democratic intermediaries to reestablish linkages between people and their governments.

Democracy and Capitalism in Crisis

For most of the twentieth century, political parties mediated the relationship of people to government and democracy to capitalism by protecting the interests of various stakeholders across society. Party mediation—the process of cultivating and nurturing the relationship of citizens to their government—buoyed the postwar growth years in which democratic capitalism flourished across the West. And even today parties behave, in many ways, exactly as we'd like them to; they vote together in the legislature; they are ideologically sorted. Parties face trade-offs in how they prioritize different tasks: maintaining local party organizations, fostering relationships with civic associations and issue-advocacy groups, selecting good candidates capable of winning elections, passing policies that might address the needs of voters.

The question of whether democracy and capitalism can coexist has long vexed scholars and revolutionaries alike. Central to this relationship are political parties, the institutions that have evolved to do most of the work of representative democracy. The relationship of democracy and capitalism was built over centuries, with political parties playing a critical role at each stage of its development. Parties are essential to long-term democratic stability and economic growth.[5] The breakdown of party systems, on the other hand, has led to democratic collapse and economic volatility.

For centuries, it was unclear if democracy and capitalism could really coexist. Critics of capitalism argued that states, even those with representative institutions, inevitably served the interests of capitalist producers. However, a nineteenth-century skepticism about the compatibility of democracy and capitalism increasingly gave way to exuberance after World War II, when democratic capitalist economies experienced record-high growth while also protecting the interests of workers. A new line of thought, modernization theory, argued that the development of a capitalist class was necessary to overthrow ancien regimes: middle-class industrialists did not inhibit democracy but instead spurred it.[6] Strong parties throughout the West provided a way for capitalism and democracy to coexist. Social democratic parties promoted social solidarity and basic guarantees for workers and citizens. Conservative parties kept the radical right in check. The result was democracy with bourgeois characteristics, in which "the state apparatus has a bourgeois class composition and the state power operates in such a way as to maintain and promote . . . the class character of the state apparatus."[7]

But the relationship of parties to citizens has changed, ushering in a period of dysfunctional parties and growing tensions between democracy and capitalism. Fifty years of deregulation and globalization have transformed power, both within and across countries. Free-market, anti-state attitudes that influenced conservative parties of the 1980s evolved into a neoliberal consensus. In advanced democracies, parties of the left elected into office as centrists accepted the limited role of the state. As a consequence, there has been a slow abdication of government from many aspects of public life. The class characteristics of state power seem like a threat to democracy.

Democracy is in retreat even where it has long been taken for granted. In the United States, for example, deep partisan polarization has fueled antagonism between the Republican and Democratic parties, among party leaders, and within the electorate. The parties seem unable to do their basic jobs, with gridlock in Congress and an extreme right attacking the fundamental legitimacy of the democratic process. The European Union has transformed European domestic politics, on the one hand fueling resentment within countries (as evidenced by the Brexit referendum and populist parties in Southern Europe), and on the other hand doing little to curb democratic backsliding in Eastern Europe (in Viktor Orbán's Hungary).

Resurgent authoritarianism provides a template for democratically elected leaders to centralize power and erode minority rights and liberal protections.[8] Digital communications technologies and social media platforms allow the rapid creation and dissemination of misinformation and propaganda.[9] Migration flows have diversified once-homogeneous populations, sparking nativist and xenophobic responses. Globalization puts pressure on governments to deregulate their economies and ease the movement of capital, goods, and people, which has generated extreme wealth for some while many communities are left behind.[10] These communities, lacking aid or social support, have experienced declining life expectancies and economic mobility.[11]

Further, rising economic inequality fuels anger about the perceived indifference of elected officials. In the United States, the top 1% of the income distribution possesses as much wealth as the bottom 90%.[12] The economic system that once buoyed domestic growth and opportunity has become a source of unchecked wealth and greed. The middle classes have been hollowed out. Economic inequality disproportionately affects communities of color that have long been excluded from the benefits of full citizenship. Corporations seem like shadowy global behemoths, operating tirelessly in pursuit of profits while working conditions and economic mobility decline. Meanwhile, the financial crisis of 2008 and the ongoing economic fallout from COVID-19—including massive job losses, business closures, eradication of savings, supply chain crises, and, now, rising inflation—have called into question the capacity of government to meet the needs of citizens.

The breakdown of democratic capitalism in the form of stark inequalities, wealth and opportunity hoarding, and growing risk and precarity are not just a signal that something is wrong with the economy. They also reveal that something is broken in the way democratic institutions are supposed to provide a counterweight to private resources and power.

The Peril and Promise of Parties

In 1796, the first president of the United States, George Washington, issued a warning about parties after serving two terms in office. The union of American states was still young, and the nation and constitution still precarious. In his Farewell Address, published on September 19 in the *Philadelphia Daily American Advertiser*, Washington made plain the foremost threat to the future of American democracy: political parties. Parties, Washington argued, had the potential to cause more harm than good, since they allowed small but "artful and enterprising minorities" to dominate the public will. They risked despotism. They weakened public administration and created formal channels for foreign influence and corruption. They sowed too much division and stoked animosity throughout the polity. At worst, parties might foment riot and insurrection.

When Washington was president, the United States did not meet any of the formal standards of democracy we now hold. Instead, democracy was something that took shape over the next two centuries. Parties began as factions in the legislature, then expanded as more people gained the right to vote. The extension of suffrage, combined with the social divisions created by the industrial and national revolutions of the eighteenth and nineteenth century, led to splits that still exist today—those between labor and capital, urban cities and rural towns.[13] Parties were built through top-down coordination of campaigns and strategies and bottom-up organization of interests in local communities.[14] Conservative parties were often loyal to monarchs or tied to landowning, aristocratic interests; liberal parties advocated expansion of political rights; and labor and workers' parties pushed for workers' interests.

Parties were often rooted in local communities, since the work of elections needed to be carried out by party agents and volunteers. Local party agents registered voters and coordinated elections. They printed election materials, provided ballots to voters, or oversaw elections conducted vive voce (aloud, by voice; it was not until late nineteenth century that countries like the United States and Britain adopted the secret ballot). Mass party organizations created multiple sources of accountability between citizens and politicians; for most of the twentieth century, parties competed by offering distinct policies and visions to voters. At the same time, parties competed over fundamental issues of state and society, including the creation of new social programs and regulatory institutions. Parties on the left, including labor, social democratic, and liberal parties, became associated with economic redistribution and social welfare policy in the mid-twentieth century. Parties of the right, such as conservative parties, were instead associated with lower taxes and less spending. While parties of course differentiated themselves on more than economic policy, there was a consistency to the way parties occupied the left-right spectrum in the United States and the policies they pursued in government.

In a healthy democracy, parties compete by offering different sets of policies to voters and cultivating a loyal base of voters whose demands form the basis of party policy. Scholars have also long acknowledged the importance of linkages between citizens and parties. This refers to the myriad relationships, informal and formal, that help to establish voters' attitudes and loyalties to parties. At the heart of today's crisis is a disconnect between citizens and leaders, a belief that politicians do not serve the interests of the public. The anxieties about parties dating to Washington's Farewell Address resonate today, at a time when parties seem to divide much more than they unite, and when antiparty sentiment has become pervasive in the United States and elsewhere.

While parties still claim to represent and speak for the people, they may have no connection to individuals. These days, joining a party might mean receiving emails soliciting campaign contributions or following candidates on social media. Campaigns are branding and advertising exercises. The parties market their candidates through a vast network of political strategists and consultants. Candidates rely on support not from residents of their districts but from far-away fans willing to donate money. While parties once reached citizens through membership and local party offices, they now rely on a political industry of pollsters and strategists who target potential voters. It is not clear to voters or even to aspiring candidates how to access their local party offices, if they exist.

Candidates and campaigns may not even need to work closely with whatever formal party organization exists. As a result, it can be very difficult to distinguish what the party actually is or who leads it. Presidents and vice presidents are often the most visible heads of their parties, but they do not occupy official leadership positions within the party. In Congress, the parties must elect leaders (the Speaker of the House and the Senate majority leader), but again, these individuals are not necessarily party leaders. The Republican National Committee and the Democratic National Committee have official leadership (chairs, vice chairs, secretaries, treasurers), but their influence is subordinate to a world of donors and interest groups that devote significant resources to their own political agenda.

The Power of Parties

Parties as connectors between society and government require us to go beyond election results and voter attitudes. Instead, we must examine whether parties are integrative (socializing people into politics), representative (claiming to act on behalf of a group interest), and responsive (shaping policy decisions in accordance with their responsibility to integrate and represent voters). Parties also have a moral component, in that perceptions of the legitimacy of government itself run through the work done by parties. It is parties that actually command the state, and then sell the public on whether or not the state is responsive and trustworthy.

We often think of the state or government as a clunky bureaucratic apparatus that is somewhat orthogonal to politics. If anything, it might be the
case that parties politicize agencies when it is in their interest to do so.

The perception that citizens have of government rests in large part
on how parties claim credit for policies. Parties have become more reluctant to tout the benefits of state action and have scaled back many social
policies as well. In doing so, they have deprived themselves of the ability to win the trust of voters or cultivate attachments based on what
a party actually provides voters. Such large-scale economic, technological, and social disruptions as globalization, immigration, extremism,
and inequality are seen as challenges that democracies must manage and
respond to. They are imagined to be external forces acting upon governments. And because governments have not responded in ways people
find satisfactory, democratic legitimacy has eroded. Antiparty sentiment
is seen as part and parcel of this erosion of trust in our democratic
institutions.

But these changes weren't simply external. Instead, internal political choices are made by parties across the political spectrum, across
successive governments. Parties have retreated from the representative
functions they once performed. As parties grew more professional and
campaign-oriented, they also became less responsive, shedding the representation and mobilization functions they once performed. Citizens
are no longer recruited and socialized into parties through active engagement and community networks. Indeed, parties have outsourced many
of their traditional intermediary and mobilization functions to outside
groups. Instead of parties, it is advocacy coalitions, nongovernmental
organizations, lobbying firms, media, and social movements that now
provide messages and information to voters. As a result, voters are likely
to hear about the failures of parties rather than hear parties defend and
justify how political decisions are made.

Changes to party organization therefore have significant consequences for representation. Parties determine which factions in society
are mobilized and whose views are taken into consideration when making policy. When parties are strong intermediaries, they can effectively

manage the relationship of democracy and capitalism, even if the result is a democracy in which the rich have more power. When parties are weak intermediaries, they lay the groundwork for serious, potentially irreparable imbalances in who democracy serves. Parties have abdicated their traditional intermediary roles, driving down trust in parties and party membership—both of which have reached historic lows.

Parties in a Neoliberal Era

While postwar economic growth required strong, class-based parties, given the economy's reliance on manufacturing and industry, liberalization and knowledge-based growth since the 1980s have instead been associated with technocratic, elite parties. These parties have little connection to their traditional popular bases of support. The decline of social democratic parties in Europe, for example, was associated with austerity and the disappearance of manufacturing jobs. As parties of the left embraced conservative economic policies in the late twentieth century, they neglected their relationships and obligations to former constituencies, such as the working class. Further, as parties reached consensus on many aspects of economic policy, debates over culture and identity became more salient. While these debates are often vicious, they do not translate into policies that can improve the material circumstances of citizens.

The new era of neoliberal policy, rooted in economic ideas that emerged in the postwar period and that gained influence and legitimacy in the 1980s, also changed the scope of politics, including the way representation happens and what citizens expect from democratic politics. Major political players in advanced democracies have "de-politicized" areas of policymaking.[15] Neoliberal growth was driven by its electoral appeal, an elite-led project that responded directly to what businesses demanded but also won votes. The parties of the left in particular changed significantly by cultivating more educated voters who were winners of globalization, who appreciated the left's values orientation.[16]

All the while, the relative balance of power between labor and capital shifted decisively in capital's favor. This was not a foregone conclusion; rather, it was the most important consequence of the erosion of the representative capacity of parties. Since the 1970s, parties have failed to fulfill a range of responsibilities: from their most basic role integrating citizens into the political system to their highest purpose of crafting and pursuing a social vision. Political parties today, while well-financed and cohesive, are nonetheless weak intermediaries, unconnected to their constituents, susceptible to capture by narrow and monied interests.

Finding a Way Forward

Thirty years ago, democracy and capitalism triumphed over seemingly all other forms of political and economic rule. Centuries-old debates about whether or not the two could coexist were laid to rest. Today, however, democracy and capitalism seem to work on behalf of only a select few. Liberal democracies have been shaken by citizen discontent and the rise—the election into power—of populist and illiberal leaders. Capitalism of the twenty-first century has produced extreme inequality and precarity, while social contracts between governments and citizens have eroded. Protests across the globe over the past decade have been rooted both in economic grievances against inequality as well as demands for greater accountability and less corruption.[17] The political power of capital signals the rise of an uncomfortable, plutocratic new normal in our democracies. Unless parties reclaim the function they once served to bind citizens to the state, we may not be able to answer the question of whether democracy is possible without them.

Understanding how the relationship of democracy and capitalism broke down requires recalling how it first came to be. The second chapter therefore discusses the scholarly concepts and theories that explain why intermediaries are crucial to the functioning of representative government. Further, it details the political economy dimension of parties and discusses how parties in the neoliberal era shifted how they govern and who they represent.

The third chapter explores how political parties emerged alongside responsive, representative democracy in the oldest modern democracies. The very idea of representation, and the use of elections to guarantee representation, was a historical innovation that required political parties. Political leaders and citizens needed to build the structure of this new system. Who would manage and oversee elections? How would candidates for office be determined, and how would they convince people to vote for them? How would voters learn which candidates were associated with what ideas, and how would they hold their representatives accountable once they were elected to office?

Across different political contexts—the limited democracy of the newly independent United States, the monarchies of Western Europe—political parties established the procedures of representative democracy while also fulfilling representative, integrative, and ideational functions. They were able to do this through a civic component to parties, one that has atrophied in recent years.

The end of the Cold War marked a shift in how parties prioritized their electoral and governing responsibilities. The fourth chapter tells the story of third-way politics, of a centrism that claimed to represent a traditional base of working-class voters but really hewed to indistinct constituencies of educated professionals. Across the United States and countries like Britain and Germany, the social democratic left adapted to an era of globalization and economic growth by reorienting their policy priorities—in particular their reliance on the state as a lever of policy. Further, many of the political trends at the turn of the century led to a *convergence*, rather than divergence, in the political economy of representation. This contributed to a sense that the parties served the concerns of corporations and the wealthy at the expense of the rest of the electorate, paving the way for more extremist politics.

Just as privatization of many public services and goods has eroded trust in government, so too has there been a corresponding privatization of representation. The rise of a politics industry that does the messaging and campaign work of parties, combined with a deregulated campaign finance system, has made parties porous to private interests. The distance between parties and their citizens is the subject of chapters 5 and 6.

The conclusion takes up the question of how to strengthen parties. Many reform proposals today either explicitly or implicitly weaken parties, which will only exacerbate problems related to democracy and capitalism. In the final chapter, the book details why reforms like third parties and open primaries are inadequate solutions to the problems of weak parties. It examines reforms such as enhancing the associational ties of parties, strengthening relationships between civic groups and political parties, funding explicitly partisan infrastructure, and enhancing the role of leaders who are party builders rather than outsiders who want to upend the party system.

In limiting this book to the relationship of parties to democratic capitalism, this analysis omits other crucial elements of party history that are worth mentioning. Political parties are themselves sites of democracy: their leaders should be accountable to members; their goals and agenda items should be the product of deliberation and compromise. But throughout history, parties have excluded marginalized groups in society, erecting barriers to women and racial minorities. For example, the Democratic Party in the post–Civil War American South used violence and repression and explicitly banned Black Americans from political participation.[18] Parties have also often been corrupt, with party machines helping to buy off politicians or exchanging favors and government resources for bribes and kickbacks. The periodization described here does not denote a golden age of parties but instead serves to explain how party organization is not fixed and how party adaptation produces trade-offs in what parties do well.

The problems that our societies face are potentially so significant that fixing a part of the democratic process—that is, parties—cannot really move the needle on the relationship between democracy and capitalism. There is a structural imbalance of power at the heart of the wealthy democracies today, owing to global capitalism, that seems insurmountable through routine politics alone.[19] Further, the antidemocratic ideas and individuals mobilizing on the far right are attempting hostile takeovers of mainstream center-right parties as well as democratic governments themselves. This looming danger makes the issue of party reform more urgent rather than more hopeless. While institutional reforms to improve democracy and better policies to tackle inequality may go far to alleviate these problems, the long-term health of democracy also requires stronger intermediaries.

A democracy of the future that is more inclusive, more equitable, and more just will require reasserting and repurposing parties rather than rejecting or displacing them. As Theda Skocpol has written, "[T]here cannot be any going back to the civic world we have lost. But Americans can and should look for ways to recreate the best of our civic past new forms suited to a renewed democratic future."[20] Pro-democracy coalitions and factions, as well as mobilization of those without wealth and power, can be sustained only through the representative, intermediary roles of functional parties.

CHAPTER 2

What Are Parties For?

In the late nineteenth century, Democratic Party politics in New York City were controlled by Tammany Hall. Famous for storied leaders like Boss Tweed and infamous for political corruption, the Tammany machine embedded party politics in everyday life for the first time. Designing and maintaining the party machine required knowing everything about voters: "their needs, their likes and dislikes, their troubles and their hopes."[1] One boss, George Washington Plunkitt, kept a journal detailing how the party machine worked—and just how intertwined local party officials' business was with people's lives. Here's his entry on a typical morning:

> 2 am: Aroused from sleep by the ringing of his doorbell, went to . . . bail out a saloonkeeper who had been arrested for violating the excise law.
> 6 am: Awakened by fire engines. . . . Hastened to the scene of the fire, according to the custom of Tammany district leaders, to give assistance to the fire sufferers, if needed. . . . [F]ires . . . are considered great vote-getters. Found several tenants who had been burned out, took them to a hotel, supplied them with clothes, fed them, and arranged temporary quarters for them until they could rent and furnish new apartments.
> 8:30 am: Went to the police court. Found six "drunks." Secured the discharge of four by a timely word with the judge, and paid the fines of two.

After sunrise, Plunkitt's day got even busier. He counseled a widow in court, paid the rent of a poor family, placed men in jobs with railway, subway, and gas companies, went to funerals that involved "conspicuously" going to the front of a Catholic church and a synagogue, presided over a meeting of election district captains, and bought ice cream for children at a church fair. At 9 p.m., Plunkitt heard from constituents at the district headquarters. He paid for a church excursion, bought tickets for a local baseball game, and listened to complaints from peddlers persecuted by the police. The day ended with a wedding reception; he had already "sent a handsome wedding present" to the bride. At midnight, he went to bed.

Party bosses like Plunkitt, Tweed, and their ilk relied on patronage, persuasion, graft, flattery, and threats to reward loyal supporters, dissuade challengers, appeal to constituents, and build their base of political power. As democracy expanded in countries that had long limited the suffrage to property-owning white men, the small cliques of people who led political parties needed to find ways to mobilize new sets of electors. One way was the provision of spoils, and patronage became a common method of engaging voters.

While American parties have roots going back to the founding era, their organizational features are often said to have originated with Andrew Jackson's spoils system in the nineteenth century. In an 1816 letter to President James Monroe, Jackson was explicitly antiparty. He implored Monroe to "exterminate that monster called party spirit" in selecting his cabinet: "[Do not] indulge in party feelings. [Your] conduct should be liberal and disinterested, always bearing in mind that [you] act for the whole, and not a part of the community. . . . [C]onsult no party in your choice."[2]

However, less than a decade later, Jackson—with the help of a senator from New York, Martin Van Buren—reshaped the party system. The presidential election of 1824 had featured four candidates representing factions of an amorphous Democratic-Republican Party, and none of the candidates won a majority of electoral votes. The House of Representatives held a contingent election, eventually awarding the presidency to John Quincy Adams. Van Buren was particularly concerned with uniting sectional interests for the purpose of selecting presidents: a stronger party would help politicians "substitute party principle for personal preference" and learn to "acquiesce in the fairly expressed will of the party." He wrote in 1827 to the news editor Thomas Ritchie about the need to

reorganize parties, arguing that presidential candidates with little principle of their own would be better off having been selected by a party: "his
election . . . the result of a combined and concerted effort . . . holding in
the main, to certain tenets."[3]

Political parties began as legislative factions within the innermost circles of government. In the United States, they were rooted in debates
between Hamilton and Jefferson in George Washington's cabinet, for
example. By the turn of the twentieth century, parties were mass organizations with the infrastructure, resources, and capacity to bring voters to
the polls. But more important, they were representative intermediaries.
Parties took on the hard work of representing varied interests—from
those of the landed aristocracy to those of the burgeoning working
class. The parties took on the role of shaping and reflecting these collective demands, such as those of workers in nineteenth-century New
York City (Democrats), businessmen and factory owners (Republicans),
or farmers in the Midwest (the short-lived Populist Party). Parties welcomed newly enfranchised voters, including waves of migrants into
cities; they worked closely with civic associations, trade unions, and
other groups that sought to bring citizens together in pursuit of common
goals.

The kind of party-building that took place in an era of democratic expansion also occurred against a backdrop of industrialization—a
massive shift from agrarian to manufacturing economies, from rural
to urban life, from disconnected communities to integrated, national
economies that required new types of state intervention. As economic
production reshaped how societies were organized, they also generated
new political demands. Translating demands into policies required party
leaders not just to retain their connections to distinct constituencies but
also to apply new ideas of *governance*. How would leaders use the state
in creative or innovative ways to solve problems generated by new modes
of economic production?

* * *

Some of this history of parties might continue to resonate today. We
think of parties along a left-right spectrum and tend to distinguish left

and right by their economic policy differences. We also pay close attention to whether or not parties can mobilize enough voters to capture
electoral majorities, and the content of parties' policy agendas. But the
party as a mass organization is now a distant memory. In the twentieth century, parties honed their electoral and campaign capabilities,
becoming more professional and centralized in the process. Many of the
structural conditions of mass party democracy no longer obtain today:
society is less explicitly class-based, with fewer integrative mechanisms
such as labor unions or churches.[4] After the economic crises of the
1970s, the new orthodoxy of neoliberalism also scaled back the scope
of government, which affected the types of policies that parties offered
voters.

These structural changes have implications for what scholars term
the *political economy of representation*—the way economic interests are
politicized, prioritized, and reflected in government. While parties have
become effective at nailing down messages and hammering home issues
that resonate with slices of the voting public, they have grown less effective at delivering the policies and governance voters seem to need. This
is largely due to the way parties have eroded in their intermediary and
organizational capacities that once made them better able to channel and
represent interests.

Why do so many people say that parties don't represent them at all
even when they loyally vote for a specific party? Why do voters in long-
standing democracies around the world distrust their party leaders and
consider them beholden to special interests rather than the public good?
Why have so many activists and reformers sought to circumvent or even
get rid of parties, whether through more direct forms of democracy or
the expansion of primaries? Worse yet, why does democracy itself seem
to be at risk, with antidemocratic extremists railing against the system?

Many problems we see today, including distrust in democratic institutions and rising inequality, stem from the growing gap between who
parties represent and what parties prioritize. This chapter draws on concepts and theories of parties—some from the distant nineteenth century
and others from a more recent shift to the neoliberal era—to better

understand parties as intermediary organizations. To understand why democracy seems less responsive, we need to understand where parties came from and how they developed as democracy expanded. We also need to expand our conceptual understanding of parties beyond organizations that exist purely to win elections.

The United States in Comparative Perspective

This book is primarily about the United States, and it is crucial to acknowledge the many unique features of the American party system. Our elections are expensive and funded by many different individuals and actors, while many other countries regulate campaign donations or publicly subsidize political parties. American parties use primary elections to select candidates, while most countries do not. We have an electoral college to select the president and a highly decentralized election administration apparatus. All of these affect how parties operate, and subsequent chapters will go into more detail about how these features contribute to ongoing problems with American democracy.

However, focusing only on the ways the United States is different—perhaps even thinking that our party system is singular, or sui generis—obscures the many important ways parties are similar across time and space. Not only is it possible to think about the United States comparatively; it is also important. Much of what we know about parties comes from observing similar trajectories of parties through history. To speak very generally, we lose something when we think about each country's democratic trajectory in isolation instead of thinking about pathways that might be common to many countries. Large-scale changes and processes, like democratization or phases of capitalism, have distinct characteristics that play out similarly in different regions of the world. Without a comparative perspective, we miss opportunities to expand our analytic understanding of politics and institutions. In order to better understand the relationship of parties to other outcomes we care about—including representation, trust, democracy, and participation—we need to look across countries rather just within them.

Scholars have developed many ways of thinking about parties comparatively. There are "party families": parties of the left and right, religious parties, green parties, and so on, which share common ideologies, policy priorities, and goals. Political scientists also study "party systems," which describe the way parties within a democracy relate to one another. There is a relationship, for example, between electoral institutions and the number of parties, with first-past-the-post, single-member district elections producing two-party systems while proportional representation tends to produce multiparty systems. Two-party systems and multiparty systems therefore help us to understand how the number of parties affect, say, coalition governments or interest representation.

Many long-standing democracies seem to be experiencing the same kinds of challenges in the twenty-first century—including resurgent factions on the right, illiberal elected leaders, and dissatisfied publics—and it is worth considering whether there are trends common across parties that help to explain democratic discontent. This chapter therefore thinks about the relationship of parties to democracy conceptually, theoretically, and historically rather than within a specific national context. In subsequent chapters, I draw on examples of parties outside the United States to illustrate important trends and patterns. For example, when parties move closer together on certain issues (say, economic issues), does that raise the salience of other issue areas? Do parties get punished or rewarded as a result? My hope is that we can use the experience of parties in other democracies to shed light on dynamics in the United States.

Political Parties in the Era of Democratic Expansion

A party is an organization that exists to coordinate politics, in the broadest sense.

The basic infrastructure of parties, with elites at the top of an organization or hierarchy comprising members, hasn't changed much since the nineteenth century. But back then, no country was a democracy as we would understand the concept today. Before republican government became the norm, monarchs ruled in concert with legislatures. Monarchs convened assemblies of representatives drawn from the landed gentry, the clergy, and the nobility. These legislative bodies met in order to bring the interests of distinct elite groups to royal courts. In 1295, Britain's "Model Parliament" convened for the first time; it included the nobility as well as representatives from each county and town. In 1341, the British Parliament separated the House of Lords, where the nobility sat, from the House of Commons, for local representatives. Parliamentary systems—from the French *parler*, "to discuss"—eventually became common throughout Western Europe.

These early legislative assemblies provided checks against royal power on issues such as taxation, spending, trade, and warfare. This consultative process led to legislators seeking out agreeable colleagues and voting in blocs. As parliaments assumed greater power over decision-making, divisions naturally arose between those with landed interests in agriculture and those with interests in trade or between the clergy and advocates of religious freedom. Early parties thus united cadres of (the few) men with political power; the French political scientist Maurice Duverger described them as "restricted electioneering organizations with loose connections to still looser parliamentary factions."[5] They served the interests of particular, small groups of notables rather than serving some amorphous public.

However, during the so-called Age of Revolutions in the eighteenth century, the notables responded to liberal and democratic ideas sweeping through the Atlantic world. American and French revolutionaries overthrew monarchs and established republican forms of government— radical alternatives to absolutist (or even parliamentary) monarchical rule. A half-century later, in 1848, revolutions swept through the whole of Europe, affecting, Denmark, various Italian and German states, the Austrian Empire, and the Kingdom of Hungary. These revolutions rarely resulted in democracy, but they were evidence of a new push for democratic rights. Over the course of the late nineteenth and early twentieth centuries, the fight for democratic rights became linked to workers' movements in favor of greater redistribution and labor protections—an important development to which we will return.

As suffrage expanded incrementally in places like the United States, Britain, and France, elite factions had to expand party organizations to include new waves of enfranchised voters. In the mid-nineteenth century, the United States began reducing property requirements to vote; by 1840, most had been eliminated—albeit only for white men. (Racial restrictions for free Black men increased during this same period.)[6] In Britain, the Great Reform Act of 1832 revised franchise requirements and expanded the electorate to 11% of the population, up from about 6%.

This slow expansion of the franchise gave parties time to develop a more expansive infrastructure, find sources of funding, and create campaign strategies. Often, parties tapped into existing voluntary civic associations like social clubs, literary societies, gentlemen's clubs, leisure groups, and mutual aid societies. These groups already had distinct structures, including written rules and membership provisions; they issued annual reports, and some charged subscription fees. The density of American civic groups impressed Frenchman Alexis de Tocqueville, who spent ten months visiting the United States in 1830–1831, then penned a famed treatise about democracy in America. Tocqueville argued that these associations created self-interest properly understood, which at the time meant citizens thought beyond their personal needs to embrace the civic good.[7]

Parties therefore developed atop a preexisting civic infrastructure as they created new democratic norms and procedures. Local party agents drafted "election registers," for example, which were an early version of party membership rolls. Party activities were conducted not only in formal offices but also in pubs, clubs, and friendly societies.[8] Party members paid dues and provided the voluntary labor to manage elections. Political parties also printed their own newspapers and pamphlets and even hosted leisure activities.

In the United States, it was only in the late nineteenth century that interest groups began to form around distinct political causes.[9] Factions within legislatures needed to articulate their principles and positions to persuade voters while also building an infrastructure to ensure citizens would actually vote. But persuading voters was not simply about campaigning; parties also sought to integrate people into their organization as loyal members. In the era of industrialization and urbanization, parties worked to build up a mass base by establishing direct ties with citizens. The benefits of belonging to a party ranged from direct and tangible rewards, like, say, jobs, to indirect or intangible rewards related to political community. The local party agent became a source of knowledge and information about voters, as well as an important node in a diffuse national party. Local party agents could distribute party literature, understand the constituency's needs, and marshal volunteers in an ongoing effort to retain party loyalists. In the words of Moisei Ostrogorski, a Russian political sociologist who studied Britain and the United States in the late nineteenth century, parties were the "foot soldiers" of democracy.[10]

Political parties in modern democracies were meant to serve as intermediaries connecting elected representatives to newly enfranchised citizens exercising political rights. The historical development of parties—from small legislative factions, to voluntary associations, then to mass organizations—is therefore the story of democracy itself. What exactly does it mean for parties to be intermediaries? As formal political organizations, they are the only entities tasked with both representing people and governing in a democracy. Advocacy groups, faith-based groups, and social movements may, to a large extent, represent people effectively, and undoubtedly they help people expand their political awareness and communities. But these groups do not seek elected office, nor can they be held accountable for governing the way parties are held to account in elections. In an era of democratic expansion, parties became the "principal means of transmitting popular will and opinion from civil society to the state."[11]

The Mass Party and Democratic Responsiveness

At the turn of the twentieth century, the mass party helped to integrate voters into democratic politics. The term "mass party" referred not to electoral majorities but to parties with extensive networks within specific but broad segments of society. These parties placed a premium on representational integrity—how well they channeled the interests of their base—rather than how savvily they conducted campaigns.

As democracy expanded, so too did the state, and parties developed governing institutions to manage the economy and develop a social contract between citizens and leaders. Demands for political rights, particularly the right to vote, became intertwined with demands for economic reform and redistribution. Social relations, as Karl Polanyi has noted, are embedded in our economic system.[12] But they are politicized only when political parties identify and organize around these social divisions. The party system from the late nineteenth through the mid-twentieth centuries was an instantiation of class in politics, with the state seen as the solution to, not the creator of, social and economic problems.

Democracy has long been associated with better economic outcomes than authoritarian governments, largely because democratic leaders are held accountable: thanks to elections, democracy has distributive consequences. And in abstract economic terms, leaders have an incentive to redistribute to new voters to win their support. But in more concrete political terms, these political relationships are nurtured and forged through the institution of the party. In her study of women's enfranchisement, for example, Dawn Teele shows that alliances between women's suffrage groups and political parties were critical to securing the vote in the first place, precisely because of bargains that women would vote for specific parties that would, in turn, legislate in their favor.[13] In the 1930s, Franklin Delano Roosevelt's New Deal wasn't just a sop to people hit hard by the Great Depression. It established a new economic and political order based on a set of promises of what the government would do for citizens, ensuring the electoral support of a diverse, cross-class swath of voters.

Democracies become more responsive to citizens through the institution of parties, and parties therefore explain how democracies produce better economic outcomes.[14] The expansion of the franchise has historically led to the greater public good, particularly in areas such as infrastructure, health, and sanitation.[15] For example, the passage of the Nineteenth Amendment in 1920, securing women's right to vote, resulted in higher rates of educational attainment in children[16] as well as improved infant and maternal health outcomes.[17] Generally, democratic competition (as opposed to one-party rule) has also been linked to greater investments in human welfare, particularly health and education, both at the state level and globally.[18] The Voting Rights Act in the United States, which finally removed Jim Crow barriers to voting, has also been associated with greater public spending and material investments in areas with Black voters.[19] It is undoubtedly the case that parties have been imperfect representatives and historically have marginalized citizens who were entitled to greater inclusion. But parties also gave substantive meaning to democratic representation by crafting policies and institutions that could deliver benefits to majorities.

From the Masses to the Center: Modernizing the Party

In the mid-twentieth century, two academic works reshaped our understanding of parties by focusing on the notion of "the center." First, in 1957, Anthony Downs, an American economist, published his *Economic Theory of Democracy*.[20] Downs argued that voters have policy preferences and that they choose candidates whose policies best match their own. To win their votes, parties use ideology, loosely defined, to package policies together in ways that appeal to majorities of voters. Then in 1966, the German academic Otto Kirchheimer described the emergence in Europe of the "catch-all party."[21] The catch-all party moved away from stark distinctions based on class toward mobilization of a political center to maximize a party's chance of winning elections, even if doing so also diluted appeals to key constituencies.[22]

Downs and Kirchheimer predicted that the world would become less, not more, ideological. Therefore, stable party systems in liberal democracies would involve parties competing for the mythical median voter. The catch-all party was not necessarily centrist, but it entailed assembling coalitions to create a broad appeal. Instead of nurturing relationships with distinct groups—like specific types of workers or adherents of specific faiths—catch-all parties were likely to appeal to voters through vague proposals that later allowed compromise or incremental changes.

A vague centrist politics is not an ideology but rather an electoral strategy, and one that can work well for parties trying to capture majorities. However, it can also entail trade-offs. It can make parties far more attentive to the work of campaigns, since messaging and positioning will help parties win elections; if catch-all and centrist messaging works, parties then no longer need to maintain local offices or engage in more direct contact with voters. It might also make parties more complacent about power relations, since they seek only to tweak their policy appeals rather than to propose ambitious agendas.

The 1970s and 1980s furthered the politics of the center and moved away from the mass organization party of the democratizing era. The professionalization of political parties that began after the Second World War severed the relationship of party officials to the public and gave rise to a politics industry that increasingly did the work of making those "connections." Thus, as parties have become professionalized, they also became more removed from the very citizens they would claim to represent. Parties disengaged from civil society and were better described as partnerships of professionals than as associations of citizens.[23]

The Italian political scientist Angelo Panebianco termed this new phenomenon the "electoral-professional party."[24] Such parties were oriented toward issues rather than ideology, and leaders rather than members. In the electoral-professional party, specialists in highly technical aspects of electioneering proved more important than party bureaucrats.

Mass media and television made campaigns candidate-centered, and as a result, parties needed to employ public relations and advertising specialists. Communications technology also made parties more dependent on pollsters, who could now gauge public opinion in more efficient and "accurate" ways. And issue-oriented campaigns required specialized knowledge to develop political messages. Eventually, these parties became more dependent on interest groups and single-advocacy groups that took over the work of representing citizens.

By the late twentieth century, scholars were increasingly concerned about the changes to party organization. Parties financed by the state operate as "cartels," characterized by "collusion and cooperation between ostensible competitors," as Richard Katz and Peter Mair have noted about parties in Europe.[25] About American parties, Daniel Shea has observed that the candidate- and service-oriented parties of the 1980s have become disconnected from the "mass base," since "the gap between what activists desire and what the voters care about is growing."[26]

Panebianco predicted the eventual *dissolution of parties* as organizations," arguing that they would become but "convenient tags for independent political entrepreneurs."[27] And indeed, voters have become wary of formal political organizations. Having reached a relative level of material security and comfort, voters identified less with blunt class categories and turned their attention to other types of issues. Rather than worry about bread-and-butter concerns, voters in the 1980s and 1990s began to show "postmaterial" concerns, those having to do with protecting the environment or increasing the recognition and representation of minority groups. Scholars at the time worried that voters would do more split-ticket voting (i.e., voting for candidates from different parties on the same ballot) or vote for new parties cropping up, like green parties. They also feared that a fragmented arena for representation—for interest groups and advocacy organizations to channel citizens' concerns, alongside parties—would make citizens more cynical and less inclined to put their faith in traditional institutions of government.[28]

A democracy in which parties retain their political power but do not effectively represent interests is one in which elections slowly lose

meaning. Their power in politics all but assured, parties might make elections little more than legitimating tactics. The state will remain obligated
to offer choices to voters, but voters will have little say in the content of
party campaigns or goals.[29] Bernard Manin described this as audience
democracy, as opposed to party democracy: parties still ostensibly run
politics, but the voters' role is subordinated to one of passive dissent
or consent.[30] The relationship of parties to voters becomes simply an
election-day transaction.

It is not simply the case that parties have changed organizationally
(although they have), nor is it simply the case that civic or associational life has changed character (although it has). The decades after the
1970s saw the party retain its electoral and political power but lose its
intermediary function. Crucially, the weakening of the party's ability to
represent interests dovetailed with the new economic orthodoxies associated with neoliberalism. As we will see, this combination has produced
a party system that is highly responsive to the economic interests and priorities of those with resources, while neglecting the bulk of democratic
citizens who constitute party supporters.

Parties through the Electoral Lens

Today, citizens do not expect to find jobs, let alone receive wedding
presents, from their local party officials. In fact, most people do not have
local party officials at all, and many state and local party offices exist only
on paper. Parties now focus on the never-ending work of fielding campaigns and winning elections. They raise money from donors and other
organized interests while working with an industry of consultants, lobbyists, strategists, and pollsters to understand which voters to target with
what messaging. They fine-tune their brands, while also stoking division
from other parties to heighten the stakes of elections.

Parties have invested in their electoral capacities at the expense of
serving an intermediary role. They market their candidates and policies
not through local and civic associations tied to the party but through

strategists and pollsters, spin-doctors and micro-targeters. Outreach takes the form of email solicitations, television commercials, and social media posts.

Parties have always needed to win elections, and democracy can be fairly understood as a "competitive struggle for the people's vote."[31] Parties are central to that struggle. Focusing on a party's electoral objectives and the extent to which it meets those objectives has been, for decades, the scholarly approach to thinking about parties. Classic academic texts like John Aldrich's *Why Parties?* (1995) define parties as teams of office-seekers or individuals united by common preferences who find it more efficient to coordinate electoral activities to win elections. More recently, scholars have viewed parties as groups of policy demanders, an aggregate of politicians and activists that coordinate and integrate activities across multiple domains of politics. Thus, a party is a rubric or umbrella under which various groups vie for their issues and candidates to reach a national agenda—a set of people who need to use the vehicle of a party to accomplish something. They think of a party as "the sum of the bargains made by the group that compose it" rather than as a separate institutional entity that exists atop the candidates and groups within it—and that, critically, exerts leverage over them.[32]

Therefore, for decades now, scholarship on parties has focused on an elite strata of party politics, particularly with respect to elements of campaigns, elections, and the legislative process. Less attention has been paid to how parties are constituted at different levels of government, especially at the local and state level. Nor do we understand much about how parties' relationships with voters are sustained across elections. To the extent that voters matter to this process, it's in their attitudes toward parties and especially their levels of turnout on election day.

Those attitudes are shaped in part by the media, which more often than not "horse-race" coverage: Which party is poised to win the next election, even if it's years away? Parties are said to be doing well when their electoral prospects are up, poorly when their electoral prospects are down. When presidents or members of Congress try to pass policies, pundits ask whether or not those policies can help parties win over specific voters. Focus falls on politics as an electoral game or marketing campaign. This often contributes to a cynical sense that parties are only trying to maneuver themselves to secure their next election victory.

As parties have focused on the electoral arena, they have neglected many of the social ties once considered integral to their work. As detailed by Russell Muirhead and Nancy Rosenblum, we now see "a failure of the elemental linkage function once attributed to parties. . . . [I]f parties cannot link the groups vying for power in the legislature with groups in the larger society, then legislatures, which are the heart of representative government, lose their connection to popular interests, wants, and passions, and representative government loses something of its legitimacy."[33] Parties have devoted more resources to campaigns and elections, developing new means of persuading voters without needing to interact with them.

Yet to see parties only in terms of elections is not enough. Thinking of parties as entities that exist merely to run and win election campaigns does not help us understand the relationship of parties and citizens, how it has changed over time, or what the consequences for representation and democracy have been. Indeed, the common assumption about parties today is that they operate at a distance from voters, removed in most ways from people's lives.

Beyond Elections, What Else Are Parties For?

Thus far we have discussed parties as vote-getting organizations and as representative institutions. But we shouldn't assume that parties are performing both of those functions effectively just because parties are winning elections. There are a few indicators that parties continue to win elections despite the fact that, notably, voters dislike them.

While people are not fleeing parties, their support for mainstream parties has declined. In Figure 2.1, showing support for mainstream parties versus support for challenger parties, voters in a set of advanced

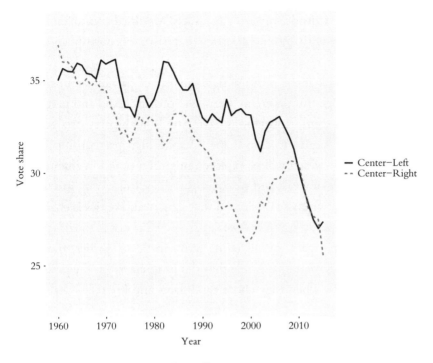

Figure 2.1 Mainstream Party Vote Shares, 1960–2015

Note: Mainstream party vote shares averaged across 21 democracies: Australia, Austria, Belgium, Canada, Denmark, Finland, France, Germany, Greece, Ireland, Italy, Luxembourg, the Netherlands, New Zealand, Norway, Portugal, Spain, Sweden, Switzerland, the United Kingdom, the United States. Authors' calculations from Klaus Armingeon, Sarah Engler, Lucas Leemann and David Weisstanner. 2024. Comparative Political Data Set 1960–2022; Giacomo Benedetto, Simon Hix, and Nicola Mastrorocco. 2020. The Rise and Fall of Social Democracy, 1918–2017; Noam Gidron and Daniel Ziblatt. 2019. "Center-Right Political Parties in Advanced Democracies." *Annual Review of Political Science* 22: 17–35.

democracies, including those in Western Europe and North America, have been voting for mainstream parties at declining rates in the twenty-first century. While voting for Democrats and Republicans remains high in the United States, a plurality of voters now identify as political independents, and extremist candidates, particularly on the right, have become much more powerful since President Donald Trump's time in office. Positive attitudes toward parties have declined considerably, not just in the West, with citizens reporting that parties are corrupt and don't serve the public interest.

If we just look at the electoral performance of parties, we might not be able to bridge this difference between voter attitudes and party performance. But some explanations having to do with party strength and weakness have begun to take shape. Despite high partisanship in the United States—which will be explored in greater depth in chapter 5— we live in an era of weak, and weakening, parties. Julia Azari, in a widely cited *Vox* article from 2018, argued that American politics is characterized by strong partisanship and weak parties.[34] She noted today's parties no longer seem capable of mediating across factional divides, and party leaders do not have the same role they did in an era when the party centralized power—when they chose candidates and brokered deals with backbenchers.[35]

This question of party strength is complicated, because parties still command large vote shares. In Congress, partisan roll-call voting has become more consistent over time.[36] However, party leadership has lost leverage over candidate selection, issue mobilization, and the policy agenda. Party strength is in part determined by the ability of leadership to coordinate these aspects of party activities. "The party" has become less meaningful as a political actor in itself and instead has become a mere label for a set of interests that are jockeying with one another for attention, resources, and power.

If we think back to the history of parties in the era of democratic expansion, and also consider how parties have changed organizationally in the postwar period, that helps us begin to conceptualize parties as intermediaries.

First, we can think about the organizational features of parties—the way they make and maintain connections to their voting base. A party can be organizationally strong even if it does not command large legislative seat shares. The brief history of parties provided here demonstrates that there are other dimensions to political parties that matter when considering party strength. As we've discussed, in the early history of democracy, parties were amorphous legislative factions that had little presence in society. In the era of parties as elite cadres, we might consider them weak on both an elite electoral dimension as well as a social organization dimension. As these parties built offices and recruited members to register and recruit the newly enfranchised, they became more grounded in the citizenry, growing stronger on both elite electoral dimensions as well as social dimensions.

What is an example of an organizationally dense party? Take a patronage party, like New York's Tammany Hall. In the past, it was common for parties to rely on patronage or corruption to reward loyal supporters and build their networks. Patronage parties are, almost by definition, organizationally dense: you need access to your local ward boss; favors are dispensed through individual relationships. There are countless examples around the world of parties built using patronage, including Argentina's Peronist Party,[37] Italy's Christian Democratic Party,[38] and India's Congress Party.[39] Patronage networks often persist even when parties have national, consistent policy platforms.

When parties compete by offering voters policies, they are described instead as *programmatic*. Programmatic parties are often associated with ideological positions that provide the basis of their specific programs. Liberal parties, labor parties, and conservative parties are unique to any given country, but we can refer to these parties in general terms because they are often associated with similar values across different national contexts. These parties can be organizationally dense, or not: because they do not rely on individual transactions to win votes, they do not need to rely on an infrastructure to monitor votes.

When programmatic parties *are* organizationally dense, however, they can develop relationships that are sustained indefinitely, beyond the mobilization required in a single election. There are benefits to devoting time and energy to growing an ongoing and local party presence. The constitutional law scholar Tabatha Abu El-Haj refers to this as *associational party-building*.[40] Importantly, these relationships are designed to foster engagement and mutual support between parties and citizens rather than to assist with any one election.

As many election activists note, the "ground game" of politics takes time. Strategists pick where to deploy volunteers for get-out-the-vote efforts, but if a party wants to become competitive in a place where it does not have a base of supporters, it needs to do more than show up every two or four years; it needs to earn recognition and trust in a tangible way. When a party is organizationally dense, it can provide information from the grassroots to the party, and it can help leaders understand what it is their citizens need from their elected officials.

As parties have become more nationalized, they have not retained a local presence; issue advocacy and the policymaking process have also become more professionalized. As a result, the parties juggle the competing demands of organized interests within their party coalition—organized interests which may or may not reflect what a party's base, as diffuse as that might be, cares about. Parties are adept at selling policies to the public and have many tools available to take stock of public attitudes, including polling and surveys. But aligning a party's message to resonate with a subset of the population is not the same as fostering a dialogue.

This brings us to another feature of parties that matter beyond elections, which is related to organizational density: parties reflect economic priorities—and parties also set economic priorities. Parties are responsible for the economic conditions in which democracy operates and are therefore economic actors in themselves; they don't just discuss the economy in campaigns but also "organize requests for the defense and transformation of the social and political order."[41] We know that democracy is supposed to regulate capital, to hold it accountable. But what that means, in practice, is that parties need to understand how people are situated economically and what the government needs to do to improve their circumstances.

We think of representation as the extent to which our values and interests are embodied in the positions of the politicians we elect. But values and interests are shaped by politicians: the issues you care about, those that activate a desire to become involved politically, are ones that elected officials also tell us to care about. It is therefore important to remember that parties both reflect people's underlying preferences, and they also, to some extent, dictate what those preferences are.

Representation is an iterative process; there is a vast set of issues that could be politically salient. It is easier to mobilize groups than individuals, and if people are already sorted into groups—whether by ethnicity, gender, or religion—you can tap into a set of identities that already exist. But the way parties developed, at least in the Western countries we have discussed thus far, was not just along lines of identity. Parties often organized along economic lines that were connected not only to specific economic classes but also to ideas about how government should rectify problems related to the market. Those problems were and are varied, related to fairness and safety of workers and consumers, of unregulated industries, of intended and unintended effects—on environments and people—of various modes of production.

So if we want to think about the political economy of representation, of which interests are prioritized when governing, we must think about parties. "Political economy" is an admittedly clunky term; an essay from 1978 noted that "the term [political economy] is once again in vogue in the discipline, and many different approaches to political inquiry have claimed it, with grandly confusing results."[42] "Political economy" can refer to the study of economics with a politics lens—the politics around economic institutions, for example. It can also refer to a line of inquiry dating to Marx, one that examines the political implications of economic relations.[43] If we think about the political economy of representation, though, we think about how well democracies embody distinct sets of economic interests, not only through what parties say but, more important, in what types of policies they pursue.

Today the interests of some large economic segments of society do not seem to be mobilized coherently into a vision of state-society relations. We might call this a problem of the left, although there is certainly an effort to mobilize the working class on both the left and the right. We might also call it a problem of antigovernment ideology (which it certainly is rooted in and related to). But this is more broadly a problem of parties that now have few mechanisms to reattach themselves to segments of the electorate they do not currently reach.

Seymour Martin Lipset and Stein Rokkan, in *Party Systems and Voter Alignments*, argued that party systems "froze" the cleavages in society engendered by national revolutions and industrialization.[44] Through parties, economic interests tied to urbanization and industry, to agriculture and the country, to national capitals or to distant towns, found political representation. The party systems of Western democracies became stable around the turn of the twentieth century, when parties of the right and left exhibited regular competition. Class-based parties in the twentieth century identified with an economic left and right, defined by contestation over redistribution, regulation, social policy, and the state's role in governing the economy.

The politics of advanced capitalism have skewed traditional left-right competition, however, because of the shifting bases of class politics. This misalignment has yet to translate into a coherent new mapping of left and right. On the right, populist leaders stoking grievance and discontent have made inroads with those considered "left behind" by the new globalized economy. The fact that the mainstream parties have not resolved a tension between governing responsibly and responsively opens opportunities to political outsiders. Realignment is an iterative process, whereby changes in society are reflected in changes to party organization, and parties then reformulate their appeals in ways that mobilize political constituencies. We are in a period today when there are disagreements about the management of political economy, and the relationship of state to society, that parties have yet to resolve.

The slow but steady erosion of intermediary capacity has produced a vacuum in democracies, one that other actors have struggled to fill— precisely because there is no other actor tasked with both representation and accountability. Peter Mair has described the void in liberal democracies of an absence of politics: parties are competitive and divided but do not actually engage in the work of politics itself. There has also been a depoliticization of policy, whereby technocrats increasingly do the work that in the past needed to be managed by parties. There has been plenty of attention devoted to, for example, the way parties became more dependent on economists and finance professionals in the neoliberal era.

Beyond the West: Party-Building in a Neoliberal Era

A party's strength or weakness might seem to rest on whether that party has lost or won votes, whether it has secured an electoral majority. Parties that are strong are those that win; parties are weak when they lose. In a democracy, parties might by connecting elections to interests, but it doesn't follow that if a party wins elections, it's necessarily representative. The combination of electorally successful parties and antiparty sentiment is rooted in a shift in how parties prioritize their different functions.

After the end of the Cold War, as many countries transitioned to democracy by adopting elections and building representative institutions, they struggled with the enormous task of party-building. Decades of research shows that parties can make or break democracy: strong parties are associated with democratic consolidation, economic growth, and the integration of citizens into politics.[45] The breakdown of party systems, on the other hand, contributes to volatility and democratic backsliding. The stakes of creating and sustaining parties is therefore much higher than simply whether or not parties can win.

Across different regions of the world, including Central and Eastern Europe, Latin America, Asia, and Africa, the fate of parties can determine the fate of democracy. In developing countries, party systems are often volatile: the names of parties may change from election to election, and parties emerge or disband quickly. Weakly institutionalized party systems are also associated with higher rates of corruption, less public goods provision, and leaders who rewrite the rules of the game to their own electoral benefit. When the party system is unstable, inexperienced or radical political outsiders have a greater chance of success. Stronger parties, on the other hand, help to align the incentives of party leaders with a country's democratic prospects. Where parties are "strong," they are "unified, centralized, stable, organizationally complex, and tied to longstanding constituencies."[46]

Reaching constituencies—a key aspect of party-building—is how a party becomes an intermediary rather than simply a group of politicians seeking election. Parties develop reputations through their campaign messaging and their performance in office. But their relationships with voters are built and sustained through personal ties as well. Professional staff, rather than volunteers, help establish a party's identity and long-term goals, which transcend the electoral goals of specific candidates. In her work on Eastern and Central European parties after 1989, for example, Margit Tavits found that parties that built "professional, specialized, and permanent central office staff" with "a large membership . . . and extensive network of visible local branch offices" had organizational strength.[47] Parties also need to reach out to local areas and recruit, retain, and integrate party members. Local offices are necessary to coordinate local volunteers and to serve as a place where voters or civic leaders can voice their issues. A wider geographic reach of parties is also critical when parties are out of power; parties must be adaptive, develop new coalitions, and reformulate their policy agendas. Further, a larger membership and geographic reach helps parties develop cross-cutting issues and diversify their bases of support.

Democratization during the 1970s through the 1990s involved party-building aimed at creating organizationally robust parties stable over successive elections and facilitating the peaceful transition of power. American and European parties served not only as models of how parties should be organized but also offered direct aid and shared organizational know-how. In an era of democratic transition across East Asia, Latin America, and Central and Eastern Europe, a network of democracy organizations (including political party institutes like the National Democratic Institute and International Republican Institute in the United States) stepped in to assist with party-building and mobilization. Party formation was considered an integral part of political development as a whole.[48]

Yet the economic realities in which party-building took place—alongside market liberalization and structural adjustment policies of the 1980s—precluded, in many ways, successful party-building. And there has been a worrying trend that parties, at least in places where democracy is less well established, have little reason to engage in party-building today.

First, parties no longer play as much of a role representing voters through associations or networked local parties. Candidates can easily mobilize voters with new communications technology, circumventing party organizations.[49] Second, in many countries parties cannot be distinguished ideologically, or parties of the left actually embrace policies of the right. Voters may thus struggle to attribute positions to parties and hold parties accountable. Another threat to institutionalization is the blurring of programmatic differences between the parties. The rise of the Washington Consensus policies in the 1970s and 1980s led many parties around the world to adopt neoliberal economic policies, including free trade, deregulation, privatization, and welfare austerity. As economic integration accelerated in the late twentieth century, many parties—in particular parties of the left—moved to the right, at least on economic issues. This led to a blurring of ideology and made it harder for voters to identify policy differences among opposing parties.[50] Classless politics is a defining feature of the party cleavages in many emerging democracies.[51]

Finally, the state has contracted in many parts of the world, owing either to economic crisis, neoliberal policy, or some combination thereof. As a result, parties have fewer policy tools available to provide resources to citizens and to cultivate programmatic relationships. As socialist regimes or regimes with large public sectors implement austerity measures, and as many public services have been privatized and public budgets slashed, parties are left with fewer goods to offer voters. Allen Hicken and Rachel Beatty Riedl describe the state's limited role as a "separate, independent factor driving party system deinstitutionalization."[52] In the 1980s and 1990s, for example, public sector budgets were slashed across Latin America, sub-Saharan Africa, and Southeast Asia. The decline in services led to growing public discontent with governance.

Markets, States, and Parties

In the era of parties as mass organizations, parties acted, however imperfectly, as equalizers of influence. They brokered a compromise between the radical left that sought to destroy capitalism and the aristocratic or industrialist right. The Keynsian-managed capitalism of the postwar period benefited from organizationally dense, class-based parties.[53] But today's era of neoliberalism and globalization requires parties to do very little, since their overriding policy concern has to do with creating a favorable environment for growth.

All these dynamics of contemporary party politics—the decline in parties as democratic intermediaries, the rise of professional political elites, the focus on electoral victories rather than legislative action, the crisis of representation, and the weakening of parties—can be linked to the de-legitimation of government and glorification of markets across many long-standing liberal democracies.

The view that the role of government is secondary to the role of markets in creating economic growth lies at the heart of neoliberalism. Many Western nations deregulated large industries, decreased barriers to trade, lowered tax rates, and scaled back social benefits. Through international organizations and conditional loans, these nations also diffused these policies to countries that were transitioning to democracy. The global order is defined by both democratization and market liberalization. Business enjoys special power in democratic regimes. Because capitalists set prices, wages, production levels, and "the economic security of everyone," the government is structurally dependent on capital, and capital, in turn, has structural power.[54] Business can also use tools such as lobbying or state capture to exert instrumental power, and at worst can leverage a public power unmatched by other formal institutions.

This has upended our traditional understanding of how parties operate in democracy. Because parties have less ability to develop distinct economic policies, and because they face constraints in the use of state resources, they have not been able to serve as democratic intermediaries linking citizens and the state.

Historically, parties facilitated the relationship of democracy and capitalism by mobilizing and articulating an interest distinct from that of capital and by bringing the state's resources to bear on societal and economic problems. But as parties have become more complex—taking on, in different ways, the roles and functions of corporations, associations, public relations firms, even identities, while also trying to remain, at their core, political membership organizations—they have changed their priorities and their strategies.

Parties are disappearing and are being "replaced by new political structures more suitable for the economic and technological realities of 21st-century politics."[55] These structures are capable of winning votes and amassing majorities. But they are not necessarily representative, nor are they able to articulate inherent justifications for the state. Given that parties negotiate the implicit bargains between those with power and those without, and given that parties are responsible for articulating the terms of the social contract, stipulating what government does or should do, it is no surprise that people feel disappointed in democracy today.

CHAPTER 3

Building the Party

In November 2021, Michelle Wu was elected mayor of Boston. A Taiwanese American lawyer and politician, Wu became the first non-White female mayor of one of America's oldest cities. In addition to her historic victory and progressive politics, she is also known for her "zest for retail politics," the kind of old-fashioned sidewalk campaigning that requires shaking hands and kissing babies.[1] As a member of Boston's City Council (she won a seat in 2012, then became president in 2015), she developed intimate knowledge of Boston's neighborhoods. A former city councilor, John Connolly, spoke of her "genius-level understanding of field politics. . . . [S]he can tell you the six places Albanians socialize in Roslindale."[2] Unlike her three competitors, Wu did not rely on outside consultants to run her campaign, despite the challenges of face-to-face campaigning during the COVID-19 pandemic.

Mayoral candidates may be some of the only remaining politicians who still cultivate the art of retail politics, which an Associated Press reporter described in 1980 as candidates selling themselves "on the doorstep, in the supermarket, at the factory gate, atop the ski lift."[3] Over the past fifty years, the need for politicians to talk to people has diminished significantly. When John F. Kennedy debated Richard Nixon on television, a new era of politics was born, one that emphasized telegenic charm and the ability to reach most, if not all, of the electorate with ease. Just as social media has played a pivotal role in recent elections, the television and communications revolutions of an earlier era profoundly shaped how parties conducted their business.

National parties devoted more time to campaigns, shifting resources from state and local parties to professional campaign activities. Politicians running for national office find it both impractical and unnecessary to represent constituents by knowing the nooks and crannies of a district or state. Candidates often campaign on national political issues; they employ pollsters and consultants to slice up voters into artificial yet meaningful designations ("silent majority," "soccer moms"). Parties that invested more in candidate service invested less in their traditional mobilization and integrative functions.

Despite the nationalization of political parties, politics itself is still—to use the longtime Speaker of the House Tip O'Neill's old adage—decidedly local. Volunteers are deployed in competitive districts and states to knock on doors and persuade people to vote. These mobilization efforts can be transformative.

The connective tissue between party organizations and local communities has long been lost, but that does not mean local politics or parties have disappeared. Instead, it creates opportunities for new or extreme political actors to mobilize support, sometimes by coopting existing (but decaying) party organs. After Donald Trump lost the presidential election in 2020, he actively campaigned on the Big Lie: the false claim that he rightfully won the election and that the election was fraudulently decided. His former political adviser Steve Bannon has used the Big Lie not only to mobilize Republican voters but also to shape the electoral process itself—not through a national strategy but through a decidedly local one. Bannon's precinct strategy uses local Republican parties to drive recruitment of far-right poll workers and election administrators. According to Bannon's website, the strategy asks conservatives to be explicitly tied to the party: "become a voting member of our Party" and, before all else, "contact your county or local Republican Party Committee, find out where and when it meets (terminology varies from state to state), and attend the meeting."[4] From there, Bannon hopes that Trump's supporters will volunteer as poll workers (or what he terms "election inspectors") to keep watch on election day. Working with lawyers like Cleta Mitchell, who was part of President Trump's legal team to challenge the 2020 election result, Bannon was training the thousands of activists (over eighty-five hundred volunteers had signed up in summer 2021) to challenge election results.[5]

Local and state politics haven't stopped mattering, but political parties are more nationalized and less decentralized today. This chapter describes how parties were once organized to conduct elections and foster party loyalty at the local level. This is a history of how parties developed, with attention to the embeddedness of parties in communities, which created direct ties between party officials and the constituencies they served. It examines this pattern across the long-standing democracies to get a sense of party development both in and outside the United States. Doing so helps us to understand how concepts like party membership and involvement have changed over time.

The many changes to election campaigns and local parties over the past fifty years have reshaped how we think about representation and party politics. Are parties membership groups that we join and that socialize us into politics? That provide us with a partisanship that translates into citizenship by helping us learn to deliberate and make political claims?[6] Or are they more akin to firms, marketing political slogans to us voter-consumers who make choices on election day but never expect the party to actually interface with us? Parties developed as mass organizations with concrete ties to the electorates they represented. They were social and civic organizations that ensured contact and engagement with local communities. As communications technologies and party organizations shifted, however, the relationship between parties and their members weakened.

Membership and Belonging: The Origins of Mass Parties

Are you a member of a political party?

Maybe you've given money to a candidate who's affiliated with a party or voted in a primary. Maybe you got roped into one or two meetings of the Young Democrats or College Republicans in school. Perhaps you've even done all of those things, and you vote regularly, and proudly, and identify as a Democrat or Republican.

Maybe you were born into a family that cared about politics. Michelle Obama's father, Fraser Robinson III, worked for the Chicago water plant and was a Democratic precinct captain. As a young girl, Michelle accompanied him on his rounds through the district. The Koch brothers, Charles and David, were raised by Fred Koch, an industrialist who was active in the right-wing John Birch Society and held its meetings in the family basement.[7] When Senator Ted Cruz was in high school, his parents enrolled him in afterschool programs teaching free-market values. In a group called the Constitutional Collaborators, Ted and other high schoolers met multiple times a week to study the U.S. Constitution, eventually memorizing a mnemonic version that captured the enumerated powers of the government.[8] There are dozens of recent or current members of Congress who come from political families, including Senator Liz Cheney, Senator Mitt Romney, and Speaker Nancy Pelosi.

But most citizens are not born into politics, which is precisely why parties built up mass organizations in an era of democratic expansion. In the historical period when parties were building mass organizations in the late nineteenth century, their ties to citizens were formalized through membership. Strong parties cultivated relationships with individuals and groups who could participate in party activities. Membership provided the backbone of party organization itself, and individual members worked to mobilize voters, oversee campaigns, and recruit candidates. When party financing and party activities (distributing campaign literature, knocking on doors) depended on actual party members, parties needed local offices and staff who could coordinate these activities. A party's territorial and organizational reach—its local offices, its members—has long been a determinant of its strength.

These days, however, elections are less about parties and members; instead, parties care about voters, who are up for grabs. Whereas parties once connected society and government, gauging the actual interests of people through direct, personal contact, they now aim instead at "electoral persuasion rather than partisan mobilization," replacing integrative activities of the past with messaging to segments of voters.[9]

From Associations to Parties in Europe

Political parties are rooted in a culture of membership and civic associations that was common throughout the nineteenth century. Religious guilds were created to promote spiritual education; leisure societies formed around such interests as literature, sports, and music; friendly societies provided local aid and charity. Trades unionism was expanding in Britain and the United States. The early party families we still have today emerged at this time: parties of the left, consisting of labor parties, social democratic parties, and (occasionally) liberal parties, and parties of the right, consisting of religious parties and conservative parties. These parties followed a "logic of constituency representation" rather than one of electoral competition, in that their priority was fidelity to the values and interests of their party's ideologies and bases of support.[10]

The century between 1850 and 1950 was when political parties evolved from small legislative factions, often in parliaments with limited legislative powers, to mass organizations at the center of modern representative democracy. At the start of this period, most of the countries among the early democratizers limited suffrage to property-owning white males. In Western Europe, the political turbulence of the 1848 revolutions led governments to ban associational activity—including that of political groups and unions. Nonetheless, people began organizing in favor of representation and suffrage or for workers' protections. Political parties were rooted in a culture of membership associations that predated formal democracy. Nancy Bermeo and Philip Nord have described "subscriber democracy" of the nineteenth century, whereby party infrastructure was built atop a vibrant civic landscape.[11]

As parties expanded, they grafted on to the associational civic infrastructure that already existed. Religious groups, for example, facilitated the rise of Catholic and Christian parties, which evolved into modern-day Christian Democratic parties of the center-right. In the 1820s, the Irish Catholic Association created networks of church groups to protect Catholic culture, which also served the purpose of building a Catholic identity. Many religious denominations followed suit. In the 1850s, the Dutch Anti-Revolutionary Party—a Calvinist party advocating religious education—became one of the first membership-based parties. Membership was used as a "tool to cultivate identity, not just (or even primarily) as a means to mobilize for elections."[12]

Voluntary associations often had written rules, regular meetings, and leadership positions. Most important, they enlisted members who participated in the associations' activities and paid subscription fees. Sometimes associations printed their own statutes and reports. The turn of the nineteenth century was a period of what the historian Robert Wiebe has called a "search for order," when collective mobilization took on a bureaucratic apparatus.[13]

In an era of suffrage expansion, political parties needed to build an infrastructure to connect the legislative factions of like-minded candidates with the newly enfranchised electorate. The British Conservative Party, for example, created the National Union of Conservative and Constitutional Associations (NUCCA) in 1867, in response to a law that reduced property qualifications to vote. The NUCCA was a federation of conservative parties across the country. Each of these local parties enlisted members and elected local leaders. As the Conservative Party grew, it enlarged its electoral capacities by registering voters, nominating candidates, and running campaigns and elections. But it also developed its social and intermediary capacities through leisure groups and friendly societies. In his study of conservative parties, Daniel Ziblatt distinguishes between strong and weak parties. Strong parties are characterized by hierarchy and a mass base—so, for example, a salaried professional leadership, local party associations with wide geographic spread, and an ability to "subordinate and contain" interest groups and radical reactionaries. Weak parties, on the other hand, contract out, meaning they have fewer local parties and little party hierarchy, and therefore become competitive with interest groups and reactionaries.[14]

The Primrose League began in 1883, at first as a society of Conservative loyalists that became a "Tory militia."[15] The Primrose League was a social organization that had cross-class appeal and included not only men but also women and children. These social clubs sponsored music, dances, and teas, and also met with Conservative Party officials at annual "grand habitations." Party leaders worked closely with the Primrose League to provide lectures or advice on how to register voters. Further, party agents worked with the Primrose League to canvass voters—to spread the word of issues important to the party "street by street, village by village, and hamlet by hamlet." From 1884 to 1901, Primrose League membership rose from 857 to over 1.5 million members.[16]

Liberal parties, which formed around causes like individual rights, free trade, and opposition to absolutist rule, also built out networks of local parties. These parties often formed in burgeoning cities to cater to the urban middle classes; they were structured with formal memberships and statutes outlining obligations of members.[17] The Belgian Liberal Party formed in 1846 with local electoral associations, and the Liberal Party in Britain held its first national meeting in 1877 with delegates from municipal parties. The Liberal model of municipal organization included local party wards, supported by members and annual dues, with locally elected ward and city associations.[18] In the early twentieth century, Germany, Denmark, and Sweden also established their own membership-based liberal parties.

Labor parties, many of which were socialist in origin and forged an alliance with trades unions, often developed their social and civic organizational capacity prior to their electoral capacity because they were excluded from political participation. By the 1860s, both the United States and Britain had national unions: the Trades Union Congress in Britain and the Knights of Labor in the United States.

France and Germany still banned unions, fearing further unrest after the revolutions of 1848 swept the continent. France banned union activity after the French revolution, and Otto von Bismarck's Germany passed the Anti-Socialist Law in 1878 that banned socialist meetings and newspapers. These associations were a hallmark of societies undergoing social and political development as the middle and working classes expanded.[19]

Labor parties became involved instead with civic groups like youth and women's organizations as well as cooperative societies. In 1875, the General Association of German Workingmen and the Social Democratic Workingmen Party merged to form what would become the German Social Democratic Party, or SPD (Sozialdemokratische Partei Deutschlands). The SPD had 24,443 members in its first year; members paid fees that supported political activities and newspapers. When Germany lifted its antisocialism laws in 1890, the SPD worked closely with national labor unions. By 1914, the party had over a million members and ninety-one newspapers; it was affiliated with an insurance company, the Volksfursorge, operated by labor.[20] Social democratic parties across Europe similarly included related social clubs and voluntary associations.

Party membership surged after the Second World War. As unionization rates rose, social democratic parties dominated elections of this period, and governments expanded social welfare policies that included universal healthcare systems, employment protections and regulations of work and workplaces, unemployment insurance, pensions, and state-funded higher education.

As political parties grew, they did not rely solely on membership dues to finance their activities. Labor unions often took fees from their affiliated trade unions, while conservative groups received funds from business groups or trade associations. Some of the parties that emerged after the war in Italy and Germany worked with these associations to signal a deradicalization and programmatic commitment to democracy.[21] But locally based parties, with active dues-paying members, formed the backbone of party operations.

Building Parties in the United States

Although the United States never developed membership parties like those of Western Europe, American party organization has nevertheless followed a trajectory similar to party development in other liberal democracies. No sooner was the nation founded than ideological factions emerged. The Federalists and Anti-Federalists, for example, were divided over the ratification of the Constitution. In 1828, the election of Andrew Jackson under the banner of the Democratic Party created a federal patronage system. With the help of political operative Martin Van Buren, the Democratic Party mobilized voters by dispensing jobs and resources to loyal supporters.[22] In the 1850s, the Northern Whigs and antislavery Free Soil Party coalesced into the Republican Party.

In states and localities, parties could be quite expansive in the ways they cultivated voters. Urban machines, for example, had legions of party workers who obtained their jobs through the party, and they were expected to help with canvassing, rallies, and other election-related efforts. The party was financed through assessments of incomes; locally, this meant that individuals receiving patronage jobs paid small sums to the party; nationally, this meant that state parties sent money to the national committee. While the heyday of the behemoth urban machine (like those of New York and Chicago) was the late nineteenth century, the machine as a way to organize the party existed in Detroit, Cincinnati, Philadelphia, and other industrial towns. In the cities, the party provided not only access to employment but also social welfare assistance and occasional charity.

At each level of government, party committees could establish regular meetings, as well as procedures for nominating and electing local and state chairs. State parties often held their own nominating convention, and rules of party activities were often specified by statute. These laws specified that party chairs needed to be elected, for example, or included provisions about when party caucuses should be held. Parties could also establish local Republican and Democratic clubs, which provided activities for members. The Republican National League, for example, which formed in New York in 1887, was created to supplement the work of parties outside campaigns. They offered musical or social programs, distributed party materials, and hosted discussions and speakers. The local party committees were therefore engaged in the active mobilization and socialization of voters. In a study of the Pennsylvania Republican Party around 1900, local party committees and their volunteer staff considered it their duty to track what we would now call public opinion. Party agents were assigned two specific populations, to track "their conduct . . . their conversation . . . any who are disaffected." When a college professor seemed no longer to support the party, local party agents made sure that he received a letter from a personal friend, who also happened to be a minister, explaining why the professor should support the party's candidate.[23]

What did these local party offices do? Much like their European counterparts, party members mobilized voters, canvassed towns, printed and distributed newsletters, and did all the hard work of campaigning—knocking on doors, phone-banking, organizing get-out-the-vote drives with local civic groups. State parties also coordinated between the local and national organizations. They helped to determine, for example, where national candidates should campaign or speak. Through the state and local organizations, parties were able to foster ongoing relationships with other intermediaries, including labor unions, business associations, and civic groups—not only for election turnout but also to gauge issues of political import.[24]

National Committees

Most of the parties were organized loosely at the local and state levels, and presidential campaigns involved massive coordination across state parties rather than a national operation As property qualifications for the suffrage were eliminated, parties expanded to conduct elections for local and state offices. The Democratic National Committee was an outgrowth of an 1844 central committee established to elect James K. Polk and George M. Dallas to the presidency. By 1848, this committee also coordinated state parties and "promote[d] the Democratic Cause" beyond the nomination and election of presidential candidates. The Republican Party was also "locally organized before national agencies were brought into use," and in 1855 a Republican Association of Washington, DC, was created. It printed a circular in 1856 "urging Republicans to organize clubs or associations in all cities, towns, and villages," with instruction to "urge upon its members the importance of at once collecting funds."[25] The chairmen of nine different state Republican committees met that year "for the purpose of perfecting the National Organization" and assembling a nominating convention.[26]

While the Republicans and Democrats were national parties by the 1850s, they had no national headquarters: The national "organization" was mainly an ad hoc, epiphenomenal committee to manage the presidential campaign every four years. State parties had leeway to organize as they wished. They came together under the auspices of the national committee by sending delegates from the states to the national conventions. Party-building was both a top-down and a bottom-up activity, owing to federalism: states not only oversaw elections within their states for state offices like governor and the legislatures but also coordinated elections for federal offices like the House and Senate.

Around 1920, the Republican Party, led by Chairman Will Hays, established continuous party operations at the Republican National Committee (RNC). The RNC, newly headquartered in Washington, DC, hired permanent staff to maintain the organization in non-presidential-election years.[27] The Democratic National Committee (DNC) follow suit after the election of 1928, when Governor Al Smith of New York called for the party to develop a program rather than "profiting solely by the mistakes and failures of the opposition."[28] The DNC chairman John Raskob hired a full-time director of publicity and convened a permanent executive committee. In theory, the committees in election years included a representative from each state party committee. Each state committee used to send one man to the national committee;

after women were granted the right to vote, states began to send one man and one woman from each state party.[29] Neither party's national committee had a constitution or bylaws when first formed, but members of the state party committees served four-year terms.

The role of the national committees began to change after World War II, with party leaders taking a more active role in fostering relationships with the state parties. On occasion, the national party sent teams to congressional districts to solve perceived problems with local organization.[30] The RNC created "policy-publicity" regional conferences where local party leaders engaged in discussions with national party officers. The national party also developed its own field men to coordinate with state and local parties in advance of election campaigns. In all these efforts, consultation was the goal: it was understood that local party leaders were familiar with local "problems, prospects, and complaints" and that national policies required local support.[31] In the 1950s, both the RNC and the DNC expanded their paid staff to over seventy members each, the numbers doubling or tripling in presidential election years. The chairman became a full-time, salaried position rather than an honorific bestowed on an elected official or wealthy donor.[32] Even so, local and state party chairs remained the critical link between the national interests of the party and the party on the ground.

Through the 1950s and 1960s, the national party committees developed the structures we are familiar with today. The RNC, for example, established various divisions, including public relations, finance, research, and a speakers' bureau. It also had divisions, deemed "less essential," related to specific constituencies: women, nationalities, minorities, labor, and agriculture. The RNC created a training program, where campaign staff were taught how to influence voters and conduct voter registration.[33] The RNC also invested in its Campaign Management College to provide advice, seminars, and training on campaign techniques; state parties and the Young Republicans and College Republicans could all take part.[34] A neighbor-to-neighbor program in the 1950s trained primarily women to fundraise in their communities and to collect neighbors' names and addresses.[35] In the 1970s, the DNC established regional directors, support services for congressional and senatorial candidates, and direct mail.[36]

Marginalizing the Local Party

Despite the creation of national committees, parties were still local and state affairs. Most state parties were arranged in a similar structure, with a state committee and chairperson, then county committees, and ward or district party committees and chairs at the lowest level of organization. The national committees were "vitally interested in fostering the strongest possible state and local organizations."[37] In 1960, at least thirty-six Republican and twenty-one Democratic state committees had permanent headquarters and some full-time staff, and a few state chairs were paid full-time positions.[38]

Today few state parties (around 30%) coordinate joint activities like registration drives or fundraising with the state party; only about half even share a mailing list with the state party.[39] Local parties get very little financing for staff, office space, or operating expenses from the state parties. State and local parties do not buy ads or conduct opinion surveys; those activities are undertaken by the candidates themselves or with the national parties.[40] The expansion of primaries made the state parties secondary players in many aspects of politics. Surveys of state and local parties through the 1970s and 1980s showed that they assisted candidates by distributing campaign literature, fundraising, and organizing campaign events. In some ways the state and local parties of the late twentieth century mirrored the national parties of the early twentieth century: they were epiphenomenal, ad hoc, with little to do outside the campaign season. There were some efforts to reform parties through the creation of new types of local party groups.

In *The Amateur Democrat*, the political scientist James Q. Wilson described new factions of politicians emerging to challenge the political establishment, and political machines in particular, in mid-century.[41] These "amateurs" were educated, upper-middle-class party activists who developed reform clubs such as the Independent Voters of Illinois. These political clubs were explicitly partisan, although they did not perform official party functions like candidate nominations or elections. In California, for example, the Los Angeles Democratic Council tried to bring local workers, a variety of endorsing councils, and party committees into one party organ in 1942. A decade later, there were 175 democratic clubs throughout the state that came together at a conference that was open to official party committee officers, precinct workers, and interested voters.[42] The conference provided information about fundraising and organizing to win primary elections (through, for example, the use of "cross-filing" candidates in both party primaries). County party committees begin chartering and regulating club activities. The clubs, after all, could charge official membership dues and provided a casual way for party members to socialize—to "satisfy the quest for community and recognition."[43] In Wisconsin, reform clubs dated to Governor Robert La Follette's Progressive Party of the early twentieth century. Both the Republican and Democratic state parties had voluntary club wings, which were given statutory party committee status in 1974.[44]

It is hard to tie these trends directly to membership. But after the Watergate scandal in 1972, many Americans started to turn away from parties. This was evidenced through lower voter turnout and lower rates of self-reported party identification. People became less likely to participate in political activities, such as attending campaign events.[45] There was also a rise in split-ticket voting, whereby voters would vote for both Republican and Democratic candidates for different offices. The national parties, in response, centralized operations toward campaigning.[46]

Parties as Service Providers: The Candidate-Centered Party

Local, grassroots party organization was necessary in the era of labor-intensive campaigns and mass parties. But in the 1970s, the advent of new technologies and forms of outreach changed how parties mobilized voters. As early as the 1930s, Carlton G. Ketchum, a Republican adviser,

established a National Republican Finance Committee with a sustaining membership program. As Cornelius Cotter and John Bibby describe
it, "Ketchum set up a sustaining membership program—precursor of
contemporary sustaining mass mail solicitation programs. He signed
up 4,738 sustaining members in 1937, who pledged specific amounts
for 1938, 1939, and 1940. A very high ratio (95.6%) of the pledges
was collected totaling $202,343 in 1938. The state quota system also
originated in this era. Under this system, each state is assigned a quota
that represents its share of national committee quota income for the
coming year."[47] By the 1960s, Republican fundraising was no longer
conducted through the states; instead, the party relied on fundraising
professionals. In 1962 the party reinstituted direct-mail solicitation of
sustaining members, which made up 40% of the party's receipts by 1965.
In 1978, the Republican National Finance Committee raised over $9.7
million, over 80% of donations averaging $37.34. By then, the party had
also added big-ticket financing schemes, such as the Republican Eagle
Program and Republican Associates Club. The Democrats, similarly,
developed a national fundraising scheme—a President's Club (established in 1961) that raised $6 million over the next five years. In 1974, the
party created a National Finance Council whose one hundred members
committed to raising $200,000 for the party.[48]

By 1979, the DNC had programs to support federal candidates,
create regional field offices, and oversee direct mail. The party enjoyed
majority control of the House of Representatives from 1933 to 1994
(with brief exceptions in 1947–1949 and 1953–1955). The Senate
was also mostly in Democratic hands until 1981. Most governor-
ships and state legislatures were held by Democrats in the postwar
period. At the local and state level, the Democratic Party was organized through political machines, unions, and social movements
and advocacy groups. But they adopted similar campaign-focused
strategies at the national level in the 1980s, including direct-mail
solicitations of small donors and a training program for Democratic candidates and staffers on fundraising and voter contact. By
the 1990s, the DNC was investing in voter files and technological

upgrades to allow data-sharing between the national party and state parties, but this was a slow process across successive DNC chairs.[49]

Direct mail increasingly became the way the parties reached out to members; this allowed parties to target specific voters and advertise issues and policies. Direct mail was used to solicit campaign funds as well; in the 1983–1984 election cycle, 15 million people donated over $500 million owing to direct-mail solicitations.[50] While not cheap, mailings obviated the need for local parties, providing national party officials with the tools to get their messages directly to voters.

Political parties adapted to these changes by redirecting their organizational priorities and resources. Rather than financing local and state offices and organizations, parties focused on campaign activities. Much of the work that parties had once done in-house were delegated outside the party. Political action committees (PACs), for example, increased in number and size throughout the 1980s.[51] PACs allow corporations, unions, and membership organizations (like trade associations) to raise money on behalf of specific campaigns and candidates. And because advocacy groups could also avail themselves of direct mail and mass communication, they provided voters with ways to get involved politically— through focused issue areas and attenuated "pocketbook" membership.

Local parties still occasionally assisted with candidate recruitment and campaigning through the 1980s.[52] However, the nationalization of parties accelerated after the 1980s, with parties concentrating their efforts on fundraising and campaign services.

Democratizing the Party: Primary Elections

One of the major tensions in parties is the relationship between a party's leaders and its members. In 1911, Robert Michels, a German sociologist, wrote about his experience in the German Social Democratic Party. The resulting study, *Political Parties: A Sociological Study of the Oligarchic Tendency of Modern Democracy*, coined the term "iron law of oligarchy" to describe the tensions inherent in social organizations. For Michels, organizations—particularly those guided by egalitarian principles and aiming to represent large segments of the populace—are inevitably led by individuals whose interests may not align with those of their members. Not only do leaders value hierarchy, but they also tend toward oligarchic decision-making. A small elite becomes entrusted to speak on behalf of the organization, while demanding acquiescence from the rank and file.

Party primaries began in the 1920s as a response to the perceived corruption of state and local parties but were not in widespread use until the 1970s, when both parties changed their presidential nomination process to allow primary voters greater say. After the 1968 election, the Democratic Party adopted the McGovern-Fraser reforms, officially the Commission on Party Structure and Delegation. These reforms opened the presidential nomination process to primary elections and therefore circumvented the role of party bosses in nominating and approving candidates.[53] Today some states allow only people who officially register with a party to vote in that party's primary; other states hold blanket primaries in which candidates of all parties compete against each other.

The internal party reforms after McGovern-Fraser were not limited to primary elections. The parties sought to make their organizations more inclusive, although they did so in different ways. The Republican Party devoted more resources to state and local parties through technical assistance, such as building up a fundraising infrastructure and providing computer services. It also created a National Black Republican Council. The Democratic Party was more active in encouraging minority participation given that its Southern faction had only recently been required to dismantle Jim Crow laws against Black participation. The Democrats created an Equal Rights Committee to combat racism in the state parties in an effort meet the McGovern-Fraser report's goal of "ensur[ing] a full opportunity for all minority group members to participate in the delegate selection process."[54] The party adopted new rules for state parties, covering public party meetings, broad registration drives, and publication of how the party would select candidates and determine qualifications for office.

The parties also continued to experiment with rules about how presidential selection would work. Primary voters select a winner of the state party primary, and the state party sends delegates to the national convention to cast votes for the state's winning candidate. The party officially nominates its presidential and vice-presidential candidate at its national convention, after all the state primary elections have taken place. Both parties have adjusted their rules to give other party members a say in the party's nominee as well. But since the 1970s, the parties have less and less of a say in selecting candidates up and down the ballot.

In 1919, the Nineteenth Amendment granted women the right to vote in the United States. In a pamphlet teaching women the electoral process, women were instructed to "join a party" by voting in its primary election.[55] Because there is no formal party membership, voting in a primary election has often been considered a proxy for membership itself. For Americans, voting in a primary election is one of the most direct ways to influence a party decision. Primary elections were initially established as a way to democratize parties, but they also erode the party's gatekeeping function. Most parties in established democracies do not use primary elections to select their candidates. Instead, party leaders choose the candidates they think will be most appealing to an electorate; they have an incentive to put forth a slate of candidates with broad appeal. It is this function of parties—to select "good" candidates who play by the rules of the game—that keeps extremism at bay, since the party has an interest in its own long-term success.[56]

Today primary elections are seen as a vehicle for extremism in elections because they allow a small number of highly motivated voters to determine the general election candidates. For presidential primary races, turnout is quite low, between 10% and 30%. And for congressional and state-level races, that number plummets to the pathetic single digits, somewhere between 4% and 10% of the eligible voting population.[57] While there are debates about the extent to which primary voters are more extreme than voters in general elections, they influence the behavior of candidates at the primary stage. Since 2010, the trend of "getting primaried"—that is, of an incumbent being challenged in a primary—has risen. In the case of Republicans, moderate incumbents have been replaced by more extreme candidates. These primary challenges tend to drive a campaign toward ideological extremes rather than moderation.[58]

During the presidential primary races of 2016, two competing and mutually exclusive narratives emerged to describe the state of the parties. The first narrative was that parties were undemocratic, with party leadership making decisions that subverted the will of voters. Specifically, Senator Bernie Sanders's stronger than expected showing against presumptive nominee Hillary Clinton set off debates about the role of convention delegates (chosen by voters) and superdelegates (chosen by the party). Debbie Wasserman Schultz, the chairwoman of the DNC, resigned on the eve of the Democratic convention after reports that party officials had tried "to sabotage the campaign of Senator Bernie Sanders."[59] Party leaders have every right to make rules about candidate selection; doing so is not a conspiracy but rather a critical element of running a party. Nonetheless, the Democrats reduced the role of superdelegates in 2018.

The Republican Party, in contrast, started the primary races with a field of seventeen candidates. As insurgent candidate Donald J. Trump racked up primary victories, the Republican establishment struggled to respond as his nomination became all but assured. The RNC explored ways to challenge the nomination,[60] and there was some discussion of what might happen at a divided convention. But ultimately the Republican establishment fell in line behind the candidate receiving the most primary votes.

These episodes point to the limits of primaries as a means of voter engagement with parties. With so few voters participating in primaries, general candidates are selected not by party leaders with an investment in the party's long-term viability but by a small subset of voters who prefer more ideologically extreme candidates.[61] Most local and state parties do not have criteria or vetting procedures for candidates who decide to run for a party's label.

Civil Society and Civic Life

Coinciding with new strategies of party organization were changes to society, at both large and local scales. Political parties are embedded in societies; they reflect divisions, concerns, and ideas within those societies and also create the political opportunities to address these. While modernizing the party seemed to provide new ways to connect to voters, these connections were attenuated: they allowed for professional management of the party's messages and very little feedback from voters themselves. The advances in communications were not an adequate substitute for direct ties through local communities and associations. This was the beginning of the end of the "zone of engagement" between citizens and leaders that parties had once provided.[62]

Support for mainstream parties was highest in an era of unionization and civic activity. After World War II, social democratic achievements in the early twentieth century had produced larger states, more coordination in industrial relations, and stronger labor organization. Majorities of citizens worked in the industrial sector, particularly manufacturing. Mass transit connected cities and towns, and the suburbs were beginning to grow. Civic life—associations, businesses, and politics—sustained local communities. Voluntary membership associations provided critical means for citizens to become engaged in their communities during the 1950s and 1960s. Fraternal organizations, veterans' groups, and religiously affiliated groups like the Knights of Columbus provided places for people of different occupations or backgrounds to spend time with one another. The top ten membership associations in the United States were large, cross-class organizations, including the American Federation of Labor–Congress of Industrial Organization, the American Farm Bureau Association, the Red Cross, the Woman's Division of Christian Service, and fraternal orders like the Freemasons and the Elks. These organizations were composed of local chapters, with dues-paying, active members who engaged in advocacy, voluntarism, or civic projects. The federated structure of these associations allowed for local chapters to connect to larger national organizations, but rather than focus on national issues, these groups served their immediate communities.[63]

Civic life helped sustain party democracy. Strong civic groups provided parties with potential volunteers and members, but as opportunities to engage in membership groups and civic associations declined, parties likewise narrowed the ways they engaged the public. The pattern of party-building in Western Europe and the United States in the early twentieth century—with strong local organizations and engagement of party members—was facilitated by associational civic life. Some groups were explicitly political, including labor groups and farmers' organizations. Others formed around free trade and currency issues or prohibition and temperance. Sometimes these groups worked with parties; at other times they organized in opposition to parties. There were complementarities among different kinds of voluntary civic associations, and they mirrored those of political parties.[64]

In the 1970s, there was an "advocacy revolution"—a shift in the way citizens came together to make political demands. The public interest advocacy movement, which organized on behalf of noncorporate interests, reflected more of a central and hierarchical structure than a social movement. While public interest advocacy sought "a collective good," it did not involve collective activity. National, professionally managed organizations established headquarters in Washington, DC, to advocate for narrow issues, including civil liberties, religious freedom, and environmental causes. They raised money through direct-mail solicitations and relied less on activities of local groups.

Members did not receive benefits for joining organizations, and the staff and leaders of these organizations pursued political strategies without input from members. These groups were "oligarchic in nature," with professional staffs working on publications and with leaders who couldn't be removed from power.[65] Common Cause, for example, was formed in 1970, organized by John Gardner, who had been the secretary of health, education, and welfare under President Lyndon B. Johnson. Common Cause did have nominal members: "educated, middle-class professionals, most of whom did little more than contribute money."[66] Common Cause's political strategies mirrored those of other interest groups; they ran ads in papers and contacted members of Congress with reform ideas. They "chose to influence policy through Washington-based activities rather than building locally based coalitions" to support goals like campaign finance reform.[67] Advocacy is conducted through what has been called organized combat, whereby well-resourced interest groups and single-issue organizations compete to secure policy goals.

This erosion of civic capacity both contributes to and is exacerbated by a weakening of parties. There are no longer "participatory institutions that enable the vast majority of citizens, particularly low- and middle-income Americans, to engage in politics and governance."[68] In 1974, 70% of White working-class voters were in at least one organization or club; by 2004, the rate was less than 40%, while membership among middle- and upper-class voters declined only from 81% to 73% in that same period.[69] While there is ample evidence that civic engagement fosters greater political interest and activity, civic groups have few local or state parties with which to engage. Further, the absence of parties removes a way that people could once interact in politics.

Political advocacy today tends to draw people likely to be politically active anyway—those with higher levels of income and education. Aside from get-out-the-vote drives during election campaign season, particularly during presidential elections, much less political mobilization happens face to face today than in an era of mass parties. Civic life is important because it is a site of small-d democracy: a place where people must deliberate and compromise in order to set and achieve their goals. The professionalization of advocacy, however, has closed off opportunities for majorities of citizens to become involved with politics. Politics is the domain of hobbyists today—people who follow the news or debate

politics online. Far fewer people get involved in political causes and mobilize others toward achieving a specific political outcome, even at the local
level.

The Decline of Organized Labor

Labor activity was particularly important to the development of political parties. In Europe, labor organization helped build parties that
demanded both political rights and economic freedoms. Many trade
unions established their own political parties or allied with liberal parties.
Labor unions were a critical vehicle for the development and trans-
mission of working-class interests, as well as for the recruitment of
candidates and leaders from working-class backgrounds.

Since the 1970s, however, unionization rates have declined
(Figure 3.1), particularly in the United States, and the erosion of
parties in local communities is connected to lower rates of unionization.
Labor unions used to be critical sources of political mobilization,
education, and training. Union workers were active participants in
campaigns and party activities, providing crucial support for the parties
of the left.[70]

Public sector workers are unionized at much higher rates (33%) than
private sector workers (6%), but union rates in the United States are at
their lowest since peaking in the 1950s. The decline of unions has also
been linked to rising economic inequality, the concentration of corporate power and wealth, and worse working conditions.[71] The decline of
manufacturing unions has been particularly stark as the economy has
shifted from the industrial to the service sector. Membership in the steel-
workers union collapsed from 1.1 million to 421,000, the Teamsters
from 2.4 million to 1.3 million, the machinists from 780,000 to 474,000,
and the garment workers from 363,000 to 133,000 in the two-decade
span of the 1970s–1990s, as global competition rose.[72]

As parties have become more economically conservative, social democratic parties have become less representative of a traditional left. Many

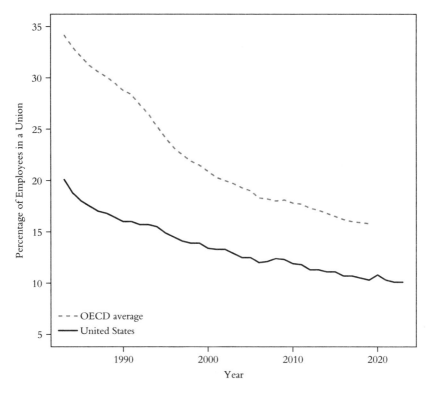

Figure 3.1 Unionization Rates, 1983–2023

Note: Data from U.S. Bureau of Labor Statistics, Union affiliation data from the Current Population Survey, and Organisation for Economic Cooperation and Development, Annual percentage of workforce members of labor unions in the G7 countries and OECD from 1960 to 2020.

have embraced pro-trade policies that separated them further from unions.[73] Lower rates of union participation have also contributed to less involvement with and trust in parties. In a study of West Germany, weakened social ties, including lower rates of union membership, lower church attendance, and less identification with the Catholic Church, was correlated with less party identification after the 1970s.[74]

Support for social democratic parties was high beginning in the interwar period, when they commanded 20% to 30% of vote shares. When in government, these parties advocated for labor goals that included paid leave, pensions, and collective bargaining. After the Second World

War, parties of the left expanded their appeals beyond the working classes. Their base of support included farmers and agricultural workers, urban professionals, and those employed in the public sector.[75] The decline of unions has had significant consequences for the ability of parties on the left to maintain supporters and activists and to maintain a pro-worker agenda. But it has also been consequential for a working class that is increasingly politically adrift, as we will see in later chapters.

Declining Membership: The 1980s to the Present

The idea of local party offices and party members seems antiquated today, yet formal membership still exists. A recent study of ten European parliamentary democracies revealed that membership requirements typically include being of a certain age and adhering to party principles. Party members tend to be older, male, highly educated, and financially better off, which aligns with the type of people who are more likely to participate in politics. Some members report acting as party ambassadors by discussing the party with nonmembers; some members hold elected office. Membership fees average €45 (with reduced fees available for retired or unemployed persons). Most members do very little: upward of 47% said their membership is inactive.[76] In the 1960s, membership rates in Europe averaged about 15%. By 1980 that number had declined to 10%, and in the 2000s, membership fell to 3%.[77]

Declining rates of membership in civic associations and new party structures also track with a shift in party financing after World War II (Figure 3.2). Governments began to regulate parties through provision of public subsidies, first to parliamentary groups, then to party organizations. Norway began to subsidize parliamentary groups in 1960; by 1970, Austria, Sweden, Finland, the Netherlands, Denmark, and Germany also provided financial support to parties, with Britain, Ireland, and Italy following suit in the 1970s. The United States also experimented with public financing during that decade. In exchange for receiving funds, states held parties accountable. Most parties needed

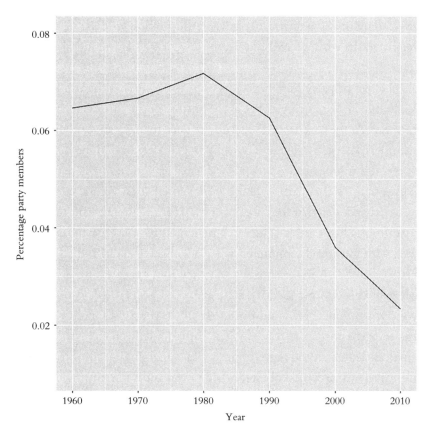

Figure 3.2 Party Membership in Advanced Democracies, 1960–2010
Note: Rates of party membership as a percentage of the total population averaged across thirteen advanced democracies.
Data form the MAPP data set, Emilie van Haute and Emilien Paulis. 2016. http:// doi.org/10.5281/zenodo.61234

to publish their budgets or report campaign expenditures. To qualify for funding, parties needed to receive above a certain threshold of the parliamentary vote share; occasionally they also needed to document official membership.

Parties in Europe are highly regulated by the state, a trend that has contributed to a "cartelization" of parties. By the turn of the twenty-first century, parties were like public utilities: they still offered voters plenty of choices in elections, but voters had no way to really challenge

the dominance of mainstream parties in the political process.[78] The more
regulated the parties have become, the fewer activists and members they
have.[79]

The loss of party members thus owes to changes at the top in party
leadership and financing as well as the bottom of the party as a mass organization. At the top, party leaders do not need to maintain or consult any
members; decision-making is done by an elite tier. And in the electorate,
voters feel more alienated from the formal structure of the party. The
consequence is that parties are solely elite enterprises. Voters' values have
also changed such that they no longer want formal attachments to stodgy
institutions like parties. The stark materialism of the past was associated with industrial economies, when a "working class" and an "upper
class" were clearly delineable in a way they aren't today. Further, as people gained economic security, scholars noted a shift to "postmaterial"
concerns beyond bread-and-butter issues. In the 1980s, political loyalties to parties began to fray as voters shifted attention to issues such as
environmentalism and rights for historically marginalized groups. Voters
were likely to be cynical of established power and authority, such as that
embodied by parties. Patterns of electoral behavior in the 1980s showed
that voters were increasingly likely to split their votes between different parties, opt for new parties (like green parties), or disavow political
participation altogether.[80]

Were locally organized parties better able to understand and respond
to people's needs? Parties had typically done the work of connecting
neighborhood associations and families to city hall. As intermediaries,
they served as "focal points of community life, and as links between the
community and the larger political world."[81] The history of the mass
party shows a relationship between parties and democracy—one that
builds upon and amplifies the impact of civic activity on social capital.
It might seem as if a citizen's relationship to a party is transactional: you
interact with a party so as to elect a specific candidate or press a certain
issue. But the party, as a permanent and ongoing association, allowed citizens to come together apart from supporting a specific interest. Party
involvement is purposive, helping to bring people "into contact with

other values and interests, compelling them to adjust their demands, and, ideally, to consider the broader public good."[82]

From Local to National Parties

Representative David E. Price has served the 4th district of North Carolina since 1988. Before that, he was a political science professor at Duke University. In his 1984 book, *Bringing Back the Parties*, he wrote, "[T]here is a social context of democracy, of the sorts of interaction and communication that are required if political efficacy is to be experienced throughout the society and if unifying notions of the common good are to emerge. Political parties may have filled these needs imperfectly, but nothing currently on the horizon promises to be an effective substitute."[83]

We take the dominance of the mainstream parties of the right and left for granted, but in recent years new parties have capitalized on the sentiment that the parties are a self-serving cabal. Despite their waning popularity and low membership numbers, the mainstream parties continue to be better funded and to command larger vote shares than newer or niche parties.[84] While the parties today share the same names and, to a lesser extent, the same values and ideologies of their prior incarnations, they are actually quite different organizationally. They retain far fewer connections to the electorates they represent. They often base their legitimacy to govern not on ties to specific constituencies but on vague promises that they will govern more responsibly than their opponents. By the 1980s, party organizations had become "bureaucratic, vertically integrated, technologically sophisticated, professionally staffed, and financially endowed."[85]

Parties were once socially embedded, local, and materially distinct. After the 1980s, they underwent a process of nationalization and professionalization, focusing their priorities solely on electoral performance rather than representative integrity or integration. As a result, voters—the people—have lost the foremost way of engaging consistently with politics, of learning the values of deliberation and pluralism, of seeing the process of interest aggregation and compromise unfold.

All these trends have contributed not only to a decline in the civic capacity of mass publics but also to vacuums in representation that make democracy vulnerable to radical extremists. The parties began to nationalize in the 1980s; over the next few decades, they became more polarized while economic inequality grew. This process was mediated by the way parties reoriented their economic positions in a neoliberal era, to which we now turn.

CHAPTER 4

Parties and the Third Way

In May 1998, leaders from the world's wealthiest countries gathered for the G-8 summit in England to discuss matters of shared concern, including sustainable growth and free trade. After a weekend of meetings, Prime Minister Tony Blair of Great Britain and President Bill Clinton of the United States left their counterparts—Russia's Boris Yeltsin, Germany's Helmut Kohl, and France's Jacques Chirac, among others—to retreat to Chequers, the country estate of U.K. prime ministers. There, they engaged in a "wonkfest," the term they coined for their lengthy political discussions, and debated the future of the left.[1]

These wonkfests were opportunities for Clinton, Blair, and their trusted advisers to discuss policy agendas they wished to develop not only within their own countries but across all industrialized democracies. They aspired to help all parties of the left reinvent themselves by navigating a Third Way in politics that combined traditional social democratic goals with conservative approaches to the state and society. They moved away from long-held party positions on welfare spending and redistribution, free trade, and regulation.

Clinton and Blair had known each other for years as self-styled party reformers and were both influenced by ideas developed through transatlantic relationships among their advisers. Soon after the Labour Party secured a parliamentary majority in May 1997, Clinton and Blair got to work advocating their new left approach. Wonkfests, Third Way dialogues, and bilateral meetings between Blair and European leaders took place over the next two years. Prior to German elections in September

1998, Blair and Gerhard Schröder, the leader of the German Social
Democratic Party, released a policy paper titled "Europe: The Third
Way" that laid out shared goals and approaches:

> We need to apply our politics within a new economic framework, mod-
> ernized for today, where government does all it can to support enterprise
> but never believes it is a substitute for enterprise. The essential function
> of markets must be complemented and improved by political action, not
> hampered by it. We support a market economy, not a market society. . . .
> We invite other European social democratic governments who share our
> modernizing aims to join us in this enterprise. . . . This requires adher-
> ence to our values but also a willingness to change our old approaches
> and traditional policy instruments.[2]

Acknowledging and celebrating "personal achievement and success"
were imagined to be critical to the creation of wealth. Likewise, state
action was seen to impede entrepreneurship, so the state should "row,
not steer." Thus Blair and Schröder renounced the goal of "equality of
outcome," emphasizing instead the "importance of rewarding effort and
responsibility." The policy document advocated lower corporate taxes,
lower rates of social spending, flexible labor markets, liberalized capital
markets, and welfare-to-work policies. It also emphasized the role Europe
would play as a political actor, as the European Union moved toward
greater integration.

Rather than rely on stodgy class politics, Blair and Schröder declared
that the left could not be an "ideological straightjacket." Instead, they
claimed, "people want politicians who . . . search for practical solutions
through . . . well-constructed and practical policies." They welcomed
the structural economic shifts taking place, including the expansion
of some sectors and the decline of others, as well as the transformation of technology and skills-based labor. By 1998, social democratic
or labor parties were in government in thirteen of fifteen European
Union countries. And while these leaders recognized that transitioning to the global economy would produce winners and losers, they
hoped that the disruptions would be minimal and ultimately worth the
sacrifice.

This chapter ties some of the changes to party organization, particularly on the left, to party decisions that were consequential for the management of democratic capitalism. While historians date the era of neoliberalism to the 1970s, the 1990s accelerated the uptake of neoliberal ideas in a few key ways. The first was the end of the Cold War and the resulting rush to liberalize markets and politics. There was no longer an alternative to democracy or to market capitalism. The second was the movement toward integrated economic trade regimes. The Treaty on the European Union was signed in Maastricht in 1992, and the EU took shape over the next few years before ratification of the Treaty of Lisbon in 1997. Canada Mexico, and the United States also signed the North American Free Trade Agreement in 1992. By 2001, China had acceded to the World Trade Organization. As trade barriers fell, easing the movement of goods, services, capital, and people, societies also began a process of transformation.

Globalization and large-scale economic changes, such as deindustrialization or financialization, are sometimes considered shocks—as if they occur externally to politics. Economic policy, however, is squarely within the realm of politics. This chapter examines how parties across the ideological spectrum signed on to neoliberal policies, and adopted more, not less, similar views on the relationship of states and markets.

Did these economic policies reflect what voters wanted? Parties of the left arguably needed to find new policy appeals after electoral defeats throughout the 1980s. But moving "to the center" does not entail a specific agenda. Centrism has no clear base. The political center is a nondescript place, a nonexistent voter—yet it looms large in the public imagination.

The end of the Cold War inaugurated a period of peace and prosperity in the countries of the West, and the leaders of left parties oversaw a period of remarkable economic expansion as well as greater global integration. The traditional ideological distinctions of left and right eroded as parties reached a near-consensus on economic management. The appeal of centrism lies in its seeming adaptiveness and flexibility. But in privileging short-term electoral gain, centrist approaches rob

parties of their purpose: to think of the long-term interests of different
constituencies and to reconcile them with short-term electoral priorities.

The End of Traditional Liberalism in the United States

Party systems are characterized by competition between parties, which
typically distinguish themselves through their policy objectives and
goals. These objectives are themselves rooted in something akin to
ideology—conceptualizing the relationship of state and society in a way
that defines the obligations between political leaders and their citizens.
Policy choices reflect not only what elected officials promise they *will*
do but also what they think the state *should* do. In the postwar period,
the choice between parties was often a choice between traditional liberalism and conservatism. Convergence was on the horizon, however, and
it would change everything.

In the 1970s, social democratic parties held fast to the three broad
commitments of traditional liberalism: a commitment to redistribution
through social policy and taxes, to job security, and to holding corporations accountable to employees.[3] In 1972, the Democratic platform
included reducing military spending, amnesty for draft evaders, and ratification of the Equal Rights Amendment. It called for busing to end
school segregation and expansion of welfare programs, including an
unprecedented call for a guaranteed income. But the economic crises of
the 1970s—the "noxious bog of unemployment and inflation"—forced
a reckoning with these positions and led to an intellectual turn away from
the economic theory and policy of Keynesianism.[4] The Keynesian consensus had long supported government intervention in the economy,
but a new wariness of "big" states called into question the role of the
government in achieving desired economic and social outcomes.

Conservative parties, which advocated paring down the size of the
state and cutting social protections, were newly ascendant. The conservative revolution unleashed new ideas about the state and markets at the
same time it called into question the nature of parties and democracy.

In 1975, a private organization known as the Trilateral Commission issued an influential report, *The Crisis of Democracy*. David Rockefeller, chairman and chief executive of Chase Manhattan Bank and a scion of the Rockefeller family, had formed the commission in 1973 to bring together commercial leaders, academics, and prominent state officials from North America, Western Europe, and Japan. The Trilateral Commission report aimed to establish why democratic governments had lost legitimacy among the public.[5]

The problem with democracy, the commission concluded, lay in governability. Democracies simply lacked the ability to address problems, despite having effective bureaucracies and institutions. Without a "reassertion of governing authority," distrust in public officials would continue to worsen. But this authority could not simply stem from public spending, since Keynesian policies and generous welfare benefits were exacerbating the economic crisis. The report called for political leaders to shrink the scope of the state, while also strengthening its administrative capacities—to do things efficiently, with less red tape.

The conservative project of shrinking the size of the state and emboldening capital was not simply the product of the Trilateral Commission, of course, but was also the result of larger societal and institutional forces. Business became better organized, particularly against regulation and corporate taxation.[6] A network of think tanks, academics, and businesses financed and coordinated the rightward shift of the Republican Party in the Reagan era.[7] Conservatives swept successive elections, with Republicans in power in the United States from 1980 to 1992, the Conservative Party in government in Britain from 1979 to 1997, and the Christian Democratic Union in Germany from 1982 to 1998. These parties did not govern identically, but Ronald Reagan and Margaret Thatcher embodied and continue to symbolize the emergence of a new conservatism that saw free markets and small government as key to growth and to liberty. Each dismantled the Keynesian welfare capitalism that had dominated politics in the United States and England since World War II.

The interests of economists calling for less regulation and greater flexibility in price and labor markets dovetailed with the ideals of conservatives espousing a doctrine of personal responsibility. Reagan's economic policies cut corporate and personal tax rates and privatized government services. The new conservatism of the 1980s curtailed social programs directing aid to the poor.[8] Reagan took aim at social spending on unemployment insurance, Aid to Families with Dependent Children, and Medicare and Medicaid; the latter two programs had grown from 1.4% of the federal budget in 1965 to 10% by 1981. As academics argued for the benefits of lowering taxes and spending, the director of the Office of Management and Budget, David Stockman, "reject[ed] the notion" that the "Federal Government has a responsibility to supplement the incomes of the working poor."[9] The Reagan administration slashed funding to federal programs for entitlements, education, and worker training, while increasing military spending.

Although Democrats kept a hold on the House of Representatives and also state legislatures, party leaders wondered how, or if, the party would be able to win national elections again.

Converging Parties and Centrist Policy

Conservative victories throughout the 1980s prompted an identity crisis among parties of the left, which could no longer advocate traditional liberalism and win national majorities. They now needed to reconsider their commitments to their core goals. The Democrats' crises of electability stemmed not only from the party's infighting over candidates and positions but also from a lack of new policy ideas. After 1980, a coalition within the party began to criticize the party's seemingly rigid adherence to New Deal ideas and constituencies. The House Democratic Caucus, led by Representative Gillis Long and his executive director, Al From, focused their energies on revamping Democratic policies and priorities. They established working groups and committees to rethink the party's approaches to government spending and economic growth in particular.[10]

In 1985, a group of Democratic politicians announced the formation of the Democratic Leadership Council (DLC). The chairman of the DLC, Richard Gephardt of Missouri, proclaimed the council a "way station or bridge back into the party for elected Democrats," emphasizing that the group's motivations lay in the party's ongoing electoral defeats.[11] It "broke fundamentally" with Democratic Party strategies, particularly the party's reliance on "minorities, New Politics issue activists, and labor."[12] By prioritizing electability concerns the DLC's strategies were avowedly *anti*party: they did not concern themselves with party-building or working with existing constituencies to develop a blueprint for party renewal. The DLC did not aim to represent anyone, but instead to position the party for greater electoral success.

This elite and technocratic approach to party governance inverted the typical way that party leaders connect with constituencies. Strong parties derive intellectual and social legitimacy from their linkages to distinct segments of society; this intermediary function is why parties are the lynchpin of representative democracy. But this new elite politics, as planned and carried out by experts, technocrats, and party leaders, disconnected parties from the public. Local party offices and ties to communities and civic groups withered. Parties privileged candidate service and fundraising, with little effort to reach out to voters. The DLC mobilized support by traveling to cities to dine with potential donors. While the DLC opened a few state chapters in the late 1990s to involve politicians sympathetic to its policies, these chapters served as a vehicle for Clinton's presidential campaign in 1992. As From describes, these chapters were shuttered once Clinton was elected. The DLC preferred to keep in touch with state officials online, "without the hassle of managing state organizations."[13]

And the policy decisions made within conservative and social democratic parties alike reflected skepticism of government intervention, austerity in social welfare programs, and pro-business, pro-trade positions. While social democratic parties still championed issues like poverty reduction, access to healthcare, and protection of the environment, their policies accomplished these goals through markets rather than states, often over the opposition of their loyal voters. Rather than embracing conflict and negotiation, the DLC eschewed it, approaching policymaking as something done by experts with little input from other groups. When From invited Virginia governor Chuck Robb to serve as DLC chair, he promised that Robb would "answer to no one but himself when proposing controversial ideas."[14]

Around the same time, a set of ideas emerged in policy circles that branded itself "neoliberal." This approach married traditional liberalism (protection for individual rights and the inclusion of marginalized groups) with a wariness of big government and disdain for interest-group politics.[15] The neoliberals aimed to solve the ideas deficit on the left; it replaced placating specific constituencies with a nonparty "collection of journalists, academics, politicians . . . linked by a common belief in the growing obsolescence of conventional politics."[16] They shared with conservatives a focus on the market as a source of entrepreneurship and freedom. Doing so would create growth and maintain America's global leadership on economic and security matters.

The DLC was the vehicle for the uptake of neoliberal ideas into the Democratic Party.[17] In 1989, the DLC opened the Progressive Policy Institute (PPI), a think tank to hone Democratic Party policy. Including the word "progressive" in the name was a way, according to From, to make it "harder for reporters to label it . . . conservative."[18] The PPI's 1989 paper, "The Politics of Evasion: Democrats and the Presidency," argued that the Democrats needed bolder policy ideas because they were losing low-income voters, particularly in the South and Midwest. On economic issues, foreign policy, and social issues like race and crime, the Democratic Party was too out of touch, losing too much ground to Republicans. The paper concluded by recommending "recapturing the center" in explicit ways; emphasizing values of "individual responsibility, hard work, equal opportunity—rather than the language of compensation," it also proposed that "the central purpose of criminal punishment is to punish."[19] The authors cited the British Labour Party and Japanese Socialist Party as examples of successfully moving from left to right.

The DLC's "New Orleans Declaration" in 1990 laid out principles for a "post-industrial, global economy." Government would replace entitlements with personal responsibility and replace redistribution with freer markets. The DLC hoped to achieve liberal outcomes through improving education, expanding job training, building infrastructure, and national service. Most important, it sought "liberal ends through market means" by conditioning government benefits on employment and by expanding opportunities for the poor by encouraging investment in markets.[20] Critics like Jesse Jackson derided the DLC as "Democrats for the Leisure Class" and continued to advocate cutting military spending, imposing higher taxes on the wealthy, and expanding domestic spending on social programs.[21] Yet Democrats had shifted decidedly to the right as a way of co-opting some of the rhetoric against the state and in favor of the market. Social democratic parties embraced market solutions, free trade, and growth through liberalization—the core tenets of neoliberalism. Democrats in the United States, the British Labour Party, and the German Social Democratic Party all made an effort to *un*distinguish themselves from their rival parties by adopting conservative economic positions as part of a growth agenda.

Party leaders elected in the 1990s ran under the banner of long-standing parties but led them in new directions that reflected changes domestically and globally. The DLC faction captured the Democratic nomination in 1992, and Bill Clinton defeated Republican George H. W. Bush and Independent Ross Perot. His administration moved the Democratic Party to the right, particularly on free trade, deregulation, and market-based growth strategies. After two early defeats, one on healthcare and another in the 1994 midterms, when the Republicans regained control of the House for the first time since 1952, the Clinton administration turned even more decisively away from traditional liberalism.

The Clinton administration relied heavily on pollsters and strategists rather than party brokers to forge relationships with the electorate. Pollster Dick Morris suggested "triangulation," a strategy for Clinton to "adopt the most popular parts of the Republican agenda . . . and claim them as his own," particularly on issues like budget deficits, the size of government, and welfare spending.[22] And this is precisely what the Clinton administration did. Reflecting on Clinton's economic policies,

Jeffrey Frankel and Peter Orszag, economists who both served on Clinton's Council of Economic Advisers, wrote that the administration's overarching vision "sought to adopt some of the promarket orientation associated with the ascendancy of the Republicans in the 1980s."[23] They were proud of "progressive fiscal conservatism," which combined "modest attempts at redistribution . . . [with] budget discipline." The party's approach to governing was to take an explicit backseat to the activities of the market. The 1993 budget agreement "substantially reduced the scope for policy-makers to create or expand" programs, and policy therefore became a matter of "small-bore" activities.[24]

In 1993 Clinton also entered into the North American Free Trade Agreement, legislation staunchly opposed by labor unions in the United States and environmental groups. At a meeting in 1993, unions vowed to defeat members of Congress who voted for the agreement, which they saw as a "life or death issue."[25] Jesse Jackson led protests against the trade agreement, while Clinton's secretary of labor, Robert Reich, touted the benefits of free trade and its potential positive impact on job creation.[26]

Other notable policy achievements of the Clinton administration included the Personal Responsibility and Work Opportunity Reconciliation Act of 1996, which reformed welfare in multiple ways. It replaced Aid to Families with Dependent Children with a new program, Temporary Assistance for Needy Families, which implemented work requirements for welfare recipients and gave states greater latitude in administering benefits. Welfare policy had long been on the Republican agenda, including in Newt Gingrich's Contract for America after 1994. Other public services were also scaled down or privatized. Clinton relied on enterprise zones—tax breaks and less regulation—to spur urban development, an approach favored by conservatives. The Clinton administration also "accelerated the scale and destruction of public housing" and, in 1999, banned public housing funding from being spent on construction of new housing units.[27]

Whereas parties had once been active in shaping policies to achieve goals related to employment, prices, or financial regulation, now political leaders delegated decisions about fiscal management to nonelected authorities. The Clinton administration's monetary policy, according to the administration's economic advisers, "was simple to state: leave it to the Fed."[28] The Federal Reserve, the central bank of the United States, has become the sole actor when crafting the nation's monetary policies. Its decisions have distributive consequences, but central bank independence has been a critical pillar of economic management.[29] Delegation to central banks was a concession to financial and business elites, a promise that workers' concerns would be secondary to the need to control inflation. This also allowed politicians to throw up their hands when faced with difficult questions of the trade-off between unemployment and inflation. While macroeconomic management used to be subject to processes of democratic deliberation, it is now solely the province of central bankers, who answer to no constituents.[30]

In 1999, Clinton signed into law the Gramm-Leach-Bliley Act, or Financial Services Modernization Act, that repealed Glass-Steagall prohibitions on commercial, investment, and insurance activities among firms. Glass-Steagall, more formally the Banking Act of 1933, had separated commercial from investment banking after the financial crises of the 1930s. The new act had the effect of encouraging consolidation in the financial industry and expanding the availability and use of financial products.

The philosophy of centrism that characterized the DLC entailed accepting much of the logic behind conservative policy and *de*politicizing economic issues. The role of parties was no longer to discern the interests of party members but instead to govern "responsibly" by pursuing policies that fostered growth—in hopes that the effects of that growth would be rewarded at the ballot box.

Across the Atlantic

The British Labour Party also struggled to define itself after Thatcher's Conservative government took office in 1979. Thatcher broke decisively with Keynesian policy: to curb record high inflation, she implemented a program to tightly control the money supply, privatize state-owned industries, and reduce income taxes while raising consumption taxes. The Thatcher government passed legislation restricting closed union shops and types of collective action; a year-long miners' strike in 1984 ended with a victory by the Conservative government and the closure of coal mines. Unemployment rose, union membership declined, and the safety net shrank. Thatcher was reelected twice more, and her legacy in Britain includes reduced social spending, deregulation of product and financial markets, and privatized public services.

Thatcher's liberalizing reforms changed both Conservative and Labour party positions in the direction of less state intervention. Like the Democratic Party in the United States, the Labour Party also struggled with "electability" in the 1980s; under Thatcher, the party remained committed to preserving unions' right to strike, greater distribution, and nationalization of industry. But young Labour Party activists sought a new direction. Future prime minister Tony Blair, then an MP from Sedgefield, organized study groups to modernize the Labour agenda. In 1993, Blair and Gordon Brown, who would later succeed Blair as prime minister, met with members of Clinton's transition team for tips on "seizing the initiative on crime . . . and emphasizing private sector growth."[31] Blair was elected leader of the Labour Party in 1994 and worked with a group of advisers—including the Labour Party's director of communications, Peter Mandelson—to rebrand the party "New Labour" prior to the 1997 general election. They took the critical step of revising the Labour Party's commitment to nationalization of industry by replacing the party's Clause IV with a commitment to democratic socialism.

In 1998, Anthony Giddens—a sociologist and then-director of the London School of Economics—published "The Third Way," a manifesto laying out a new social democracy that combined commitments to equality with personal responsibility, autonomy, and cosmopolitanism.[32] He became a trusted adviser to Blair as the Labour Party embraced egalitarian rhetoric "better suited for a neoliberal age." To address social problems like health inequalities, Blair relied more on markets and less on government.[33]

The Labour Party won the 1997 general elections with a decisive majority. Blair followed the lead set by the Democrats in the United States and enacted economic policies of liberalization and deregulation. The Labour government reneged on campaign promises to raise taxes on top income earners and raise pensions, and instead extended the Conservative tax cuts and spending plans.[34] Blair and Brown, now chancellor of the exchequer, prioritized macroeconomic stability by delegating authority over interest rates to the Monetary Policy Committee and Bank of England. Depoliticizing monetary policy was seen as critical to enhancing the credibility of financial markets and signaled that Labour would hew to fiscal and monetary stability rather than run up deficits through social spending.[35]

After changing Labour's commitment to nationalizing industry, the government pursued further privatization through private finance initiatives, which contracted public services to private providers. While Labour remained committed to investments in health and education, it also delegated more authority and control over public services to the private sector. The government's Working Family Tax Credit increased benefits available to families with at least one adult in employment, and Labour's approach to poverty reduction relied on encouraging or compelling work. Rather than expanding the social safety net, Labour saw "the state's role as stimulating re-entry [of the unemployed] into the labor market."[36] Labour did not reverse Thatcher-era limits on collective bargaining and strikes, although it did implement a national minimum wage and greater protections against workplace discrimination. These protections accelerated a trend toward individual, rather than collective, claims against employers. The net result of Labour policies was further de-unionization of the workforce and greater power in the hands of employers.[37]

With respect to party organization, the Blair government relied on advisers and consultants to formulate policy. Blair, Brown, and advisers like Mandelson and Giddens felt that policy formulation was best left to experts rather than consulting with internal party stakeholders, much like the DLC. In 1997, the party's National Executive Committee and Cranfield School of Management implemented Partnership in Power, a new procedure for policymaking. This procedure replaced policy debates at party conventions with narrow consultation procedures. Policy-specific committees, composed of ministers and party leadership, would develop policies and consult with party members who had questions or concerns, rather than debate and deliberate in settings like party conventions. Thus the autonomy of party leaders in setting decisions expanded, while party activists were sidelined.[38]

In Germany, on the eve of the 1998 election, Schröder's Social Democratic Party (SPD) adopted Neue Mitte—a "new center." Like Blair, Schröder embraced liberalization. He had positioned himself as a moderate in the early 1990s and an ally of business, particularly industrial sectors like biotechnology and computer software. The 1998 elections brought an end to five successive governments helmed by the Christian Democratic Union/Christian Social Union set of conservative parties and the long reign (since 1982) of Helmut Kohl as chancellor.

Schröder's centrist positions on the economy were at odds with other factions in the SPD. The German finance minister, Oskar Lafontaine, was a Social Democrat of the traditional ilk; rather than embracing deregulation, he advocated greater spending to increase demand and reduce unemployment. He called on the German Bundesbank and European Central Bank to lower interest rates and also supported tax harmonization, leading newspapers to anoint him "red Oskar."[39] He pushed back against the provisions of the Neue Mitte approach but courted enough criticism that by March 11, 1999, he resigned. Schröder appointed Hans Eichel the new finance minister; Eichel vowed immediate budget reductions.

Schröder implemented an austerity budget with spending cuts and reduced corporate tax rates while raising consumption taxes on gas and electricity. His budget cut funding to all ministries, including social welfare and pension programs. In 1999, the SPD lost regional elections and faced pushback from trade unions and blue-collar strongholds.[40]

Union leaders spoke out against policies backed by Eichel and Economics Minister Werner Mueller that would reduce corporate taxes and state spending. The president of the German Labor Federation, Ursula Engelen-Kefer, declared that this was "not what we elected them for," while Roland Issen, head of the white-collar German Salaried Workers' Union (*Deutsche Angestellten-Gewerkschaft*, or DAG), called the Neue Mitte "a clear contradiction of the SPD election program."[41]

Nonetheless, the SPD was reelected in a coalition with the Greens in 2002. A year later, Schröder presented Agenda 2010, a set of reforms to labor and social welfare policies. Following the recommendations of the Hartz Commission, chaired by Volkswagen executive Peter Hartz, Germany rolled out four stages of reforms between 2003 and 2005. These reforms created agencies to place people in jobs and new categories of part-time job opportunities plus cut unemployment benefits for the jobless. Opportunities expanded in temporary, contract-based employment, while thresholds for accessing social benefits were raised.[42] Trades unions opposed the reforms, which have been linked to growing income inequality in Germany, and Schröder resigned as leader of the SPD in 2004.

Parties in a Global World

The Third Way was a transnational effort to transform political parties led by the left, and this global orientation legitimized the project of a political move to the right. When Blair was elected in 1997, he recalled his notes from a 1993 meeting with Clinton: simply the words "opportunity, responsibility, community."[43] At meetings in 1997–1998, the Clinton and Blair teams met to strategize making Third Way approaches permanent in their respective parties. Delegates from the United States included Al From, Larry Summers, Andrew Cuomo, and the journalist Sidney Blumental, while Labour sent Anthony Giddens, Peter Mandelson, and David Miliband. Official Third Way conferences over the next year included the Italian premiers Romano Prodi and Massimo d'Alema, the Netherlands' Wim Kok, and Sweden's Göran Persson.

On the eve of European Parliament elections in June 1998, Blair and Schröder released a new policy paper laying out a Third Way for Europe itself. The paper, authored by Bodo Hombach from the SPD and Peter Mandelson from the Labour Party, argued that the success of the European Union would lie in breaking with traditional positions of the left. Europe's left-wing family of parties should embrace a supply-side agenda of fiscal responsibility, deregulation, corporate tax cuts, and labor market flexibility.[44] Equality of outcome, public spending, and state management of market failures were no longer appropriate for societies undergoing rapid change: "The ability of national governments to fine-tune the economy in order to secure growth and jobs has been exaggerated. The importance of individual and business enterprise to the creation of wealth has been undervalued. The weaknesses of markets have been overstated and their strengths underestimated. . . . The past two decades of neo-liberal laissez-faire are over. In its place, however, there must not be a renaissance of 1970s-style reliance on deficit spending and heavy-handed state intervention."

The Blair-Schröder efforts to sell a Third Way agenda was not only an attempt to reorient their own domestic politics but also a call to parties of the European traditional left to steer their countries (and Europe at large) in a more centrist direction. At the time, it seemed like an eminently achievable goal. After the rollout of the Euro, the European Union's policies have relied on a liberalized internal market and central bank independence. Debates about the economic policy agenda in Europe create a tension between the citizens within countries and the supranational leaders who determine EU policy, since backlash to liberalization policies that are not set by domestic governments nonetheless takes place domestically.

The Third Way as a political force did not last. It was so closely associated with individual party leaders in the 1990s that successors struggled to take up the banner. In 2000, a conference of fourteen liberal leaders in

Berlin embraced "Progressive Governance of the 21st Century," with no reference to the Third Way. At the conference, Schröder called for new social compacts to balance free markets, while the Socialist prime minister of France, Lionel Jospin, advocated "globalization with a human face."[45] But the social democratic parties were unable to develop a true philosophical or intellectual alternative to the neoliberal ethos of globalization, with significant effects on their party systems. Robert Taylor, employment editor of the *Financial Times*, wrote in 1999 that the Third Way committed "to a liberalising, market-driven agenda in financial, product, and labour markets," virtually eroding the distinctions between right and left.[46] Ralf Dahrendorf, a German sociologist and former director of the London School of Economics, wrote in *Foreign Affairs* that the shifting policies of Third Way politicians were designed to "deflect criticism as if wearing an oilskin made of a curious mixture of diffidence and dogmatism."[47]

Yet the economic project of the Third Way, of neoliberalism, endured and became inseparable from the process of globalization. As the global economy became more integrated—as barriers to trade fell and corporations expanded their operations across national borders—the contours of domestic politics also changed. In 1952, John Kenneth Galbraith wrote that American business was subject to the countervailing power of government and labor. This was the case when American corporations needed to rely on an entirely domestic business environment: American workers, American consumers, and a national regulatory regime. Globalization and market liberalization altered these dynamics, since states were no longer the site of political power. Political leaders in this period of liberalization prioritized international capital over constituents.[48] To compete in international markets, governments needed to step aside and ease access to credit and to markets, rather than intervene. As a result, globalization "neutralize[d] economic accountability" and generated similar policies across parties.[49]

Globalization shaped party politics and inspired an approach to economic management that prioritized the free flow of goods and capital and less state intervention in the market. Since the 1970s political leaders have adopted the language of governing "responsibly," that is, in a way that delivers consistent growth and stable macroconomics. Problems with few easy or short-term solutions, including economic inequality and climate change, went largely unaddressed. As countries liberalized their economies and signed free-trade agreements, democratic governments promised that capitalism would generate growth regardless of its short-term distributive costs: a rising tide was said to lift all boats. The Western economies at least were well positioned to benefit from globalization: corporations could take advantage of cheaper labor markets or supply chains outside the United States and tap into new consumer markets.

The trend across all the economies of the advanced industrialized democracies has been a process of market liberalization. The 1990s were a critical period in which opposition to liberalization fell away. Instead, party positions across the left and the right reflected what the sociologist Stephanie Mudge has called a "market-centric political logic . . . a cross-partisan *neoliberal politics*."[50] These politics were characterized by macroeconomic reforms, fiscal discipline (through spending cuts), and lowering barriers to trade and financial flows. Indeed, these policies were central to the Third Way approach, producing a greater consensus across the parties on the meaning and utility of government. Rather than using the state to make determinations about redistribution or employment, markets were, in effect, left to make allocative choices under the guise of neutrality.

A stark example of this dynamic can be found in Europe, where the European Union became a powerful supranational actor. In 1992, the Maastricht Treaty brought together twelve member states of the European Communities to form a shared currency, citizenship, and defense. The Euro was adopted as a common currency in 1999, and the European Central Bank sets fiscal and monetary policy across the member states. The EU establishes criteria for inclusion in the union, particularly governing national fiscal and monetary policies. Countries are required to control inflation, deficits, and exchange rates; they also must loosen restrictions on the flow of capital, goods, and people. EU membership has impacted the domestic policies of the EU countries in a direct way: since the major parties cannot really differentiate themselves on economic policy, there is far more convergence between the parties of the left and right than there once was.[51] When countries join the EU, they become more likely to amplify differences on cultural and symbolic issues rather than play up economic positions.[52]

Declining levels of trust in parties and governments are rooted, in part, in the economic consensus between the parties that emerged at the end of the twentieth century. Party convergence—the embrace of neoliberalism and globalization—has contributed directly to "anti-system" parties in Europe, which are more likely to stake out clear positions on redistribution, EU membership, and immigration than are the mainstream parties.[53] In a study of voters across sixteen European countries from 2001 to 2013, convergence among the mainstream parties led voters to reject those parties in favor of non-mainstream parties.[54] Therefore, while voters may still perceive that there are important differences between the mainstream parties, convergence nonetheless creates opportunities for new parties or factions—particularly at the political extremes.

Blurring Political Distinctions

Other parts of the world where parties have adopted similar neoliberal policies and embraced globalization have experienced a backlash against all mainstream parties. In Latin America, for example, structural adjustment programs in the late 1980s and early 1990s wiped out distinctions between parties of the left and the right. In some cases, leaders elected on socialist platforms implemented austerity and liberalization. Convergence has led voters to reject party leaders and, in some cases, undermined the entire party system.

The Latin American experience with liberalization shows how economic policies affect party systems. Parties that veer too far from their traditional constituencies can erode the trust they've built with their bases—a process of "brand dilution" that makes it hard for voters to know where parties stand on issues.[55] In Latin American party systems, the blurring of traditional differentiations between left and right was pronounced when parties of the left, like labor parties, implemented structural adjustment and economic reforms. Left and right became increasingly meaningless, and voters were left with the impression that none of the parties represented their interests. Worse yet, convergence can destabilize the party system as a whole by creating voids in representation and opening opportunities for extremists. Regardless of the content or effects of the policies themselves, the mere fact that parties on one side of the ideological spectrum move to the center can make the party system weaker overall.

In the postwar period, many countries in Latin America pursued economic development through state-led, rather than market-based, strategies. Policies of import-substitution industrialization in the postwar period relied on nurturing domestic industry through high tariffs and state intervention in large industrial sectors of the economy. When Latin American governments experienced an ongoing series of debt and fiscal crises in the 1980s, the international community responded with demands for market liberalization. The economist John Williamson coined the term "Washington Consensus" to describe the ten policy areas that Western governments and international lending institutions believed were necessary to address the Latin American debt crisis. They included fiscal discipline, reducing public expenditures, reducing barriers to trade (i.e., tariffs), privatizing state enterprises, and deregulating many aspects of the economy. These policies emphasized the need for "positive real interest rates, competitive exchange rates, and more secure property rights" to attract foreign direct investment and deter capital flight.[56]

These reforms had a significant impact on parties and party systems. In countries where the major political parties agreed on neoliberal reforms, there was less differentiation between parties in the party system. The situation was the same in countries where parties on the left, with deep ties to labor unions, adopted neoliberal programs. The economic policies adopted by the parties had the effect of weakening the party system as a whole, because they eroded the basis of representation for huge swaths of the population— particularly those who felt economic dislocation as a result of structural adjustment.

The party politics of this era have been characterized by "bait and switch" policies.[57] As Susan Stokes argues, "it was not always the era of economic liberalization via democracy . . . [because] the neoliberal economic revolution was not approved ex ante by popular mandate."[58] Instead, leaders who campaigned explicitly on leftist platforms took office and implemented liberalizing reforms in the late 1980s. Because there was not stable opposition to economic policies, voters had no ability to channel their grievances into the political mainstream. These party systems faced backlash from the public, as citizens took to the streets to protest many of these reforms. Further, in the long run the parties lost voters, since "uncertainty as to what parties are likely to do in public office can inhibit the creation or reproduction of name-brand loyalties among the electorate."[59]

In Argentina, Carlos Menem was elected president in 1989 after a campaign promising higher wages, state ownership of industries and utilities, and potential non-repayment of Argentina's debts. Menem was a Peronist candidate, and the Peronist party (Partido Justicialista) was a populist party with long-standing ties to labor unions. His campaign promises ran counter to those of the candidates from the incumbent center-left party as well as the conservative party; both of those candidates called for liberalization of trade and privatization of industry. Once in office, though, Menem appointed a conservative as labor minister and a vice president of a large conglomerate, Bunge & Born, as finance minister.[60] His chief debt negotiator with foreign lenders was the presidential candidate from the party of the right. Menem's cabinet implemented strict austerity measures, including currency devaluation and privatization of telecommunications, airlines, media, steel, and other industries. In the immediate aftermath of reforms, economic dislocation left many working-class voters worse off: wages declined, and unemployment rose. Over time, Menem's strategy appealed to middle-class voters; he appointed technocrats and business leaders to government positions, and dismantled labor unions (while also offering concessions to unions).[61] Throughout the 1990s, public support for parties and the legislature declined. Ultimately, the strategies of the Peronist party reshaped the party system in Argentina over successive economic crises around the turn of the century.[62]

A similar dynamic happened in Venezuela, which was one of Latin America's stable democracies. The Democratic Action Party was traditionally aligned with labor and competed against the conservative Independent Political Electoral Organizing Committee. In 1988, Carlos Andrés Péres, who had once been vice president of the Socialist International, was elected president from the Democratic Action Party. While he had long been aligned with policies like a minimum wage and state intervention, he implemented a "Great Turnaround" in 1989 that included privatization and trade liberalization. Pérez stopped price controls, floated the nation's currency, and passed reforms supported by the IMF. As prices for gas and bus fares rose, however, citizens protested, culminating in Venezuela's first-ever general strike.[63] The public lost faith in the governing parties, neither of which successfully responded to the economic crisis or opposed neoliberal reforms. In 1992, a young military officer named Hugo Chávez attempted a coup; in 1998, he was elected president. Widespread opposition to the policies advocated by both of the main parties led voters to reject the parties altogether and to embrace a candidate who vowed to transform the political system.

The Latin American experience of structural adjustment was stark, involving a complete restructuring of the economy. But market liberalization had serious consequences, and when parties seemed inattentive to those consequences, they left citizens with no way to articulate their needs or grievances. Unsurprisingly, the result was widespread distrust of the parties overall.

The Once and Future Left

The dynamics of centrist, Third Way politics in the liberal democracies of the West were less dramatic than the upheaval in Venezuela but followed a similar pattern. Parties of the left abandoned long-held positions that severed ties to loyal constituents and moved the parties of the left and right closer together on economic issues. The platforms of the mainstream left and right parties became less differentiated on issues like trade, regulation, and redistribution at the turn of the twenty-first century.[64] When the mainstream parties all signed on to the neoliberal orthodoxies of the 1980s, they removed from public deliberation the policies most fundamental to everyday well-being: those that governed people's access to jobs, their incomes, their opportunities, their mobility. Over time, they left people with little faith in the ability of ruling parties to address their concerns.

Yet the electoral success of the Third Way parties showed just how effective a policy of triangulation could be. After all, the American electorate had changed significantly since the 1970s. The "traditional constituencies" of the social democratic left—blue-collar, unionized workers—were only a small proportion of the workforce by the 1990s. In 1975, 25% of the labor force in the United States worked in manufacturing; by the 1990s, the rate was only 15%. More workers pursued college, and women began to constitute a greater share of the workforce. Because of these changes, the political scientist Herbert Kitschelt wrote in *The Transformation of European Social Democracy* that social democrats would no longer answer primarily to the working classes. Instead, "education, occupation, gender" would shape "political consciousness . . . in more powerful ways than class."[65] The Third Way parties changed long-standing alignments of class and party, particularly the alliance of the left with the working class. Parties of the left adopted a policy agenda that, in many cases, left the working class worse off. Parties could afford to do this because they were actively courting new constituencies within the electorate, including highly educated, skilled workers in professional or managerial roles.

Class is a muddled term to begin with, but growing differentiation within sectors of the economy makes it even harder to establish solidarity along class lines. The fastest-growing employment sector has been the service sector, which obscures traditional class divisions by encompassing so many types of employment: personal services, retail, hospitality (restaurants and hotels), as well as healthcare and law. Services account for 70% to 80% of the American workforce, but "there is no unity to [this] vast residual category."[66] People working for globally competitive corporations may orient themselves toward libertarian politics of lower regulation and taxation to favor greater corporate profits. Over the 1980s and 1990s, educated and skilled workers with preferences for growth voted for social democratic parties but exhibited "left-liberatarian" attitudes, creating challenges for social democratic party leaders. Social democratic parties might be able to cater to pro-capitalist, libertarian constituencies while also supporting public sector workers, but Kitschelt argued that they could not do this *and* support blue-collar workers—especially in industries requiring protection from trade. Social democratic parties have lost the votes of unskilled and semi-skilled workers.[67]

At the same time, centrist and Third Way politics have attracted salaried workers in skilled employment, especially managers and professionals whose incomes steadily rose over time. Third Way policies favored a growth agenda, one that let markets decide which industries were productive and profitable. In an increasingly interconnected global economy, corporations could move some of their operations to places with cheaper labor and less regulation through processes like offshoring. In semi-skilled and low-skilled jobs, wages began to stagnate; workers hoping for government relief or inclined toward redistribution found little reception in any of the mainstream parties. Left parties did little to compensate their domestic workers whose opportunities were hurt, rather than enhanced, by global competition. The political left has expanded its middle-class vote share since the 1990s, while the working classes have become politically adrift.[68]

The electorate has changed not only in the composition of the work-force but also in the preferences of younger, educated voters. These voters are more inclined toward issues like environmental protection, social justice, and identity and recognition (women's rights, LGBTQ+ rights, etc.) than traditional tax-and-spend issues.[69] In response to these trends, parties differentiate themselves more on *values* issues—for example, traditional values associated with law and order, religion, and family versus cosmopolitan issues associated with rights protections and inclusion.[70] Values differences have increasingly supplanted economic differences, and Kitschelt predicted that without new ways of discussing questions around distribution—with no alternative to market liberalism beyond something like "socialism"—social democratic parties would find it increasingly difficult to respond to competing left-libertarian demands.

Further, the parties themselves have changed. As the educated upper-middle classes saw their incomes and opportunities grow relative to those with less education, labor parties—which, in the past, had been channels for recruiting and electing working-class representatives—became more elite themselves. Increasingly, representatives came from highly edu-cated, professional backgrounds, with incomes far above those of their constituents.[71] In 1945, 56% of representatives in the House and 75% of senators had college degrees, while in 2021, 94% of House members and all senators graduated from college—and 66% and 75%, respectively, had graduate degrees.[72] In Britain, 40% of Labor MPs had working-class jobs in 1960; by 2005, that number was down to the single digits, and only 1% of Labour MPs had worked for a union in 2015.[73] It is therefore unsur-prising that a significant change in parties of the left was not only a shift in policy but also a rejection of the language and necessity of class politics. The Labour Party's manifesto in 1997 called for setting aside "the bitter political struggles of left and right. . . . Many of these conflicts have no relevance whatsoever to the modern world—public versus private, bosses versus workers, middle class versus working class."[74]

The Third Way parties were instead more likely to couch issues in terms of "working families," "human capital development," and "social investment" rather than in terms of class divides, labor unions, or even "the unemployed" and "the poor."[75] By accepting the logic of the market, by embracing wariness of the state, and by delegating decisions about economic policies to nonelected bodies, party leaders effectively shed their responsibility to consider the needs of their former constituencies.

The organization of Third Way parties was top-heavy, as party leaders honed their ability to deliver messages rather than to receive them. Peter Hall argues that the neoliberal "growth regime" privileges more elite parties, which must sell an agenda of liberalization to constituencies that may not support them.[76] Demands for neoliberalism were not going to come from citizens themselves, even middle-class ones. Parties replaced the input of members and civic groups with consultants and strategists who could promote these policies to the public. Through new techniques of representation, like polling and message targeting, parties obviated the need to consult with voters.

Finally, as parties across the political spectrum adopted similar approaches to economic management, they accelerated the integration of the global economy and the movement of goods, capital, and people across national borders. This has had dramatic consequences for domestic politics, producing new cleavages around immigration, nationalism, and redistribution. There may be realignments along new class-party lines, with working-class voters choosing parties of the right that are anti-immigration and protectionist (antitrade). Parties that carry the banner of centrism, on the other hand, may continue to support globalization, skilled workers, and more immigration.[77] The material distinctions between the parties have not disappeared since the turn toward centrism in the 1990s. Rather, they have reemerged in a new political context, sometimes under the rubric of "cultural" or "values" differences.

Parties Today

In the 1990s, parties of the left were elected to power across many of the liberal democracies. In many cases, they inherited a new kind of conservative politics, one that eschewed state intervention, redistribution, and regulation. In response, parties of the left modernized themselves, combining neoliberal economic approaches with social commitments. Accelerating trends of party decline outlined in previous chapters, the factions styling themselves as new versions of old parties (New Democrats, New Labour) required very little party infrastructure. They privileged an elite and technocratic decision-making favoring globalization and growth and sidelined the voices and views of opponents. As the political scientist Peter Mair explained, this was an abdication of politics itself—of the negotiation, compromise, and mediation of competing interests that once characterized party leadership.[78]

Not only did the politics of centrism reduce the contestation critical to party systems, but it had another important effect. Through austerity and deregulation, parties deprived themselves of critical levers they used to respond to the demands of citizens. Healthy partisan attachments are the product of what scholars call "programmatic linkages": if you need something from the government, a party wins your loyalty by providing it through policies. But as party connections to local groups and citizens eroded, public perceptions that politicians were willing to act on voters' demands diminished. Economic inequality rose under both conservative and liberal governments, and party leaders have been likely to attribute this to "forces" beyond their control—those related to globalization or corporate interests. The primary beneficiary of centrism turned out to be the private sector itself—those whose economic and political advantages grew as the state receded. Parties became increasingly porous to those with money and closed off to those without.

CHAPTER 5

Selling the Party

Only a few decades ago, the similarities between the Republican and Democratic presidential candidates occasionally overshadowed their differences. In 2000, George W. Bush, the governor of Texas, seemed affable, if not quite serious; Al Gore, a two-term vice president, was known as a policy wonk. But both men were political scions: Bush was the son of former president George H. W. Bush, and Gore's father was a long-serving senator from Tennessee. Both were from the South, both from political families, and both establishment members of their parties. As governor, Bush's signature policy achievements included education reform (allowing high-performing high-schoolers admission to Texas colleges) and tort reform. Gore was passionate about the environment and the development of a high-tech sector.[1]

During the 2000 presidential campaign, the two candidates made promises to voters largely in line with the centrist visions of their parties at the time. Bush dubbed himself a compassionate conservative who would cut taxes and pursue school accountability. Gore promised fiscal discipline and targeted tax cuts, while protecting social programs like Medicare and Social Security. In the presidential debates, their efforts to distinguish their policy agendas were often fodder for parody. Each employed image consultants to burnish his credibility and appeal, and to make the candidates distinct one from another.

The issues at stake in the 2000 election were soon eclipsed by the administration of the election, the result hanging on a ballot recount in the state of Florida. The Supreme Court's decision in *Bush v. Gore* halted the recount process on December 12, 2000, and Gore conceded the presidency to Bush. Thus the 2000 election is best remembered for the court battle rather than the campaign. But the election revealed just how much parties had changed over time—particularly in how they use campaign consulting, communications technology, and digital outreach to curry support. This chapter traces how the economic consensus of the third way dovetailed with party priorities that increasingly devoted resources to campaigns rather than linkages with citizens

The Third Way changed the parties of the left, steering them away from traditional social policy or pro-labor orientations and toward a free-market, deregulated, and depoliticized stance on economic issues. Enabling this shift was a technocratic turn in the parties themselves related to the communications revolution of the late twentieth century.[2] Parties have increasingly come to rely on professional strategists who find ways to make policies appealing to different segments of the electorate. The role of the politics industry, including campaign consultants and public relations specialists, has been to displace the role once played by local parties.

The number of consulting and strategy firms has exploded, blurring the lines between advertising, politics, and data science. Often, these firms are started by people with experience on political campaigns. But the firms apply techniques of marketing to corporate and political clients alike and have become a lucrative line of work. Given the wealth of information about voters that is readily available, it would be silly for political operatives not to use it. However, some of the consequences of shifting to the technologically sophisticated campaign have been to change the meaning and nature of party relationships with voters. One difference between consultants and party operatives is that consultants don't have to win elections for their candidates. Most are paid on a fee-for-service model; very few receive bonuses for victories. Their goal is therefore to spend as much of the candidate's money as possible and bring further awareness to the campaign in order to draw in more money. By providing commercial services, Adam Sheingate argues, consultants hone their own craft—a type of political work characterized by appealing

to individual opinion rather than partisan identity alone.[3] They bor-
row strategies from the business world and have become more deeply
institutionalized as a profession. In 1987, Neil Fabricant and Stanley
Kelley—a former ACLU lawyer and Princeton professor of political
science, respectively—created the first graduate program in political
management at the City University of New York. The first trade publication for consultants, *Campaigns and Elections*, began publishing in
1980.

The growth of politics as an industry fosters deeper relationships between elected officials, their campaign staff, and the private sector. Campaign spending has increasingly gone to consulting and strategy firms to create ads through traditional and social
media.

Consider that the 2000 election was the most expensive in history up to that point, costing around $2.4 billion. (For compari-
son, the 2020 presidential election cost $6.5 billion.)[4] In 2000, the
top soft money donors to the Democratic Party included seven
labor unions, whereas the top Republican soft money contribu-
tors were corporations, including AT&T, Philip Morris, and phar-
maceutical companies Bristol-Myers Squib and Pfizer. In addition to
these traditional sources of funds, the parties now solicited individual donations. Individual donors have become much more prominent in campaign financing, with sectors like finance, real estate,
electronics, and single-issue advocacy groups dominating campaign
spending.

Institutional investments in the national party committees have
focused on the capacity to raise money, while delegating issue advocacy
and "outreach" to the private sector—albeit a subset of the private sector that is invested in political outcomes.[5] The development of policy
is increasingly the purview of experts drawn from industry, business,
and think tanks. And while campaign finance reforms are mostly aimed
at party spending in elections, the diffuse world of policy itself has
also become more responsive to well-resourced groups with a policy
agenda.

From Members to Respondents: The New Science of Partisan Attachment

Party membership, either formal or informal, used to be the way people became connected to parties. Membership is distinct from *affiliation*, which is a mere psychological sense of attachment to a party. The attachment may be based on something like alignment of party priorities or even alignment of values, but attachments may also be indistinguishable from fandom. The way that party membership differs from party affiliation is in the practice of politics, the investments of time and energy that turn you from a supporter of a candidate or a cause into more of a stakeholder. While party membership has traditionally been the heart of a party's organizational structure, today parties are top-heavy. There has been a sidelining of meaningful participation in favor of outreach. This helps parties target likely voters in elections, but does nothing to make people feel connected beyond the ballot.

Parties have many ways of reaching voters today: mail, television ads, email, digital ads. As parties have centralized their activities in their national offices, they have reduced reliance on local parties. The way parties assess what voters want has been fundamentally shaped by the party's way of selling its candidates. As campaigns utilized new communications technologies, so too did parties increasingly rely on communications specialists to determine voter preferences. How do parties assess what their members or base want? How do they navigate competing or conflicting preferences? Alternatively, how do they assess what voters, writ large, want? How do they then go about determining how to respond to these interests? While many political consulting firms are associated with a major political party, consulting has displaced the party as the place where campaign messages are crafted and honed. The rise of a politics industry has gone hand in hand with a nationalization of parties, but has also, somewhat paradoxically, facilitated disjuncture between what candidates do and what parties may want candidates to do.

Selling the President

Over time, as parties developed their fundraising and marketing apparatus, they co-opted the work once done locally by party members. For example, groups like the National Committee for an Effective Congress (NCEC), established by Eleanor Roosevelt in 1948 to elect progressive candidates, had specialized in understanding voters and data to help candidates with targeting. But in the age of television and the associated ascendance of advertising, campaigns changed. In the 1952 presidential campaign between Adlai Stevenson and Dwight D. Eisenhower, television networks were hesitant to broadcast political campaign advertisements. Stevenson chose to give thirty-minute speeches on air, eschewing slick advertisements, reasoning, "I think the American people will be shocked by such contempt for their intelligence; this isn't Ivory soap versus Palmolive."[6] Eisenhower, on the other hand, worked with Madison Avenue advertising firms and Hollywood producers on ads like the famous "I Like Ike" animated spot. This was a "sea change in politics [that] elevated the role of advertising experts and media consultants in campaigns as it simultaneously debased the content of their messages."[7]

An advertising executive named Rosser Reeves, famous for the "M&Ms melt in your mouth, not in your hands" slogan, decided to create "spox" for Eisenhower—one-minute spot ads that ran between television programs. To determine the content for these ads, Reeves mailed inquiries to tens of thousands of *Readers' Digest* subscribers asking for their concerns. He also met with pollster George Gallup, whose polling company regularly surveyed American public opinion. Reeves then determined that the Eisenhower campaign would focus on three issues: the cost of living, political corruption, and the Korean War.[8]

In 1951, Clem Whitaker and Leone Baxter started Campaigns, Inc., the nation's first political public relations firm. They had worked on political campaigns on behalf of trade unions and companies in California, helping candidates and political causes by honing messages, mailing pamphlets and postcards, and advertising through newspapers and radios. By 1968, the International Association of Campaign Consultants had formed; in 1969, so too did the American Association of Political Consultants (AAPC). Within twenty years, the AAPC had grown from forty to eight hundred members.[9] Candidates for the Senate or for governor hired full-time directors of research and polling.

In the 1970s, the NCEC began geomapping—combining information on who had voted (which they obtained by contacting election boards) with maps of districts. A decade later, the NCEC specialized in developing indices of precincts to predict how well Democrats would perform, how they could persuade, and how get-out-the-vote efforts would fare.[10] The relationship between the party and the party base was increasingly top-down and one-way; parties controlled messaging, relying on political consultants and public relations specialists to sell policies to segments of the public.

Marketing the Party and Targeting Voters

Hiring a consultant has become crucial to political campaigns. In 1990, around 46% of candidates for the House of Representatives hired at least one consultant; in 1998, candidates hired at least five consultants and incumbents averaged at least seven. The work of political consulting has also become very specialized, with media consultants to help with radio and television advertisements, direct-mail specialists, and consultants who conduct opposition research.[11]

Consultants have taken over much of the work previously done by local parties, in particular. A study of congressional campaigns through the 1980s found that local precinct captains used to oversee public opinion and mobilization by working with party volunteers; canvassing involved building trust with voters, learning neighbors' attitudes, and conveying information to county and state party leaders.[12] Now consultants for hire make it easier for candidates to develop their own campaigns. Although they still run under a party label, the party plays little role in recruiting or selecting candidates or financing their campaigns.

Because the locus of campaign activity has shifted to the national party, candidates rarely even contact their local party. They are "better off distancing themselves" from parties to cultivate a personal following or to show that they are outsiders.[13] Local parties find themselves with little to do besides occasionally providing volunteers for campaigns or distributing campaign materials such as lawn signs and posters. Only 15% of local parties report receiving any kind of financial or operational assistance from state parties.[14]

National parties and political consultants use personal information to create profiles of likely voters or donors using data. This entails a buildup of the parties' likely-voter databases. In the 1980s, the Republican National Committee established its Voter Vault; the Democratic National Committee established Datamart. These databases of voters contained such information as voting histories, census data, and data from consumer marketing companies. Data-mining techniques became more sophisticated after the Motor-Voter Law of 1993. The National Voter Registration Act required states to digitize and integrate databases on voter information that included full names and addresses and personal information like birthdays, party affiliation, and political activity (i.e., political donations). Data-mining firms like Aristotle, Inc. combined this information with consumer data and email addresses to sell to clients. The early days of campaign consulting involved bringing in advertising experts; by 2000, thousands of people called themselves campaign consultants. In his study of political consulting, Dennis Johnson describes the evolution of "targeting" over time and the way consultants use personal information to create profiles of likely voters or donors; for example, in the 1970s a Republican consultant noted that families with daughters enrolled in Brownies (young members of the Girl Scouts) were likely political targets.[15]

For political parties, direct mail became an effective way to reach voters and solicit funds. Direct mail had the advantage of allowing parties to go back to known donors or to find likely ones by triangulating consumer information with voter information. Because parties could create profiles of likely voters and target them directly, they could in effect create their constituencies, whether "suburban moms" or "urban professionals." Yet direct mail was expensive, given that mailing lists needed to be purchased and there were costs associated with postage and processing.

Email outreach is considered the modern-day version of "grassroots politics," given how little actual grassroots politics there is. There has been a rise in face-to-face contact for voter mobilization, with evidence that talking to a party volunteer can increase voter turnout.[16] While party volunteers knock on doors in the weeks leading up to campaigns, there is little party presence at the local level otherwise. Further, the data analytics game usually ensures that the same profile of voter is contacted repeatedly rather than reaching out to people who might require persuasion. Those who volunteer for these campaigns tend to be more extreme and demographically unrepresentative than the voters they reach.[17] Finally, the consulting industry has its own goals, related to profits and industry competition, that may be at odds with what candidates need.[18] Communications technology has made it easier to reach voters and to guess how they will vote.

Voter Lists and Campaign Donations

As technology became more sophisticated, the need to fundraise dovetailed with cheaper ways of soliciting funds. In 1996, Bob Dole was the first presidential candidate to ask people to visit www.DoleKemp96.org, his campaign's official website; the site received 2 million hits the next day.[19] By the early 2000s, Voter Contact Services and a partnership of companies calling themselves the Voter Emailing Company merged their databases to match email addresses to voter lists. The political strategist Max Fose, who was the internet manager for John McCain's presidential campaign in 2000, noted, "Now, we not only have TV, radio, print advertising and direct mail, but we can send several emails for a fraction of the cost."[20] For the cost of one piece of direct mail, campaigns could now send one hundred emails to 1 million voters. The *New York Times Magazine* warned that the consequences of microtargeting could be significant: "[T]he candidate knows everything about the voter, but the media and the public know nothing about what the candidate actually believes. It is, in effect, a nearly perfect perversion of the political process."[21] A data-mining firm called Labels & Lists acquired Voter Contact Services in 2011 and created an online subscription service at VoterMapping.com to geomap its data and allow instant geotargeting.[22] In 2008, Barack Obama's campaign hired a national targeting director who worked closely with Harold Ickes's Catalist data management firm to reach Democratic voters.

In 2012, strategists pointed out that because many television viewers were using DVRs to record programs, they were no longer watching commercials. The presidential campaign that year, between Barack Obama and Mitt Romney, responded by focusing on email and internet ads instead, becoming the first digital campaign.[23] Candidates, parties, and super PACs paid over $3.6 billion dollars to consulting firms to handle the new approach.[24]

Campaigns continue to rely on the strategies of companies like Democratic DSPolitical, CampaignGrid, and Targeted Victory, which honed microtargeting techniques. Using a rich trove of data on individual habits, hobbies, interests, and internet activity, these companies assemble fine-grained profiles of voters. They work with companies that track personal internet activity via millions of cookies, including Yahoo, Microsoft, and Experian. Their explicit aim is to craft specific messages for voters that might move the needle in very close races; for example, in one Democratic race among four liberal candidates in 2012, a company called Precision Network helped state legislative candidate Morgan McGarvey target "voters under 35" and "women who voted in the past 3 of 5 elections."[25] Companies increasingly specialize in matching consumer preferences to political preferences; they've found that Levi jeans, Subarus, and clear liquor are associated with Democrats, while Wranglers, Cadillacs, and brown liquor are associated with Republicans.[26]

As campaigns have moved online, voter outreach now takes the form of highly targeted messaging over email and digital platforms. In 2016, the firm Cambridge Analytica illegally hacked the Facebook profiles of millions of users to create a database to sell to political campaigns. The Trump campaign then hired Cambridge Analytica to conduct "psychographic microtargeting" of likely Trump voters. However, at issue in the Cambridge Analytica scandal was far more than just campaign techniques. The company had done work for the British Conservative Party and the Brexit campaign and was associated with conservative figures; its principal was Robert Mercer, one of the top donors to Trump's campaign. Mercer's daughter Rebekah Mercer and Trump's later chief strategist, Steve Bannon, both served on its board. For Trump's campaign, Cambridge Analytica harvested data on as many as 87 million Facebook users to build psychological profiles of voters, although Facebook's terms disallowed apps from selling such data.[27] Cambridge Analytica was interested in using personal Facebook data to identify five personality types, each of which require tailored messages.[28]

Although there is little evidence that psychographic targeting is an effective political strategy, campaigns have always been a game of inches.[29] Digital strategies are able to do many things at once: reach many voters, while knowing a great deal about them, plus raise money, while also spending money on advertisements to highly segmented slices of the electorate. A study by the British think tank Demos concludes that digital strategies will become the primary way campaigns reach out to voters.[30] Polling is also changing, increasing the use of cell phone (as opposed to landlines) and online polling.[31]

People are aware that politics is a game of messaging. Adam Sheingate argues that there can be cynicism toward political consulting, a sense that one is being manipulated: campaigns now are part of a "media-intensive politics born from an unending search for more precise measures of public opinion and more effective means of political persuasion."[32] These strategies have become influential outside the

United States, with political consulting a routine part of services performed by public strategy conglomerates. The politics industry may be
value free; it is not a pure political project. Dennis Johnson also notes
that outsiders, like super PACs, can and do utilize these digital strategies themselves. Candidates may be "drowned out by outside voices,
hyperbole . . . massive spending . . . fake websites," but they are also
engaged in "7,000 variations of their basic message" rather than a set of
policies.[33]

Politicizing Civic Activity

Political strategies are not just limited to professional lobbying. Policy advocacy overall has also been shaped by the professional politics industry. Edward Walker notes the rise of public affairs consulting, which provides "third-party allies or grassroots recruitment"
to lobbying firms pursuing political goals. For example, for-profit
universities worked with advocacy professionals to create an organization called Students for Academic Choice. This organization
recruited students from for-profit schools to lobby against the Obama
administration's gainful employment rule, which examined whether
or not graduates from for-profit universities made enough income
to pay back their student debt, threatening underperforming private universities with a loss of federal funding. (The rule passed but
was later overturned by President Trump's secretary of education,
Betsy DeVos.) Students for Academic Choice collected signatures for
a Department of Education petition and spoke on behalf of the
universities.

    As Walker details, these kinds of professional advocacy services create
what he calls a "subsidized public"—an ad hoc mobilization of specific types of people who tend to be politically active and educated
in order to "help elites win legislative, administrative, and other policy issues."[34] This work expands traditional lobbying beyond campaigns
with the goal not simply of persuading elected officials or bureaucrats

to adopt certain policy positions but of serving as "mediator[s] between corporations, organized interests, and the state." Professional political advocacy provides the veneer of legitimate political participation where none existed before.[35] As policy campaigns, such efforts have the effect of collapsing the distinction between professional advocacy and interest groups.

The expansion of a private sector for politics therefore has changed how parties operate while also amplifying preexistent inequities in political participation. Democracy has long been favorable to the wealthy. Most, if not all, democracies are stratified along lines of income and socioeconomic indicators like education. In a seminal study of American pluralism, the political scientist E. E. Schattschneider claimed that the "heavenly chorus" of civic activity "sings with a strong upper-class accent."[36] Casting a ballot, attending a political rally, contacting your representative: all forms of political participation require time and energy, and it has long been the case that people with more education and income are more politically active. Voter turnout, for example, has long been biased toward higher-income, more educated voters. This bias in participation is amplified by the growing porousness of parties to influence from well-resourced groups. Parties have come to rely on the private sector to supply financial resources for campaigns and elections, as well as technical know-how for policymakers.

Parties increasingly think of voters as data segments to be captured, and they devote resources to the technology of campaigns. This amplifies problems with money in politics, since everyday citizens have limited means of intersecting with parties. We now turn to the world of campaign finance, which creates incentives for parties to cultivate well-heeled donors and interests. According to a recent report by Nathaniel Persily, Robert Bauer, and Benjamin Ginsberg, "individuals with means can associate more freely and efficiently in collective efforts to influence the political process. Moreover, they may now do so with greater opportunity to arrange their participation with limited or no public disclosure."[37]

Wealthy Donors

Wealthy donors have always been an important source of financial support for parties, and today there are many more avenues for wealthy donors to influence elections beyond candidate campaigns and party committees. In the 2016 presidential election, both campaigns benefited from billionaire largesse: by the week before the election, nineteen billionaires had donated $70 million to the super PAC Priorities USA Action to support Hillary Clinton, while at least $18 million raised from four billionaires went to super PACs supporting Donald Trump.[38]

Wealthy influence in elections is not simply the result of direct financing of individual campaigns, because there are still legal limits on how much people can donate to candidates. There are no limits, however, on how much can be given to outside groups working on campaigns. According to reporting from the *Wall Street Journal*, some fifty-six donors who gave $1 million to campaigns in 2016 gave $200 million to the outside groups backing the candidates.[39] Labor unions and their affiliated groups gave about $33 million. By the time of the November election, the campaigns had raised $685 million ($56 million coming from Trump himself to fund his campaign), and super PACs raised another $205 million.[40] Individual donor families have eclipsed organized and corporate interests in their campaign largesse; the Adelsons and Mercers were critical backers of Republicans in 2016, just as the Steyers, Pritzkers, and Soros families were for Democrats.

Billionaires were even more important to the 2020 election. Together, the top twenty donors spent over $2.3 billion.[41] On the left, Michael Bloomberg alone gave over $1.2 billion in total campaign contributions, and donors from tech and finance like George Soros, Dustin Moskowitz, Reid Hoffman, and Sam Bankman-Fried gave tens or hundreds of millions. More billionaires donate to the Republican Party, although more money was raised in 2020 for Joe Biden. The Adelsons, Richard Uihlein, Kenneth Griffin, and Stephen Schwartzman also gave tens of millions.[42]

Examining campaign finance is critical to understanding how parties have become weaker over time. Not only does money amplify the voice and influence of the wealthy in politics, but it also subordinates the work of the party to the activities of outside groups. Small donors, like large donors, are also ideological.[43] Together, these trends make parties reliant on money that does not come from a representative cross-section of society and makes it harder for parties to prioritize issues and candidates from their large bases of supporters.

While many candidates usually run with a party label, the effect of money in politics has been to scramble what the party label actually means. When parties exert seeming influence in elections, their candidates are more likely to win.[44] But campaign finance allows anyone—whether or not they reside in a district—to have a say in primary and general elections. Part of this contributes to an overall nationalization of election campaigns, whereby national issues and leaders become important to even local and state campaigns.[45] Further, the more donors come from outside a candidate's district, the more responsive that candidate tends to be toward a national donor base.[46] Many donors have expressive motivations; they are not interested in access to a candidate but instead in ideological affinities. One study found that senators' preferences and votes are much more aligned with the ideology of their donors than of their constituents.[47] PAC money is becoming more ideological as well. Increasingly, novice candidates receive a growing share of funds from single-issue or ideological PACs in primary elections.[48]

While incumbents used to have a tremendous advantage in elections, easily winning their seats even when facing primary or general challengers, that pattern has recently begun to change. Since 2014, experienced candidates have won fewer than 50% of their primaries, compared to the period 1980–2014, when they won 73%.[49] More money has flowed to outsider candidates, particularly those who articulate a position distinct from that of the incumbent. An early notable primary loss was the defeat in 2014 of Eric Cantor, the House majority leader in the Republican Congress. Cantor was widely considered a successor to John Boehner, then Speaker of the House, but was defeated by the economics professor David Brat. Brat's primary campaign took aim at Cantor's insufficiently conservative stance on immigration, and although Cantor spent millions more on his campaign, Brat won the primary—and the congressional seat. (He held the seat until 2018, when Abigail Spanberger, a Democrat, defeated him in a general election.)

Financing the Party: Regulations and Democratic Tensions

One of the reasons parties and policy are so influenced by the preferences of the rich is because campaign financing has become one of the foremost ways of participating in politics. Because American parties are not financed by the state, they are dependent on donations from individuals, corporations, unions, and other groups to fund party activities. Americans are wary of this relationship—of the way campaign finance might create biases or quid pro quos between elected officials and donors—and rightly so. Campaign donations are associated with greater access to legislators.[50]

The effort to regulate campaign finance dates to the early twentieth century. In 1907, Congress passed the Tillman Act, prohibiting corporations and banks from contributing to federal election campaigns. The Federal Corrupt Practices Act required parties to disclose their campaign receipts and established limits on campaign contributions. Progressive-era reforms like the Hatch Act limited the ability of government workers to engage in political activities. But between loopholes and lack of enforcement, early reforms did little to regulate campaign finance.

In the period after the Second World War, state party committees still conducted most of the party's activities. They received contributions from the wealthy, many of whom were executives at corporations, but corporations themselves could not directly contribute to parties.[51] Labor unions, in response, organized PACs. In 1955, the American Federation of Labor and Congress of Industrial Organizations merged and created a Committee on Political Education (COPE). Union members could donate to COPE, whose funds were distributed to candidates or for educational purposes. By the mid-1950s, there were 17 national and 155 state and local union PACs.[52] They were seen as a necessary counterweight to the money of wealthy donors, which went largely undisclosed and unregulated into the parties.

Over the next two decades, the national parties began to coordinate more campaign activity. Campaign expenses grew, particularly because television ads were costly, and parties devoted more resources to innovating their financing strategies. In addition to direct mail, parties began to cultivate donors by offering expensive dinners with political leaders or by allowing companies to sponsor party conventions. Professional and trade associations also began to form their own PACs: the National Association of Manufacturers PAC dates to 1963, and the American Medical Association PAC to 1961.[53]

A series of regulations in the 1970s and in 2000 led to procedural changes to party organization that shifted the balance of power between formal party organizations and external groups. Parties underwent a series of reforms to reduce corruption (or the perception of corruption) and open the party decision-making process to those outside party leadership. These reforms weakened state patronage networks and led state parties to lose influence in the nomination and primary process.

The Federal Election Campaign Act of 1971

The modern campaign finance regime was created by the Federal Election Campaign Act (FECA) of 1971 and amendments to FECA in the early 1970s. This legislation implemented disclosure requirements for candidates, parties, and PACs. It also created the Federal Election Commission (FEC) and mandated caps on amounts that individuals could donate to campaigns and parties. A few years later, the Supreme Court invalidated FECA's limits on campaign donations in *Buckley v. Valeo*, which set the standard that money is speech and that nonparty

groups can spend unregulated and undisclosed money on issue advocacy
and voter mobilization.

Nevertheless, parties remained central to campaigns in the decades
after FECA. The FEC allowed parties to raise unlimited amounts of
soft money for party activities that were not directly related to the election of specific candidates. Soft money could be used for party-building
activities, including funding state parties, voter mobilization, and registration. Trade associations and corporations developed more PACs,
which allowed them to pool donations from individuals. Under FEC
rules, parties, campaigns, and PACs must disclose their donors' identities
and donation amounts.

The Bipartisan Campaign Finance Reform Act

As the cost of campaigns rose in the 1980s and 1990s, parties came
under fire for using soft money as a conduit for political corruption. Parties developed regular donation programs, like leadership councils and
large fundraising dinners. Some were big-ticket programs—the Republican Eagles, for example, committed donors to $10,000 annually; by
1984, at least 865 people were signed up. Democrats expanded their
small donor base through telephone solicitations and direct-mail programs. Throughout the 1990s, as soft money receipts grew, campaign
finance became a political issue; for example, Republicans in Congress
accused Bill Clinton of offering stays in the Lincoln Bedroom of the
White House to large donors. In 2000, the parties collected a total of
$500 million in soft money accounts, amplifying fears of corruption,
and by 2000 soft money totaled almost 40% of all party receipts.[54]
Public opinion was decidedly negative, 85% of Americans reporting in
1996 that PAC money was too influential and that parties were out of
touch.[55] Congress passed campaign finance reform in 2002 with the
Bipartisan Campaign Finance Reform Act (BCRA), which placed limits on party financing of candidates and elections, closing soft money
loopholes.

BCRA changed the relationship of parties to outside groups in the world of campaigns and elections. With limits on soft money, BCRA achieved its goal of stemming the money raised and spent by the parties. But as the constitutional law scholars Samuel Issacharoff and Pamela Karlan have written, campaign finance reforms have a hydraulic effect: reforms cannot reduce the amount of money in politics, only redirect where it goes.[56] After passage of BCRA, spending shifted to 527s (so-called because of their tax status), political organizations regulated by the IRS but not the FEC. Outside groups began spending more money. In the presidential campaign of 2004, groups on the left like MoveOn and America Coming Together raised over $20 million.[57] Between 2000 and 2008, independent expenditures in federal elections went up by 425%. The immediate effects of BCRA were evident in the presidential election of 2004, when Swift Boat Veterans for Truth ran national ads against Senator John Kerry, the Democratic candidate. The election law scholar Nate Persily noted that BCRA was likely to empower nonparty groups, giving leaders "less ability to aggregate the different interests groups into a party" and weakening party ties to voters.[58]

Citizens United and Political Expenditures

These days campaign finance may seem like an unregulated free-for-all of fundraising and spending. The 2020 presidential election, the most expensive in history, cost a whopping $14.4 billion. The presidential contest alone cost $6 billion (Figure 5.1).

The Cost of Campaigns

While parties have undoubtedly gotten richer in the twenty-first century, the money they spend on politics has since been dwarfed by groups outside the party, particularly after the landmark Supreme Court decision *Citizens United v. Federal Election Commission* (2010). The Court

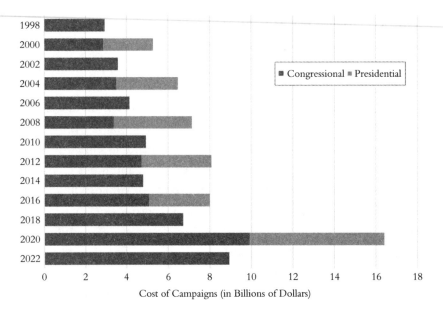

Figure 5.1 Campaign Costs, 1998–2022
Note: Data form Opensecrets, accessed December 2023.

ruled that corporations and unions can donate unlimited amounts of money to independent expenditure groups engaging in advocacy for or against specific candidates. Corporations, nonprofits, and groups such as PACs could now make unlimited independent expenditures. The decision and its ramifications have shifted the center of gravity away from parties, accelerating the divisions between party and electorate.

The combination of campaign finance laws and *Citizens United* has expanded the scope of what *non*party groups can do to influence campaigns. Rather than a set of campaigns run by the parties themselves, what we have seen is a rise in what scholars have called "shadow parties" or "extended party networks" that do the work of parties.[59] They raise money to help certain candidates (or to campaign against candidates); they can engage in their own issue mobilization and get-out-the-vote drives. There has been a proliferation in the types of entities engaged in campaign activities, expanding far beyond formal parties and PACs.

In a short span of twenty years, super PACs, 527s, and 501(c)4s have almost surpassed parties in the amounts they have raised and spent on campaigns. Whether or not these groups help or hurt parties depends on one's perspective on a party's goals. If the only goal of a party is to win seats in the next election, then in theory these groups are helping to achieve that goal.

Prior to the *Citizens United* ruling, twenty-three states banned independent expenditures by companies; sixteen of those banned independent expenditures by unions as well. After the ruling, states repealed their bans, and independent expenditures rose by 127%. While the share of corporate independent expenditures prior to *Citizens United* was about 44% of corporate and union independent expenditures, after the ruling the share of corporate expenditures rose to 68%. Campaign finance deregulation after *Citizens United* has been associated with changes to policy, such as lower corporate income tax rates and a reduction in civil litigation standards that benefit plaintiffs.[60]

The rise of groups capable of mobilizing their own campaigns, running their own ads, and cultivating their own email lists and donors makes these para-party organizations seem an awful lot like parties in their own right. Yet because parties are office-seeking, they are also held to account in a way these new political entities never are. At least in theory, parties have an interest that goes *beyond* a short-term electoral goal. For party labels to have meaning, they must be identified with a history, with a set of ideas, and especially with particular policies. Parties are distinct from personal campaigns, because party leaders need the party to persist beyond the time any one candidate holds office. Instead, parties are necessary for legislators to act collectively; they coordinate a policy agenda across branches of government and across levels of government.

The political organizations springing up today do not have direct parallels to historical movements for social change or even to earlier pressure groups. Today's 501(c)4s and super PACs are purely campaign-financing entities. Many super PACs are affiliated with former elected officials and staffed by people who are experienced campaigners; 527 organizations are often formed on behalf of parties or in support of electing candidates from a party to a specific office (i.e., the Republican and Democratic governors' associations). Both exist to raise money and to spend it on politics, not to seed ideas in the population or to win support for a cause. Further, unlike civic groups or movements with actual members, these political entities do not answer to the public or to any sort of base. They are solely vehicles created for short-term goals, funded by well-heeled donors who exert tremendous influence in the political process.

Take the example of how candidates raise money today. In the House of Representatives, people are elected to serve a congressional district that is tied, perhaps obviously, to a geographic constituency. In the past, parties had more say over which candidates ran, and parties assessed whether or not candidates were viable within their districts. In a study of state-level parties, Ray La Raja and Brian Schaffner found that states that funneled money through the parties elected more moderate candidates than states that allowed more outside money.[61]

If parties were the ultimate arbiters of which candidates could run or which issues should prevail in a campaign, then they would need some way to hold these outside groups accountable or to reject their views in the political process. But parties cannot aggregate and mediate interests if they are beholden to these interests. When aspiring candidates or well-organized factions within a party can simply accumulate their own resources and know-how, the party, as a broker or player, becomes almost irrelevant. For parties to work effectively, other groups, including financing vehicles, personal campaign committees, and interest groups, must answer *to* the party—not the other way around. As the legal status of parties has changed through reforms and Supreme Court rulings, parties have outsourced their vital political functions. They are no longer able to direct funds to candidates who better represent the party or who work with the party.[62]

Para- or Antiparty?

The post-BCRA world of campaign finance is highly decentralized. Candidates increasingly rely on financing from outside the party system, such as highly ideological donors. Outside money was critical to early Tea Party victories, for example, as they "primaried" establishment Republicans. To the extent that candidates build institutions, they can easily build para-party or individual organizations rather than graft on to existing parties.

Obama's presidential candidacy in 2008 is often cited as a modern grassroots campaign that mobilized millions of supporters through digital outreach to propel the candidacy of a one-term senator against that of the seasoned Hillary Clinton. In 2008, Obama's team created My.BarackObama.com, a social networking site that allowed users to access campaign information and organize their own meetups, much like the model of MoveOn.org. As the campaign heated up, there were debates about how Obama's organization would relate to the Democratic National Committee. His team also created Obama for America (OFA), an organization that reached out to potential supporters and small donors online. Campaign lawyers focused on battleground states rather than working through the state parties. Once Obama was elected president, there was conflict over the future of OFA. Christopher Edley Jr., a policy adviser to Obama, suggested that the organization needed to be disconnected from the Democratic National Committee in order to be "authentic and entrepreneurial."[63] Paul Tewes, a political consultant who had directed Obama's Iowa campaign, replied, "[A]s a lover of 'Party' I really don't like this. . . . [I]f the first step is to move outside the party with your organization, the political ramifications and 'future' ramifications need to be thought through."[64] At stake was the fate of the 13 million email addresses and the millions of donors Obama's campaign had collected in 2008. The Democratic National Committee sought to integrate OFA into its activities, arguing that OFA was a de facto list of Democratic voters. But OFA leaders sought to keep it independent of the party and turned it into a vehicle to mobilize support for the Affordable Care Act instead.

In 2010, the Tea Party movement within the Republican Party began fielding candidates to compete against Republican incumbents. Paul Ryan's affiliated super PAC, the Congressional Leadership Fund, is now a grassroots organization with its own in-house research unit, offices in congressional districts, and thousands of volunteers to elect Republicans to the House, with the potential for more influence on campaigns than the Republican National Committee or National Republican Congressional Committee. And Trump's presidential bid in 2016 included no ground game whatsoever; he relied heavily on outreach via social media.

Parties have outsourced vital political functions, including campaigning, fundraising, educating, and mobilizing voters, to outside groups, rupturing many forms of accountability once available to voters. Extrapartisan political organizations, such as Americans for Prosperity, the Koch brothers' advocacy group, also bring significant resources—including money and volunteers—to bear on elections. Super PACs, which are nonaffiliated PACs that can make only independent expenditures rather than contribute directly to candidates, can accept donations of any size and do not have to disclose their donors. Super PAC spending in elections has risen dramatically across the past few elections (Figure 5.2).

Many super PACs are affiliated with former elected officials or political parties and staffed by people who are experienced campaigners. In a study of House of Representatives races from 2004 to 2010, scholars found that candidates who were supported by a network of partisan political groups outperformed candidates who had bipartisan or otherwise "moderate" support, largely because this network of ideological donors and organizations lent credibility to a candidate's party label.[65]

Some 501(c)4s are likely closely aligned with the major parties. Crossroads GPS, formed by Karl Rove and Ed Gillespie, spent $17 million in 2010 and $71 million in 2012, all to support Republican candidates. American Crossroads, their super PAC, spent $105 million in 2012, most funds going to TV commercials.[66] Other 501(c)4s have been behind challenges to establishment Republicans. The conservative Club for Growth, for example, vets conservative candidates and supports a small-government, antitax agenda. The Club for Growth has spoken explicitly about its disappointment with party leaders in Congress, including Senator Mitch McConnell and former speaker Kevin McCarthy, to put pressure on the parties.[67]

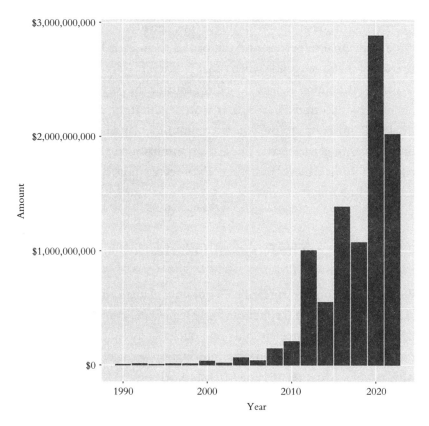

Figure 5.2 Outside Spending in Elections, 1990–2022
Note: Spending by nonparty groups including super PACs and political nonprofits. Data from Opensecrets.org.

As money moves away from parties and toward nonparty groups *at the expense* of parties themselves, parties have lost ground, competing with "ideological nonprofits, wealthy individual donors, and Super PACs for influence over candidates."[68] The goals of these organizations are altogether different from those of the party in that they value ideological purity above all else. The purpose of the organization is not, in other words, compromise or even candidate viability. Thus the rise of nonparty politics has fueled partisan polarization, which results from ideological coordination *within* the parties and fragmentation *outside* the party. Outside groups with single-issue agendas have become much more influential to parties, and the parties themselves have fewer ways to control the issue agenda when other political players can do the work of parties. If political money now flows outside the party, power itself is no longer concentrated in the party as an organization. Meanwhile, parties lose connections to the voters, communities, and civic groups that once constituted their base. These relationships used to be critical to a party's ability to achieve "pluralist goals of aggregation, compromise, and coalition-building."[69]

The Roots of Polarization

One of the defining features of contemporary American politics is partisan polarization. The Republican and Democratic parties seem bitterly divided, unable to agree not only on policies but even on the problems themselves. They disagree on facts, information, science; they disagree on fundamental issues related to citizenship, nationhood, and belonging; they even seem to disagree on the meaning and practice of democracy.[70] It is not just our leaders and parties who are polarized but also society: partisans show hostility toward members of the opposing party, and this "affective polarization"—whereby partisanship becomes part of your social identity—can influence friendships, employment, the news you consume, and where you live.[71]

Party systems require some degree of polarization: voters need to discern one party from another, and parties provide different sets of choices to voters. For party labels to be meaningful, they must be associated with distinct ideas and policies. However, the divisions between the parties today seem, at worst, to be an existential threat to our democracy itself. And the idea of strengthening parties, or making them more responsive and representative, may in turn seem unrealistic—even irresponsible. This section details the nature of contemporary polarization, which has more to do with high-stakes elections than with strong parties.

Ironically, the ideological division between American parties today was much desired at midcentury. At that time, the two parties were composed of various factions that held together Republican and Democratic coalitions. However, these factions were a product of historical circumstance and made it difficult for the parties to articulate ideological differences; as a result, the party system tended to organize around a moderate, but muddled, center. There was a widespread scholarly consensus that healthy party systems needed parties that were easily distinguishable so as to make it easier for voters to identify parties' policy positions and to hold them to account. American parties were considered not partisan *enough* rather than too partisan: they contained too many factions, there was too much split-ticket voting, and there was not enough unity in roll-call votes in Congress.

In 1946, the American Political Science Association created a Committee on Political Parties, which was tasked with developing proposals to strengthen the American party system. Its report, "Toward a More Responsible Two-Party System," was released in 1950.[72] The committee determined that opposition was critical to a responsible party system: voters needed to be able to associate parties with their policies and to use elections as a means to hold parties responsible for their promises. By building a centralized and national party organization and by attempting greater programmatic differentiation, the American party could become "stronger," meaning more "democratic, responsible, and effective."[73] The report has received renewed attention recently because it advocates that parties adopt more differentiated public policy positions, in effect advocating stronger polarization between the parties.[74]

The report's concerns—that American parties were too weak—were echoed in subsequent decades. In 1971, the political scientist Morris Fiorina argued in *Daedalus* that American politics had experienced a "decline of collective responsibility."[75] Noting that scholars as varied as Woodrow Wilson, E. E. Schattschneider, and Austin Ranney had all written about the need for greater responsibility in American politics, Fiorina laid out a case for strong parties. A strong party was one that gave leaders the ability to discipline members, and therefore to pursue programs that were "actually intended to solve a problem or move the nation in a particular direction."[76] David Broder's *The Party's Over* called for more "unvarnished partisanship."[77] The subordination of individual candidates to the party line, according to these scholars, would ease party decision-making and make it easier for voters to assign blame or credit to parties.

Nor were political scientists the only people concerned with the ideological incoherence of the parties. Groups like Americans for Democratic Action and Americans for Constitutional Action began to assess the liberalism and conservatism of the Democratic and Republican parties, respectively. These were not arms of the parties themselves but rather ideological pressure groups that sought greater consistency in the positions taken by the parties. Interest groups devised ways to measure the ideological commitments of legislators. In 1985, Grover Norquist, a conservative tax activist, created an organization called Americans for Tax Reform to support President Ronald Reagan's agenda of tax reform; it received financing from corporate sponsors that included Kraft and Dart.[78] In 1986, Norquist created the Taxpayer Protection Pledge, which asks candidates and elected officials to "oppose any and all efforts to increase the marginal income tax rates for individuals and/or businesses."[79] The pledge was a way to have conservative politicians commit to tax reform and to call out Democratic candidates for raising taxes (or, more specifically, for not opposing taxes being raised).

By the 1980s, the various internal factions within the parties representing different regional, economic, and single-issue interests began to sort themselves into the Democratic and Republican parties along more ideological lines. The Southern Democrats, once a powerful bloc within the Democratic Party, began to shift toward the Republicans. This made the Democratic Party a more reliably liberal party and made the Republican Party more reliably conservative.

Reagan's victory in 1980 ushered in a newly competitive Republican Party and signaled the slow unraveling of the New Deal coalition. The Senate flipped to Republican control that year, and a process of ideological sorting began. While the South was politically conservative, the Democratic Party had been dominant there since the end of the Reconstruction period. This had started to change long before Reagan, particularly over issues related to race. In 1948, Strom Thurmond, a segregationist from South Carolina, opposed President Harry Truman's executive order to desegregate the military. A group of Southern politicians split from the Democratic Party and formed the States' Rights Democratic Party, which was colloquially branded the "Dixiecrat party." The Dixiecrats drew support from Southern states (Alabama, Mississippi, South Carolina, and Louisiana) and fielded Thurmond as a presidential candidate. Although the Dixiecrat faction was short-lived, Southern Democrats continued to block progress on civil rights. The same Southern states that supported Thurmond in 1948 (with the addition of Georgia) supported Republican Barry Goldwater for president in 1964; that year Thurmond switched to the Republican Party.

As conservative Democrats in the South switched to the Republican Party, both parties became more ideologically cohesive—more consistently liberal and consistently conservative. And Republicans also became more competitive electorally. In 1994, the "Republican Revolution" led to party turnover in the House of Representatives for the first time since 1952: 10% of Democratic House incumbents lost their seats, and the Republicans won most of the open House seats, as well a majority of Southern House seats. Republicans also gained in state legislatures: before 1994 they controlled 31 legislatures; after 1994 they controlled 50, and also won 24 of 36 gubernatorial races. Newt Gingrich, the new Speaker of the House, inaugurated an era of heightened partisan rhetoric and firebrand Republican politicians.[80]

Razor-thin margins for the majority in the House of Representatives have increased the stakes of elections. Every two years, members of the House must recapture their seats; this permanent campaign contributes to more uncivil and vitriolic rhetoric.[81] In this era of highly competitive elections, the parties have become more likely to vote along party lines in Congress and more willing to embrace hardball tactics against the other party. This is particularly pronounced during periods of divided government, when the majority party in Congress can block the president's agenda. Polarization has been described as "asymmetric," driven more by the right than the left.[82] There are many factors that have contributed to polarization, including partisan media (particularly cable news and talk radio) and social media, primary elections, and redistricting.

The campaign finance environment has changed since the passage of the Bipartisan Campaign Finance Reform Act, also contributing to polarization. More campaign money flows outside rather than through the party, which limits the ability of parties to control candidates and messages. But there has been a partisan bias in campaign finance as well: many studies have found that after *Citizens United*, Republicans at the state level have received more financing—and won more elections— than their Democratic counterparts.[83] While donor money often goes to Republican candidates, the money is not going to the Republican Party per se. Money collected by super PACs (which can raise unlimited funds from donors they must disclose) and 501(c)4 organizations (social welfare organizations that do not have to disclose donors) can be spent directly on candidates and issues. Not only are more Republicans benefiting from "outside" money, but these Republican candidates are also more conservative than the Republicans they replace and embrace a more conservative policy agenda.[84] Further, the states have been active in driving the rightward movement of the more conservative party.[85] State party platforms, for example, have shown a sharp partisan divide beginning in the 1990s, when Republican and Democratic parties started using different language to discuss political issues. Social issues are particularly charged, with the parties sharply divided on rights (e.g., abortion rights, civil rights, constitutional rights, and workers' rights).[86] Parties are therefore polarized at both the state and national level over similar issues.

How does polarization interact with the trends of party organization discussed in this book? First, the way parties mobilize citizens today—through messages and outreach—gives voters few choices except to respond to the divisive messaging. As elections became more expensive, with television advertising and direct mail serving as the main ways candidates reached voters, parties needed to develop different organizational capacities. They invested in fundraising, public opinion research, and branding and messaging. The centralization and professionalization of campaign activity replaced the party's maintenance of local activists, state parties, and civic ties. A diffuse world of interest groups and donors became important in shaping party priorities. Over time this made parties more ideological—but not necessarily in ways that reflected the preferences of an actual voting base or set of citizens.[87]

Today parties rely less on direct relationships with voters and much more on communications methods that allow the party exclusive control over how to frame issues and sell their positions to voters. They reach out to voters likely to sympathize with the party's messaging through targeted advertising, but mobilizing voters is not the same thing as delivering policy goods. To the extent that parties engage at the grassroots, they focus on volunteers in battleground states and districts in presidential campaigns.[88] The people who receive phone calls and emails from the party are those who are likely to be politically active and to support the party.[89] Direct-mail and telephone outreach are more likely to reach people with stable addresses and with landlines, who tend to be older. While the internet has allowed more access to voters, the people who provide their email address to campaigns are, unsurprisingly, more politically active, and therefore more likely to have higher socioeconomic status and political interest.[90] It is rare, in other words, for parties to reach out to people who are disinterested or marginalized.

Since the passage of the Bipartisan Campaign Finance Reform Act, there are few ways to actually engage citizens at the local level. The state and local parties are no longer a locus of any significant party activity. Over the forty-year span of the 1980s through today, the national party committees have successfully taken over activities like fundraising and public opinion research. These days, local parties may consist of a few individuals who set up a website or a presence on social media, but they are not institutionally connected to the national party. Candidates have little incentive to engage with party committees, since they can simply develop a personal following—particularly when a candidate is challenging someone with the same party label.[91] Yet state parties might be a helpful way for parties to reassert themselves. Seventy percent of state party leaders say they'd prefer more centrist candidates. State parties are the "political equivalent of civil society, building connections, trust, and cooperation."[92]

In theory, polling might have the potential to help parties understand voters. But as parties have deepened their reliance on the politics industry itself—the network of pollsters, consultants, and strategists—this has affected how parties relate to the electorate. The goal of the party is to message issues in the right way during campaign season rather than to integrate the views of party members through an organic process of policy discussion or formulation.

As polling and survey data has become more widely available, it has also led to a shift in how scholars think about parties and the voting public. Conceptually, we collapse survey responses—how citizens feel about parties—onto representation. We assume that if people feel an affinity with a party, they are being adequately represented. The parties, as brands or even as identities, are able to stoke divisions that are undermining our institutions and perhaps even our social fabric. At the same time, they are less representative than they once were. They are more elite; they are more vulnerable to powerful nonparty factions. Parties have lost control over many aspects of politics: nonparty groups organize interests and mobilize voters, and the primary electorate, along with a wide network of donors, select candidates.

In the early days of public opinion surveys, the political scientist John C. Ranney questioned how polling might affect governing. Even if polls could provide politicians with complete knowledge of their constituents' attitudes, including information about the intensity of those attitudes, Ranney noted, this was an inadequate substitute for participation. Political engagement needed to involve deliberation, one component of "an education experience." The polls provide "no mechanism on the popular level for promoting discussion, for reconciling and adjusting conflicting sectional, class, or group interests, or for working out a coherent and comprehensive legislative program."[93]

One paradox of today's polarized climate is that people are not actually engaged in partisan politics itself—in fact, more and more people are turned off by the party system entirely. The political scientist Eitan Hersh describes "political hobbyism" among partisan loyalists, who may be fans of certain candidates or devotees of partisan social media but whose political involvement may be nonexistent (or limited to actions like small online donations).[94] This breeds teamsmanship and high-stakes rivalry but does not lead to higher rates of political participation or involvement; fewer people are actually developing ways to spend their time or energy in productive political activities. According to the Pew organization, more and more Americans find polarization to be a problem. Unsurprisingly, independents are more likely than self-described Democrats and Republicans to dislike both parties. But upward of a third of the American electorate now views both parties unfavorably, which is the highest proportion in the past three decades.[95]

The partisan polarization that has been on the rise for the past fifty years obscures the fact that fewer people are identifying with parties at all. While partisans may feel deeper hostility toward the other party, many Americans are turned off by partisanship *itself*. People who are not strong partisans to begin with are identifying as independents—and not just because they don't like labels (Figure 5.3).[96] In their study of independent voters, Samara Klar and Yanna Krupnikov find that independent voters are not just voters who "lean" toward one party another or another but dislike labels. Instead, the authors find that independent voters are more cynical toward politics, less likely to vote or to become politically active, and more likely to see parties and elected officials as corrupt.[97]

The outside groups that have an outsized influence in elections and campaigns may often work on behalf of a party's candidates, but they are also working at cross-purposes with party strength. As state parties

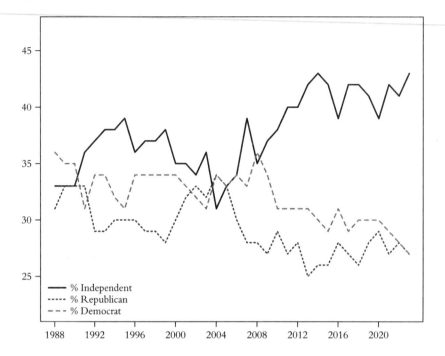

Figure 5.3 U.S. Party Identification, 1988–2022

Note: The graph shows the percentage of respondents to the question "In politics, as of today, do you consider yourself a Republican, a Democrat or an independent?" Accessed at Gallup.com, June 2024.

have lost ground to outside groups, for example, there is a misalignment of goals: while state parties help amplify a party message or reach voters directly and help them get to the polling station, outside groups—often from outside the district or state itself—work only in their own interest. Over time this can cause reputational damage to the parties, as well as brain drain from a pool of potential party activists.[98]

CHAPTER 6

Parties in a Global Economy

While democracy requires political parties, it is not always the case that parties serve democracy. Ideas about what democracy should be, and whom it should serve, evolve over time—and parties, in turn, must also adapt. Throughout history, parties have been central to the tension between what democracy is and what democracy can or should be: they are often the target of criticism when democracy is falling short, but they are also an instrument of change, carrying new values and demands into institutions of power. Parties create a direct link between citizens and governments, but they operate in a broader political and economic environment that is constantly shifting. When social movements, activists, and civic groups need the government to take action on new issues, they pressure parties to take up their cause. Citizens' livelihoods and economic opportunities are determined by an amorphous set of factors, but citizens go to parties to voice their concerns.

Parties do not respond to the many demands of their citizens simply by discussing them or even advocating for them; instead, they must use the tools of government and governance to implement new policies. This ongoing, iterative cycle of responsiveness through policymaking is precisely how parties demonstrate their commitments to supporters and how parties are then held accountable.

Thus far, this book has described how changes to party organization across the twentieth century made it harder for parties to connect to the interests and needs of their bases. The shift from mass organizations with local networks and members to professional and centralized

organizations focused on national campaigns allowed parties to keep
winning elections but over time undermined their ability to connect
with voters. Many of these changes were subtle and gradual. Discontent has also been gradual, with citizens showing a growing disaffection
toward parties but not an outright rejection of them.

In the early years of the twenty-first century, the changes to party organization dovetailed with a bigger reorganization of the relationship of
states and markets. The shorthand for these developments was the rise of
a neoliberal consensus around the role of the state in the economy. While
there were still distinctions between parties of the left and the right,
many debates about the role of markets and states were laid to rest. Parties across the political spectrum embraced free trade and globalization,
which came with its own domestic political agenda, emphasizing less regulation and state intervention in the economy. Although this agenda was
not explicitly branded as such by the parties—politicians championed
growth in general terms—it nonetheless contributed to a perception that
political elites were concerned, first and foremost, with the interests of
economic elites.

Further, parties both explicitly and unwittingly turned toward markets not only to achieve growth but also to provide solutions to problems around employment, housing, education, and community development. They did so by privatizing the provision of many government services and also by placing faith in the private sector to solve
not just economic but also societal problems. This logic of the market replaced the logic of governance: parties no longer championed
government, and therefore deprived themselves of their foremost lever
to respond to citizens. By embracing a method of governing that pri-
oritizes markets and the promise of private sector solutions, parties
exempted themselves from responsibility to respond to the demands
of citizens. And across wealthy democracies—but particularly in the
United States—there is ample evidence of a growing gap in responsiveness. Legislators and party leaders across the political spectrum are
more responsive to the interests of affluent voters than lower-income
voters.

This chapter argues that the discontent with democracy today—often in the form of a far-right challenge to the mainstream parties—is rooted not only in a failure of parties to connect to their constituencies but also in a shared approach to economic governance that renders parties somewhat indistinguishable to voters. The neoliberal consensus of the 1990s–2000s hastened the development of advanced capitalism, with clear economic consequences such as rising inequality and economic insecurity. Economic discontent has inspired a political backlash rooted in a perception that the state itself is oriented toward the protection of special interests rather than the common good.

This chapter takes up an argument from earlier in the book about the relationship between the economy and political parties. The combination of elite party organizations alongside a changing political economy has sown deep antipathy toward parties overall. Economic inequality has not manifested in politics into clear or cross-cutting demands for, say, redistribution (despite a long-standing conventional wisdom that it would).[1] Instead, diffuse discontent with few channels for political participation has evolved into anger. When parties are weak, they become vulnerable to outsiders who stoke resentment and grievance and who mobilize support against democracy by promising to upend the system.

Parties and Economic Consensus

While the previous chapters focused on the activities and priorities of parties over the past fifty years, we now turn to the way domestic and global economics shaped, and were shaped by, the parties. The final decades of the twentieth century saw a reordering of capitalism and a delegitimation of development approaches that relied on centralized or command economies. After the end of the Cold War, the advanced industrial nations, alongside international institutions, oversaw efforts to liberalize markets and politics throughout the rest of the world. These reforms included privatization of state-owned enterprises, reduction of state spending, and tighter macroeconomic and fiscal policy. Neoliberal policies were often administered together, as a means of so-called shock therapy.[2] As governments implemented austerity and structural reform to liberalize their economies, they were also under pressure to liberalize their politics: to establish free and fair elections and the institutions of representative democracy.

These two industries worked in parallel, but not together; to reform economic systems, Western-trained economists (associated intellectually with the University of Chicago and thinkers like Friedrich Hayek and Milton Friedman)[3] advised governments on how to stabilize and modernize their economies. To reform political systems, Western governments, democracy-promotion organizations, and monitoring and watchdog groups provided technical assistance and expertise. They helped with writing constitutions, monitoring elections, and empowering civil society. There was widespread optimism that capitalism and globalization could reduce poverty and produce economic growth in the developing world, and that democratization would allow citizens to hold their leaders accountable. Together, economic growth and democracy had the potential to create lasting prosperity and peace.

Meanwhile, the Western countries that promoted a free-market and pro-democracy agenda around the world were not immune to economic and political changes in their own countries. The historian Gary Gerstle argues that the United States from 1970 onward was characterized by the rise of a *neoliberal order*, a "constellation of ideologies, policies, and constituencies . . . grounded in the belief that market forces had to be liberated from government regulatory controls that were stymieing growth, innovation, and freedom."[4] Neoliberalism was not simply a set of Republican policies, in other words, although Gerstle does point out that "a key attribute of a political order is the ability of its ideologically dominant party to bend the opposition party to its will."[5]

Just as the developing world was being asked to reconfigure its economic and political system to grow their economies, so, too, were advanced industrial democracies undergoing fundamental shifts in how their governments approached economic policymaking. Beyond the actual economic consequences and distributive effects of neoliberal policies, there were also consequences for how parties think about governing. When parties across the political spectrum increasingly embraced the *same goals* (irrespective of partisan commitments) related to economic policy, they became less distinguishable on economic grounds—and more vulnerable to perceptions that the party system, as a whole, catered to corporate or economic interests.

Three dynamics were particularly consequential for political parties: (1) the prioritization of pro-market and antistate policies to prioritize growth above other partisan goals, (2) declining responsiveness in major policy areas, and (3) reliance on the private sector to solve problems.

Party Adaptation and a New Economy

The trade policies of the 1990s created a global economy that was far more economically integrated. Corporations headquartered in one country had supply chains reaching across many others. They increasingly employed people in other countries and sold goods to people in other countries. Writing in *Foreign Affairs* in 2006, Samuel Palmisano, then-CEO of IBM, argued that "state borders define less and less the boundaries of corporate thinking and practice."[6]

Globalization was, for the most part, a nonpartisan or cross-partisan project. By the 1990s, there was little left and right disagreement on whether or not economic integration would produce economic growth. Growth, after all, seemed beneficial and unobjectionable, even if it might not be uniform. The postwar social safety net established in most advanced industrial democracies seemed capable of protecting against the short-term costs of, say, sectoral change. As national governments took on the goal of making their economies more competitive in the global market, they deregulated financial flows, labor, and goods and services. This further entrenched neoliberal ideas, imbuing a logic of the market—of loosening capital rather than regulating it—across democracies.[7]

Although political parties are sites of contestation over ideas and policies, the globalization agenda was shaped and implemented by economists from the academy and financial industry. The Republican Party's ties to organized business and lucrative industries had long aligned its goals of small government with goals of economic growth. But even in parties of the left, rank-and-file party members or representatives from traditional labor interests were replaced by a technocratic elite.[8] Given the parties' "separation from society," characterized by party organizations with little substantive relationship to voters beyond elections, there was little popular objection to technocratic governance of the economy.[9] Instead, these policies enhanced the leverage of corporations vis-à-vis domestic governments. Globalization itself undermines national regulatory authority, making basic functions like taxation, arbitration, and industrial relations difficult for domestic governments to perform.

The structure of the economy, and capitalism itself, is often described as a force that acts *upon* governments rather than as part and parcel of a governing agenda. And in the emerging economies of the post–Cold War era, neoliberal policies were often demanded of governments regardless of their partisan orientation. As Adam Przeworski wrote in 1992, the neoliberal "'cure' is a painful one, with significant social costs . . . independently of public opinion and without the participation of organized political forces. . . . [I]n the end, the society is taught that it can vote but not choose."[10] This dynamic, to a much lesser extent, was also present in the advanced industrial democracies that ushered in the era of globalization. Globalization did generate growth, but it also had significant distributive consequences that took many years to materialize. Przeworski noted that representative institutions would suffer as a result of neoliberal changes: not only were politicians constrained in what they could offer voters (in terms of alternative economic and social policies), but the traditional institutions of countervailing power—those of labor or civil society—would also lose ground relative to the growing power of capital.

The parties of the left and right in the advanced democracies are not at all the same. But over the past three decades, they have certainly become more similar on a pro-globalization dimension and, to a lesser extent, on a pro-market dimension as well. As a political class, the leaders of left and right parties are concerned with macroeconomic management and low interference—in terms of regulation or labor protections, for example— in the market. Opposition to globalization therefore does not manifest very clearly among the mainstream parties.[11]

Responsiveness

The neoliberal consensus—characterized by little partisan differentiation on economic management, globalization, or intervention in the market—is an example of the way parties have become less responsive to voters. In theory, parties should reflect what voters want; throughout history, parties organized to channel and articulate the interests of voters. Democratic elections give citizens the ability to hold politicians to account for their policy goals. This may be a naïve view, but it is nonetheless the foremost way parties have operated, particularly in prior eras of democratic expansion and economic change. Citizens themselves do not just make demands on governments; they also work through representative intermediaries to align their material interests with a party's governing and electoral goals.

In many of the long-standing industrial democracies, however, there is growing evidence that government policies do not reflect the preferences of citizens.[12] Studies comparing policy outcomes with surveys of what majorities of Americans prefer find that government policies, across both parties, overwhelmingly reflect the interests of economic elites.[13] These economic elites include wealthy individuals as well as organized business. It is not surprising that these actors have significant political influence, but it is deeply problematic for democracy if there is no way for majorities of citizens to get their policy preferences enacted. At worse, a pattern of affluent bias in democracies renders elections nearly meaningless. One problem is a structural imbalance in who commands power. Corporations and wealthy donors have multiple avenues to influence politics, including campaign finance and lobbying.[14] Beyond direct electoral politics, capital—that is, private money—is also increasingly important to the work of government itself and to financing democratic civil society. The scholars Jacob Hacker and Paul Pierson refer to the contemporary right as "plutocratic populists," in combining policies that favor the wealthy with populist rhetoric.[15] Studies have shown that policies tend to reflect the preferences of high-income voters even in other affluent countries,[16] including Sweden,[17] Spain,[18] Germany,[19] the Netherlands,[20] and Denmark.[21]

The Fracturing of the Right: Capitalism and Economic Populism

The problem of democracy today stems not from a consensus between the parties but instead from a loud denunciation of the political class as corrupt and undemocratic. Support for mainstream parties of the left and right has been in decline for decades; their vote shares have declined, as have their rates of party identification. However, until recently, it was hard to make the case that these trends were indicators of party weakness; the mainstream parties faced very few competitors to their electoral power. Since the 2008 financial crisis, however, there is a rising challenge to democracy from the right, not the left. The fracturing of the centrist right given the growing popularity of an extreme right has produced stark and high-stakes political conflict. It is therefore important to distinguish conservatism from variants of ideas on the right, including populism and antidemocratic extremism.

In his study of conservative parties in Britain and Germany, Daniel Ziblatt describes the emergence of conservative parties in the early democratic period. These parties were composed of upper-class, propertied economic elites; they often had ties to the predemocratic ancien regime.[22] The conservative right was particularly important to establishing the democratic rules of the game, since it needed to contain radical elements opposed to democratic practices while also competing with socialist or labor parties that sought to upend capitalism. Over the twentieth century, there has been heterogeneity among parties of the political right. Conservative parties tend to embrace traditional values, less state intervention in the economy, law and order, and religion.[23] An electorally competitive, mainstream, moderate conservative party has been critical to democratic stability historically, while conservative parties that give in to extremism make democracy far more vulnerable to collapse.

In the United States, the Republican Party's coalition expanded in the 1970s and 1980s to include former Southern Democrats as well as organized religion (particularly evangelical Christians). Its economic positions were increasingly defined by the party's relationship to organized business. The backlash to Nixon-era regulations, including the Environmental Protection Act and the Occupational Safety and Health Act, led businesses to become more united against regulatory overreach.[24] The Republican Party became the primary vehicle for new economic ideas into politics, and an era of deregulation, lower taxes, and greater global trade brought the party closer to businesses as well.

The Republican Party's donor base and intellectual base were closely aligned on matters of economic policy. Candidates for the Republican ticket touted their pro-business bona fides, both at the national level and in the states. The party benefited from partisan think tanks (such as the conservative Cato Institute and Heritage Foundation) and business lobbies (like the U.S. Chambers of Commerce) that wrote policy proposals and helped to staff Republican administrations. More important, a network of well-heeled donors with a libertarian, antiregulation, and free-market bent seeded economic ideas among candidates and policymakers at all levels of government. The Koch brothers, for example, through their State Policy Network and American Legislative

Exchange Network, brought a business-friendly economic agenda, complete with model bills, directly to state legislators.[25] At the national level, the Republican Party built close ties to organized interest groups such as the gun lobby and the antiabortion movement.

Some fissures within the party emerged during the Obama administration. While the party unified behind opposition to President Obama's Patient Protection and Affordable Care Act, insurgent candidates and a nascent Tea Party faction began to challenge Republican incumbents in primary races. The Tea Party, funded in part by the Koch network, was avowedly antigovernment (opposing, for example, Obama's Troubled Asset Relief Program), although Tea Party supporters tended to support existing social programs such as Social Security and Medicare.[26] Tea Party politicians embraced a libertarian, antigovernment agenda, although one that was connected to traditional conservative ideas. The movement provided an early indication of a deeper disaffection toward the political establishment, particularly among people living in rural or marginalized areas.[27]

In 2012, the Republican Party's presidential ticket reflected its long-standing relationship with conservative economic interests. The presidential nominee, Mitt Romney, was a former governor of Massachusetts and successful businessman. Paul Ryan, a congressman since 1998, was part of a cohort of self-stylized "young guns" who advocated limited government couched in terms of individual liberty and economic freedom.[28] While Romney was considered moderate, a popular governor of a liberal state, Ryan appealed to economic conservatives who advocated more privatization and less state intervention.

After Obama won a second term, the Republican Party conducted an autopsy of its messaging and appeal with voters. Commissioned by RNC chair Reince Priebus, the Growth and Opportunity Project Report acknowledged that the party seemed out of touch with voters: too rigid, too White, too old, and too in thrall to the wealthy. The report admitted that the party might need to soften its stances on immigration, labor, and gay rights to make inroads with younger voters. And finally, the authors of the report argued that the changing world of campaign finance—particularly the growing ability of organized interests outside the party to finance their own issues and candidates—would make it more difficult for the party to nominate credible moderate candidates.[29] The report concluded that the Republican Party needed to work harder to combat the idea that the "GOP does not care about people." However, the recommendations of the report were decidedly *not* the direction the party took. In 2016, the Republican Party nominated Donald Trump for president, taking the party in a decidedly more incendiary and extreme direction.[30]

It is not just American conservatism that was changing at this time. In Europe, far-right politicians and parties gained ground in elections to their national legislatures as well as to the European Parliament.[31] After the financial crisis of 2008, a wave of populism produced a set of political entrepreneurs who capitalized on discontent toward the political establishment. Populism is not itself an ideology; rather, it is a political style that combines a sweeping critique of the political and economic establishment with a claim to represent the will of the people as a whole.[32] While conservative parties are often defined by their adherence to the status quo, populist leaders seek to change it.

In Europe, parties at the extremes became more competitive after 2008. These parties, referred to as "challenger" or "antisystem" parties because of their stated opposition to the mainstream left and right, mobilize around narrow issues that they argue are unaddressed (or underaddressed) by the elites.[33] These parties benefit from two dynamics. One is the economic consequences of globalization; global trade, for example, has led to deindustrialization in the West. Two, those communities left behind from the benefits of trade have experienced higher rates of unemployment and reduced economic mobility. These dynamics have given rise to more anti-internationalist sentiment that advocates protecting domestic industries and reducing exposure to trade.[34] Extremist parties have also mobilized around anti-immigration sentiment and welfare chauvinism, with far-right parties advocating social protections but only for the "rightful" citizens.

The working class remains salient to politics but does not now consistently vote with the left as it has in previous eras. Support for social democracy has declined as the general workforce in manufacturing and industry has declined, since fewer workers occupy standard working-class jobs associated with manual employment.[35] Lower rates of private-sector unionization have also impacted traditional allegiances to the left. Industrial workers and public-sector employees are a voting bloc that is increasingly up for grabs rather than integrated squarely into a political tradition. Populists often appeal directly to voters who feel maligned and marginalized by the political establishment. Working-class voters opt for populist and extreme-right parties on issues related to immigration and law and order, *particularly* when the mainstream parties downplay the salience of economic issues.[36]

New parties can also utilize technology and win votes without building a traditional party infrastructure. The election of Silvio Berlusconi, the owner of the Mediaset empire, as prime minister of Italy in 1994 showed how easily candidates could mobilize on the basis of celebrity, without need for a party infrastructure.[37] Populist parties often exist on paper but serve only one candidate. They can use social media to reach the public and mobilize supporters online. Geert Wilders's Freedom Party in the Netherlands was a personal association; Wilders broke from the conservative-liberal People's Party for Freedom and Democracy in 2006. Without party members or any formal organization, the only real party presence was a website, a party foundation that accepted private donations, and Wilders's Twitter feed.[38] In Italy, the Five Star Party began partly on the comedian Beppe Grillo's blog in 2009. It created a digital platform, Rousseau, designed to allow party members to vote on policy issues alongside candidates, and to facilitate meetings of supporters.[39] The far right tends to mobilize on such issues as immigration, globalization, and opposition to multiculturalism. Further, rather than couching their appeals in material concerns, they often use xenophobic and nationalist rhetoric. The axes of political competition have become increasingly defined by these issue dimensions rather than by materialism or economic differences.

Unfettered Capitalism and the Privatization
of Representation

Governing in an era of neoliberalism has produced a set of parties that seems highly responsive to capital, while lacking mechanisms to translate majority preferences into policy priorities. Beyond the obvious stressors to the party system, capitalism today presents another challenge to parties through the slow eclipse of the public sector by the private sector. Through decades of austerity measures and state contraction, parties have left policy implementation to contractors and companies outside the public domain. This deprives parties of the policy levers they have historically used to mobilize and sustain their base, while contributing to the perception that only businesses—not government—can manage complex problems. The scope of policies available to parties seems to have narrowed just as the challenges presented by advanced capitalism have grown.

   In recent years, neoliberal capitalism has been subject to numerous critiques related to declining economic security and rising inequality throughout the advanced democracies.[40] While postwar capitalism saw the rise of large and medium businesses that created "good jobs"—those that could provide middle-class living standards and upward mobility— the economic bargain has steadily worsened for workers since then.[41] The most profitable industries have shifted from corporations manufacturing consumer goods to new sectors like finance, tech, and services. These sectors represent a departure from the managed capitalism of the postwar period, characterized by industrial corporations that produced consumer goods.

   While productivity has risen among workers, wages for low- and middle-income workers have stagnated for the past thirty years. Further, because companies have undertaken excessive cost-cutting, wage reductions, and benefit cuts, work has become more precarious.[42] Corporations rely increasingly on outsourcing and contracting, which further severs ties and obligations to employees.[43] The United States has the

highest levels of income inequality of all the nations in the Organisation for Economic Co-operation and Development (OECD), although
inequality has also risen in other liberal democracies over time. The billionaire class's influence in campaign finance is a mere microcosm of the
larger problems related to the fact of the billionaire class itself, and the
perception that America is becoming more akin to an oligarchy than a
democracy. Wealth is tied up in an economy that has stripped Americans of opportunities and mobility. And this wealth is related directly
to trends like financialization and globalization, which accelerated after
parties converged on economic policy at the end of the previous
century.

Neoliberal capitalism makes it difficult for social policy alone to bridge
widening wealth and income gaps. Highly lucrative sectors, like finance,
have grown dramatically, with uneven gains. By 2001, financial sector
profits represented more than 40% of total U.S. profits.[44] These profits often accrue from the indebtedness of consumers, a phenomenon
Colin Crouch has termed "privatized Keynesianism."[45] Wages have stagnated or declined for low- and middle-class workers, while executive
compensation has risen. Income among the 250,000 or so individuals
who run banks and firms in the finance industry has doubled their share
of annual total income in the past two decades, driving income concentration of the top 1%.[46] Salaries for workers in finance are the highest in
the country.[47]

The 2008 financial crisis and its aftermath exposed both the dangers
of financialized capitalism as well as the state's inability to successfully
regulate the industry. Finance remains poorly understood by the general public, even by politicians; meanwhile, the profits from finance
are highly valuable.[48] The economic inequities that result from changes
in capitalism therefore translate into political inequality as well. The
financial industry's deep pockets and lobbying activity result in policies favorable to it but largely hidden from public view. Lax regulation
and financial market innovations make it particularly challenging for
governments to anticipate market failures or mitigate their effects. Economic growth in the twenty-first century has been driven not only by

the transition to a service economy but especially by finance and technology, a knowledge economy dependent on a small and highly educated segment of labor. As corporate profit margins have risen, their political power has grown.

In October 2019, a decade after the global financial crisis and merely months before a global pandemic, Marc Benioff, the CEO of Salesforce, wrote in the *New York Times*, "As a capitalist, I believe it's time to say out loud what we all know to be true: capitalism, as we know it, is dead."[49] Like many other concerned capitalists today, a group that includes Warren Buffett of Berkshire Hathaway, Larry Fink of BlackRock, and Jamie Dimon of JP Morgan, Benioff argues that what we need is a new kind of capitalism, one that works for all stakeholders. Corporations should do more than simply raise the bottom line for shareholders; they should ensure their goals align with those of consumers and workers.[50] High-net-worth individuals have therefore become more socially engaged, through, for example, philanthropy and corporate social responsibility, filling a void left by parties and governments.

Parties have overseen a slow, but deliberate, transfer of power from the public to the private sector. The erosion of parties as intermediaries between citizens and the state has coincided dangerously with a growing turn toward the private sector to achieve desired social and political outcomes. We now expect enlightened billionaires to step in when governments cannot or will not. Faith in political institutions has been replaced by faith in markets. Yet no modern democracy has been able to survive without parties, and the twenty-first century is showing us why. Without effective representative institutions, there is no effective opposition to capital. Those with resources will increasingly dominate political ideas and policies.

Reclaiming the State

The problems of democratic legitimacy today are related both to problems of capital and to problems of politics. While social and public policy is the foremost way that parties typically demonstrate responsiveness, governance in a neoliberal age has been associated with a retreat of the state. The constituencies mobilized through policy are enduring because they rely on ongoing, sustained linkages—on the promise and delivery of benefits from party organizations.[51] But the long-running project to dismantle the state has been phenomenally successful, making it harder for parties to claim credit for policies. The future of parties will rest in large part on a reclamation of the state as a necessary, and beneficial, part of democratic life.

This is a tall order given the increasing encroachment of private capital in the public sphere. Historically, policy has always been a combination of public and private. Insurance, for example, was initially adopted by companies before countries enacted national insurance programs. However, the extension of social policies in the early twentieth century created a new social contract between citizens and governments, and indeed between democracy and capitalism more broadly. While capital would be responsible for large swaths of economic life, including the creation and allocation of jobs, the dispensation of wages, and innovation that would produce better economic opportunities, governments would protect against risk. They did so through the provision of welfare, health, and unemployment protections; they also subsidized or created housing, education, transit.

In the era of austerity, however, governments did more than scale back social services. They also privatized them and relied more on private-sector contractors to implement them.

In the United States, much of the work of policymaking is done through diffuse and complicated networks of contractors and public and private organizations or through public-private partnerships. Privatization can make it difficult to attribute policies to the government or to hold government accountable for service provision.[52] Social policy is "hidden" through payroll taxes and tax expenditures, such that citizens do not attribute the benefits they receive to government activity.[53] The number of bureaucrats in the federal government has remained the same for a half-century, while the number of lobbyists and contractors has ballooned.[54]

Politicians have distanced themselves from the state for decades, furthering public distrust in government as a capable service provider. While conservative parties have been far more vitriolic in their attacks on the state, parties of the left have also preached market solutions and been reluctant to embrace a robust public sector. This has the effect of eroding faith in the state overall, making it very difficult for parties to make credible assurances that they are willing to use government for the public good.[55] Further, it entrenches the power of businesses that rely on state contracts, in effect making governments dependent on the private sector to fulfill its basic functions.[56]

* * *

The neoliberal consensus among mainstream parties reshaped the relationship of democracy and capitalism through a growing reliance on the market, rather than government, to address social problems. The promise of globalization was not only that corporations would generate wealth but also that "government leaders will find in business willing partners to reform health care and education, secure the world's trade . . . and commerce, train and enable the displaced and dispossessed."[57]

In early 2020, a novel coronavirus emerged in Wuhan, China, and spread quickly to Europe and the United States. In March, California and Washington on the West Coast declared shelter-in-place orders to stop the spread of the virus. Many other states followed suit, but the federal government and President Trump opposed these restrictions, denied the severity of the virus, politicized responses such as mask mandates and bans on gatherings, and marginalized the Centers for Disease Control and other public health experts. Governors worried about how to proceed, given the risk of retribution or withholding of resources from the federal government. And mayors worried about how to proceed, given the risk of retribution or withholding of resources from their governors.

While the government dithered in its response, the private sector stepped in. Individual businesses could develop their own policies, and they did: in states with no mask mandates or social distancing requirements, retailers, grocers, and other private entities enforced them. Philanthropists contributed to the pandemic response; the Bill and Melinda Gates Foundation developed a public campaign to mitigate the virus and spent $300 million by June 2020.

There were other ways that business became important. Trump appointed his son-in-law Jared Kushner head of an informal task force to coordinate the pandemic response; Kushner drew extensively on connections in the private sector to consider questions of supplies, logistics, and contracts from the government. Reporting by the *New York Times* showed that Jerome Powell, Steven Mnuchin, and Larry Kudlow—the chairman of the Federal Reserve, the treasury secretary, and the director of the White House National Economic Council, respectively—communicated extensively with Larry Fink, the chief executive of Black-Rock, when the federal government was developing its emergency rescue programs at the start of the pandemic. They also consulted with many other financial firms and Wall Street banks in order to understand the market response. It was a stark example of how reliant the government has become on industry experts.

The private sector remained critical as the national election of 2020 drew closer and private resources once again became critical. Facebook CEO Mark Zuckerberg and his wife, Priscilla Chan, gave over $400 million to help with election administration efforts, including educating voters about voter registration and polling locations. After the January 6 violence at the U.S. Capitol, businesses became even more vocal on voting rights issues. Corporations have denounced state legislation that makes it harder to vote and have embraced a new business activism unseen in the past fifty years. They have signed letters opposing state bills, have worked with legislatures to change the provisions of voting legislation, and have demanded stronger democratic protections.

Through philanthropies, policy engagement, and corporate social responsibility, business is called on to police itself and, where possible, to be visionary when government cannot. Many corporations have signed on to environmental, social, and governance goals precisely because of government inaction on these fronts. In policy areas such as gun control, racial justice, immigration, healthcare, and election administration, corporations and philanthropists have established policy initiatives in the face of party inaction.

The new activism of business allows consumers to channel their demands and values through the private sector without changing any of the underlying profit mechanisms that produce inequality and plutocracy. Well-intentioned billionaires and socially conscious corporations may very well be able to bring about desirable outcomes but are also accountable to no one. The rise of "plutocratic philanthropy" also gives wealthy individuals and corporations an outsized role in shaping civil society, advocacy, and even capitalism itself.[58]

The tradition of philanthropy and charitable giving has a long history in the United States. The Carnegie Corporation, Rockefeller Foundation, and Andrew W. Mellon Foundation were seeded with Gilded Age wealth; today, over 100,000 private foundations have combined endowments greater than $1 trillion.[59] Outside of foundations, there has been a trend of billionaires committing to giving away their riches in their lifetime. The Giving Pledge, Patriotic Millionaires, and other groups try to channel the immense resources of the wealthy into societal and political causes.

New foundations are savvy and modern, noteworthy for their combination of business model with their interest in civic and public issues.[60] The Bill and Melinda Gates Foundation, one of the most prominent actors in the world of development, is focused on investing its resources where governments and corporations are unlikely to—what they call "catalytic philanthropy."[61] The Gates Foundation has been a success and has undoubtedly saved lives and raised public consciousness. But the sheer amount of resources available makes the Gates Foundation its own political player, affecting the direction of research and levels of funding of public agencies.[62] Foundations also fund a variety of civil society actors, advocacy groups, and local policy initiatives.[63]

In the absence of regulation or government policy, corporations have driven a new set of standards among themselves. Milton Friedman's well-worn dictum that corporations are responsible only for creating profits for shareholders has received pushback not only from the left but from the business community itself. The corporate social responsibility movement encourages businesses to act responsibly and provides many different avenues through which corporations might signal their desire and willingness to do so. In 2019, the Business Roundtable announced a commitment to all stakeholders in response to "how corporations can and should act today."[64] But the notable thing about trends in business organizations is that corporate action to raise wages, negotiate with laborers, and commit to environmental and social goals is happening precisely because political parties have left much of the work of corporate regulation to the private sector.

Philanthropic giving and foundation resources are surely better than oligarchies in which wealth is hoarded or stolen; they are forms of redistribution that try to get resources where they are needed. It is not just corporations that are to blame for the retreat of the state but an erosion of the ability of democracies to serve the people through robust intermediary organizations. The public good cannot be divined by technocrats and political leaders whose fortunes are intertwined with those of the economic elites they serve. Citizens can organize, they can advocate, they can protest and march. But the structural advantages in our economic and political system work in favor of capital. Only parties and governments can address this imbalance.

CHAPTER 7

Conclusion

Building a sustainable democratic future requires strong parties. These parties must play a meaningful and substantial role in politics, but not simply by wielding and maintaining power. Instead, as this book has argued, parties need to be intermediaries, networked to the constituencies they serve; they need to do the work of mediating by negotiating among the competing interests within their ranks. Beyond rebuilding their intermediary capacity, parties also need to govern—meaning they need to prioritize a role for government in people's lives.

However, rebuilding parties cannot happen in a vacuum, and doing so requires both short- and long-term investments. Party leaders need to realize that the many strains of discontent within democracies today, even those related to support for antidemocratic leaders or anger at corporations and economic elites, are rooted in large part in the failure of representative intermediaries. They can no longer throw up their hands in helpless capitulation to external "forces," nor can they continue to rely on stoking division to win over supporters.

Similarly, anyone who is invested in democracy—journalists, activists in civil society and social movements, and those fighting for higher living standards and economic security—should see parties as part of the solution rather than part of the problem. It is easy to demonize parties, but many of the so-called problems with parties today are routine politics. Parties are characterized by faction and division and by an ongoing process of deliberation and compromise. Parties must respond to powerful interests, such as big business and global economic partners, but they also should be able to defend and channel cross-cutting interests that are diffuse in the population—those of workers, families, and consumers. When parties are adjudicating among different interests, they are not hopelessly riven; when they compromise, they are not forsaking the public good. They are, instead, doing what is required of them.

For parties to be strong, they need to be robust organizations connected to communities, and they need to articulate economic approaches that channel countervailing power—interests distinct from those of capital. Throughout this book, there are indications of how parties might do that. Campaign finance reforms that centralize more party authority over funding could mitigate the influence of ideologically extreme donors. Rebuilding local and state parties and recruiting party volunteers to get involved in local community-building and policymaking would develop a practice of democratic citizenship and create more robust ties to the party beyond election campaigns.[1] Explaining what government does and how it plays a productive role in people's lives would help to rebuild some trust in democratic institutions.[2]

There are other ways parties might establish connections with members or supporters. Some parties, like the Liberal Democrats in the United Kingdom and the Partido Popular in Spain, provide multi-level membership. Dues-paying members have rights in the party itself, including decision-making in the party conference, while supporters have no voting rights but are allowed to attend. This allows members more of a say in the party's candidates and policy positions, but also circumscribes internal party democracy to those who are formally affiliated. European parties have experimented with cheaper memberships or direct benefits to supporters, including credit cards and corporate discounts, access to party leaders, and members-only websites.[3] The French party affiliated with Emmanuel Macron, La Republique en Marche, coordinates party chapters through Telegram; it also uses online platforms that are monitored by party staff as spaces for policy deliberation and proposals.[4] Joining a party can also be motivated by traditional incentives, such as a desire to run for public office, an expressive sense that the party aligns with your values, or an opportunity to socialize and talk politics. Party membership is not a thing of the past; instead, these efforts to expand benefits to members can actually make parties *more* representative. For example, in a study of ten European democracies, higher membership benefits were associated with more demographically and ideologically diverse party members.[5] More inclusive manifesto-writing procedures also create more stable policy goals, established through consensus rather than elite dictum.[6]

Parties of the future need not look much different from parties of today. However, parties are operating in a different context for democracy, and party-building may feel like swimming upstream. The challenges to party-building today include the threat of democratic backsliding, the diffuse nature of critiques to capitalism, and an antiparty reform community. These are not insurmountable challenges and instead present a welcome opportunity for a new generation of party leaders.

Democratic Backsliding and Democratic Renewal

Parties may seem like a parochial concern in this era of democratic crisis. Democracy watchdogs like Freedom House and the Economist Intelligence Unit Democracy Index have noted alarming declines in the state of democracy worldwide. These organizations measure many dimensions of democracy, including the strength of formal democracy—that is, whether or not there are checks and balances and rule of law, free and fair elections, and accountability—as well as protections for civil liberties, minorities, and journalists. They have used the term "democratic backsliding" to describe the trend of democracy deteriorating from within, and date the downward trend in democracy to 2005.

Since 2005, events such as the financial crisis and the COVID-19 pandemic have furthered democratic decline. Seventy percent of the world's countries fared worse on democratic indicators during the pandemic, and the United States, for the fifth consecutive year, was ranked a flawed democracy.[7] Freedom House recorded the fifteenth straight year of diminishing freedoms, "shifting the international balance in favor of tyranny."[8] The declines in democratic indicators have taken place against an insurgent authoritarianism worldwide, led by dictators such as Russia's Vladimir Putin and China's Xi Jinping.[9]

Democratic erosion has many causes, ranging from attacks on liberal institutions like the press and political opponents to the centralization of executive power and manipulation of elections. The International Institute for Democracy and Electoral Assistance adds that the "struggl[e] to guarantee equitable and sustainable economic and social development" further undermines democratic outcomes.[10]

What role do parties play in either contributing to these trends or, alternatively, providing a backstop against them? Political parties are not inherently democratic, after all. Authoritarian leaders build parties that help them maintain power, for example, but these parties can also lead democratic transitions and remain competitive in democratic elections.[11] While the mainstream parties in long-standing democracies of the West have remained committed to democracy, they have not been able to effectively curtail illiberal populism.

The fall of the Berlin Wall in 1989 and the collapse of the Soviet Union soon thereafter ushered in a new global consensus on democracy and capitalism. Authoritarian regimes held democratic elections, and international democracy-promotion organizations worked to assist the process of transition. Francis Fukuyama famously declared the end of history: liberal democracy and capitalism were the political and economic systems, respectively, that would characterize the world. The twentieth century, marked as it had been by ideological battles and destructive wars, was ending with the "unabashed victory of economic and political liberalism."[12]

Democracy promotion was a feature of the liberal international order. Many Western countries expanded their commitments to democratic activists and opposition groups, lending financial resources as well as technical know-how. The Democratic and Republican parties in the United States, the Swedish Social Democratic Party, the German Social Democratic Party, and others expanded their support for party-affiliated organizations. They did this through vehicles like the

National Democratic Institute and International Republican Institute, two arms of the political parties of the United States that were created in 1983 shortly after Congress established the National Endowment for Democracy. These organizations assisted parties in emerging democracies, teaching them how to recruit members and candidates, how to run elections, and how to coordinate their legislative activities.

These efforts were important to democratic success. Empirically, party affiliation is critical to developing citizen attachments to politics and to democracy writ large. The Pew Research Center found that in thirty-five countries, lower rates of affiliation with political parties was associated with lower levels of support for representative democracy.[13] This might strike American readers in particular as surprising, given that party affiliation has become so polarized and divided in the United States. The example of democracy promotion is a useful reminder, however, that we have long taken our parties and representative institutions for granted. We think of them as a fixed characteristic of our politics rather than as something that might be strengthened or changed.

Democracy advocates and think tanks such as the Wilson Center, the Brennan Center for Justice, and the International Institute for Democracy continue to analyze the crisis of parties today. Noting the long history of parties and democracy, their reports examine ways to "strengthen parties." They advocate giving parties a more central role in decision-making, whether that has to do with allocating campaign funds and choosing candidates or enrolling and maintaining memberships. They focus in particular on how parties can "grasp the main concerns and claims of society" and point out that "if [they] do not aggregate . . . concerns and ideas of society, they cannot fulfill their function."[14]

We should not be overly pessimistic that this period of democratic backsliding is either inevitable or unstoppable. Rather, parties need to move toward democratic renewal. The basic commitment that all political parties need to make is to the first principles of democracy: free and fair elections and guarantees of individual rights. Democracy cannot be stable when political parties take positions challenging the fundamental precepts of democracy.

Political parties have been the primary stewards of democracy, but they haven't always—or maybe even ever—been popular. Parties have therefore adapted as conceptions of democracy and representation have evolved. In the late nineteenth century, Britain and the United States adopted the Australian ballot, a ballot printed by the state, not by parties, that listed candidates of all parties on one sheet. Voters then selected their preferred candidate in secret, rather than by picking up a party ballot or by saying their vote choices out loud. In the Progressive era, reformers fed up with party control over politics advocated reforms that weakened patronage and limited political activities by those with public sector jobs. Plebiscitary reforms, like the recall, referendum, and ballot initiative, gave voters a way to remove leaders or to implement policies directly, circumventing party control.

In consolidated democracies, citizens can trust that election procedures are consistent, that election outcomes are decidedly fairly, and that the same parties compete in each election. Further, in consolidated democracies, political parties lose elections: the party with a majority in the legislature or the party holding executive office changes through peaceful, uncontested transfers of power. After the Cold War, scholars spoke of democratization in terms of a transition paradigm. Some societies were "transitioning" to democracy, which is to say they were slowly becoming accustomed to competitive elections, alternation in power, and holding leaders accountable, while other democracies were "consolidated."

While international democracy organizations developed many strategies to support countries moving from democratic transition to consolidation, there is no similar playbook for countries now experiencing democratic backsliding. The 2020 U.S. presidential election did not produce a peaceful transfer of power in the United States, for example. Instead, the outgoing president and the Republican Party claimed the election results were illegitimate; their refusal to acknowledge that Joe Biden rightfully won the election led directly to an attack on the U.S. Capitol on January 6, 2021, when Congress was certifying the election results. The Republican Party blocked legislation to investigate the January 6 attacks and passed laws at the state level curtailing voting rights.

It is no surprise that other national leaders are decrying election outcomes, arguing that their losses were due to fraud or refusing to concede. Jair Bolsonaro of Brazil and Keiko Fugimori of Peru made similar claims in 2021. And it is unclear what the international response should be to these claims. Viktor Orbán's Fidesz Party had long been a part of the main coalition of centrist and center-right parties in the European Parliament, the European People's Party (EPP). Although Orban has overseen a stark turn against democracy in Hungary, it was only in 2019 that the EPP suspended Fidesz's membership in its group, prompting Orbán to leave the group in 2021. Democracy itself seems to be working, as recent elections in Brazil and Poland indicate. However, leaders in the long-standing democracies need to do more to reassert their democratic commitments.

Citizens are not staying silent amid evidence of democratic backsliding. Since 2010, they have increasingly turned to mass protests and civic activism to signal dissatisfaction with the regimes that govern them. There have been protests in every region of the world, ramping up from 2017 to 2019. Popular demonstrations toppled the regimes of dictators like Omar al-Bashir in Sudan and the twenty-year presidency of Abdelaziz Bouteflika in Algeria. There have also been lengthy protests in Iran, France, Chile, Hong Kong, and Israel calling for rights, democracy, or economic protections. In the absence of effective democratic institutions that channel and respond to people's grievances, public protest is becoming one of the foremost methods of political participation.[15]

While committing to democratic principles may seem merely symbolic, party efforts to denounce and exclude antidemocratic candidates and to establish the rules for political engagement—whether by informal agreement or by law—would be a step toward making democracy somewhat less vulnerable to hostile takeover. Further, the more party leaders can do to recognize threats to democracy *overall* rather than ignoring those threats that do not directly affect their electoral prospects, the more they might be able to forge a cross-partisan coalition of pro-democracy politicians who demonstrate to the public that values can trump partisanship.

Another promising pathway for parties is to rebuild through the civic activists and associations. Americans have become engaged politically, not just through protests, but through activism around social justice, the environment, working conditions, and race, gender, and inclusion. In the run-up to the 2020 election, many of these groups got involved in local, state, and national campaigns.

The cross-cutting social organizations and membership groups that once dotted urban and suburban landscapes have waned. There are opportunities for parties to lead the way in renewing civil society. The Scholars Strategy Network, a membership organization of academic researchers invested in democracy, recommends that parties rebuild at the local level. A local party can hold meetings, register members, and work with other community organizations to hold events of interest.[16] In her work on associational party-building, the constitutional law scholar Tabatha Abu El-Haj argues that political parties are not private groups electing candidates; they are associations of individuals and voters, connected through common activities and interests. Courts can help parties develop their associational linkages and ensure pathways of communication up and down the party hierarchy, in order for citizens to hold party leaders accountable for their policy promises.[17]

In 2020, the American Academy of Arts and Sciences released a report from its Commission on the Practice of Democratic Citizenship. Titled "Our Common Purpose," the report was the culmination of a two-year listening tour across the United States. In addition to calling for institutional reforms to government, the report recommended dramatic expansion of civic "bridging activities"—community activism that brings citizens into active engagement with municipalities and nonprofits.[18] The report echoes calls for civic nationalism as an antidote to revanchist nationalism, a way to encourage Americans of all stripes to transcend their differences and commit to the principles of constitutional democracy. Building pro-democracy coalitions at local and national levels can also strengthen communities against authoritarian risks.[19] While vibrant civic life alone may not be able to rebuild trust in government, it can certainly help citizens feel more invested in their communities and their futures.

It is not enough for parties to show that they are committed to democratic principles or allied with civic organizations; they must actually demonstrate responsiveness to voters' demands. Parties have both intentionally and unwittingly empowered the private sector and markets, which compounds problems associated with government inaction or gridlock. On a range of issues, including climate change, gun control, immigration, and fair labor practices and wages, parties across the political spectrum have been unwilling to pass policies even when majorities of Americans support them.

What parties therefore need to do is reclaim the levers of government available to them—to show that they are not afraid to think of government as the solution rather than the problem. They need to think about their relationship with citizens not as a set of overlapping identities but as a social contract for the twenty-first century. Citizens demand, and are entitled to, party leaders who establish fair and just societies, who pursue government policies to maximize opportunities and make society livable.

This may entail a reconfiguration of the traditional left and right to better reflect contemporary class alignments. On the right, this might mean trying to appeal to the working class with economic policy rather than appeals to grievance alone. Some Republicans have moved away from a strict antistate view of social policy. Mitt Romney, for example, proposed the Family Security Act to replace childcare tax credits with direct cash payments to parents of young children; Marco Rubio encouraged Amazon workers to unionize.[20] In a Republican Study Group memo, Representative Jim Banks from Indiana said the Republicans should hold working-class roundtables to inform a proposed Working Families Task Force.[21]

There are also voices from the progressive left calling for robust social policy, such as universal basic income, single-payer health insurance, progressive and redistributive tax policy, subsidized childcare and family

leave, and greater private sector unionization. However, given that much
of the left draws support from a highly educated, cosmopolitan base,
left parties will need to find ways to develop cross-class coalitions. President Biden has tried to move the left into more innovative approaches to
industrial policy, antitrust, and labor, and it remains to be seen if these
win back working-class voters.

Parties that can successfully pass and implement these policies will be
more successful, in terms of reclaiming support for the party, if they
marshal these policies into a more coherent ideological alternative to
neoliberalism. Within economics, a new generation of scholars has been
eager to push back against the free-market principles associated with the
Chicago school. A group under the umbrella of Economists for Inclusive Prosperity, for example, has called on economists to orient their
discipline toward finding solutions for problems like inequality, technological change, and globalization in order to create inclusive growth.[22]

Philanthropic foundations are also devoting resources to rethinking capitalism. The Hewlett Foundation and Omidyar Network have
together pledged over $40 million to research institutions tasked with
devising alternatives to neoliberalism. Larry Kramer, former president of
the Hewlett Foundation, argues that free market orthodoxy has not only
produced inequality and dislocation but also "has become one of the
principal sites of hyperpartisan conflict."[23] The grants are going to academics to think about interventions in the economy that might improve
capitalism. They include, for example, how to solve the problem of bad
jobs in an increasingly polarized labor market defined by expansion at
the top (among professional workers) and at the bottom (low-skilled
jobs), while jobs that once supported the middle class (i.e., sales, clerical,
and manufacturing jobs) have disappeared.[24] These might include ways
to bring productive economic sectors to rural or postindustrial areas or
to enhance worker productivity rather than replace workers. This line
of research goes beyond economic redistribution as a tool for solving
inequality, beyond influxes of cash—what we might think of as "emergency Keynesianism"—after crises.[25] Instead, it envisions a new role for
the state in aligning incentives between industry and society.

Whether it is Democrats who wish to build something distinct from centrism or Republicans who wish to build a more protectionist yet nonetheless small-state agenda, all parties would benefit from coherent ways of describing their vision for the state and society. A new language and set of values about social solidarity, after fifty years of staunch individualism, would help to build political coalitions. The scholar Margaret Levi stresses that because humans are social beings, governments should be concerned not only with how wealth is created but also how economies can generate human flourishing.[26] Rethinking capitalism can happen in corporations or among businesses, but it will also require our democratic institutions to commit themselves to outputs and outcomes beyond economic growth.[27] What remains to be seen is how realignments around education and class will solidify into long-term changes. Parties of the future may not map onto the traditional liberalism and conservatism of the twentieth century but will nonetheless require parties to reassert materialism—to specify how government can and should serve to mediate democracy and capitalism.

Reforming American Political Institutions

When the Democrats won the House majority in 2018, their first order of business was HR1, the For the People Act. This legislation sought to create a federal floor for American elections standards, and also implemented (or permitted) a variety of reforms in areas such as campaign finance, redistricting, and electoral systems. The legislation failed, but President Biden made political reform one of his agenda items, and the legislation was reintroduced in 2021. Although it failed again, along with a bill to protect voting rights (the John Lewis Voting Rights Advancement Act), the bills nonetheless showed that political reform is on the table today in a way it hadn't been for decades.

"Reform" can mean any number of things in a democracy, and the landscape of political reform is limitless. Public discontent with democracy often fuels a desire to upend the system in some way, though translating amorphous demands for change into actual proposals is a challenge. There are many reforms on the table to strengthen American democracy today. Some of them target a specific problem, like gerrymandering or "dark money," with solutions like independent redistricting commissions or transparency in campaign disclosures. Others may try to ease voting access (through mail-in ballots or an election day holiday). There are also reforms that take aim at the system more broadly. Some try to change the electoral system—the way we elect candidates and translate votes into seats—to make it easier for a third party to win. Others want to introduce preference-ranking on ballots, or ranked-choice voting, so that voters don't have to pick just one candidate.

Reforms are hard to achieve because parties with power are reluctant to give it up, and any change to the system might generate new winners and losers. In general, those who support reform are likely to benefit from it, while those who oppose it see no upside. While the political parties in the United States may be weak in some ways, they are certainly not weak electorally. Our first-past-the-post, winner-take-all system makes it very difficult for third-party candidates to win, which therefore makes it all but impossible for a third party to compete on a national level. Some laws, like "sore loser" laws that preclude the loser in a primary election from running in a general election, guarantee that the two parties will remain in power.

Nonpartisan Primaries

There have been recent calls for a "nonpartisan" approach to political reform that take aim specifically at this perceived two-party "duopoly."[28] As one of these nonpartisan groups describes it, they seek "a robust competition of numerous political parties and independents, and a level playing field on which that can occur."[29] The implication here is that the two parties skew the playing field, that they write the rules in their favor to block other would-be candidates.

One solution they advocate is nonpartisan primaries. Alaska recently adopted a "top four" primary, which allows candidates from all parties to compete in a primary. The top four candidates then advance to the general election in November, where the winner is selected through ranked-choice voting. California, Washington, and Louisiana also have primaries that allow all candidates to compete, and the top two advance to the general. In top-two or top-four primaries, it could be the case that two (or four) candidates from the same party compete against each other in the general election. By abolishing a party primary, this reform hopes to preclude extremists winning against moderates.

The party primary was developed as a way to address perceived corruption among party elites. It was initially established in the Progressive era, alongside other reforms like the initiative, recall, and referendum. All of these reforms sought to democratize parties by taking power out of the hands of party leaders and allowing party members—or regular voters—a way to hold party leaders to account. Primary elections are now routine; they are used to elect the president, members of Congress, and most state leadership positions. After the McGovern-Fraser reforms, the United States became the only large, long-standing democracy that leaves candidate selection almost entirely up to voters. Recently, parties in other countries have experimented with primaries, but they often limit voting to dues-paying members and also give leaders a final say.

Although primary elections are low-turnout events, they nonetheless have high stakes and increasingly draw financing and support from outside the party. This dilutes the nature and intent of an election that is explicitly designed to determine *a party's candidate*. The traditional purpose and method of conducting primaries are to select someone who is a good representative of the party itself. (In closed primaries, one must be registered with a party to vote in that primary; open primaries allow any voter to vote.) Parties exist to do the hard work of coordinating among all the would-be candidates to determine the ones who will be good legislators. They often combine this responsibility with recruitment and training, so they can identify experienced candidates who will be good standard-bearers for the party itself.

The move toward nonpartisan primaries may have the effect of sending more moderate candidates to the general election. But resources and financing will follow the political incentives, and there is no reason to believe nonpartisan primaries will be immune from the factors that drive extremism in party primaries. Further, unless coupled with much more mobilization, primaries will continue to be skewed by low turnout. What is more likely to help rein in extremism is parties' reassertion over primaries and candidates. For the Republican Party, for example, this will require debates among party leaders about which candidates qualify to run on the Republican ticket—perhaps as a broader discussion about the party's values. Further, the recent example of the Democratic incumbent, Joe Biden, stepping down and the party coalescing around Kamala Harris show that parties can do the work of candidate selection without primaries. At best, nonpartisan primaries are unlikely to create the responsive governance that democracy requires, and at worse, nonpartisan primaries might even exacerbate the trends that are rendering parties weak today.

Another nonpartisan reform includes support for a third party, particularly a "moderate" or "centrist" one that somehow transcends partisan divides. There have been plenty of times that a candidate ran in a presidential election behind a specific cause; some were able to command significant vote shares. (Ross Perot's 1992 candidacy got 19% of the popular vote.) However, an exhortation to moderation is hardly the same as a set of compelling issues that resonate with people. As articulated in earlier chapters, centrism is itself elusive. Polls may tell us where majorities of Americans stand on distinct issues, but building a party on top of polling results is not the same as, well, building an actual party. In other words, many of the efforts to establish a third party capitalize on exhaustion with partisanship without doing the groundwork of figuring out what it is people actually want from government. As Steven Teles and Robert Saldin argue in their essay, "The Future Is Faction," politics is about identifying distinct positions around which leaders can mobilize constituencies.[30]

* * *

As democratic governments endeavor to reclaim trust, and as they build policy programs suitable for twenty-first century capitalism, activists will call for change—new institutions, new organizations, new leaders. However, the aspirations toward a moderate or reasonable politics that puts the ugliness of partisanship aside are naïve at best. At worse, they are dangerous, imposing a top-down sense of what people "need" without ever doing the hard work of listening, ideating, and mobilizing among citizens themselves. Democratic politics *requires* conflict, and reforms cannot, and should not, erase it. We cannot pretend our differences don't exist; society is defined by its segments, not by its uniform homogeneity. But what our institutions and leaders must do is take those various segments and build upon them a politics that speaks to our hopes and dreams, to the ability to live the lives of security and dignity that everyone deserves. The institution of the party is neither antiquated nor adverse to democracy. For better or worse, accepting and working within parties—improving them, modernizing them, and strengthening them—will be a necessary and important part of building a democracy for the future.

Notes

CHAPTER 1

1. Lee Rainie, Scott Keeter, and Andrew Perrin. 2019. *Trust and Distrust in America*. Pew Research Center; Howard J. Gold. 2015. "Poll Trends: Americans' Attitudes toward the Political Parties and the Party System." *Public Opinion Quarterly* 79(3): 803–819.
2. Tabatha Abu El-Haj. 2018. "Networking the Party: First Amendment Rights and the Pursuit of Responsive Party Government." *Columbia Law Review* 118(1): 1–76; Adam Bonica and Maya Sen. 2020. *The Judicial Tug of War: How Lawyers, Politicians, and Ideological Incentives Shape the American Judiciary*. Cambridge: Cambridge University Press; Nicholas Carnes. 2013. *White-Collar Government: The Hidden Role of Class in Economic Policy Making*. Chicago: University of Chicago Press.
3. Samara Klar and Yanna Krupnikov. 2016. *Independent Politics: How American Disdain for Parties Leads to Political Inaction*. Cambridge: Cambridge University Press; see also James N. Druckman, Samara Klar, Yanna Krupnikov, Matthew Levendusky, and John Barry Ryan. 2024. *Partisan Hostility and American Democracy: Explaining Political Divisions and When They Matter*. Chicago: University of Chicago Press.
4. Ingrid Van Biezen, Peter Mair, and Thomas Poguntke. 2012. "Going, Going, . . . Gone? The Decline of Party Membership in Contemporary Europe." *European Journal of Political Research* 51: 24–56; Ingrid van Biezen and Thomas Poguntke. 2014. "The Decline of Membership-Based Politics." *Party Politics* 20(2): 205–216.
5. Steven Levitsky and Daniel Ziblatt. 2018. *How Democracies Die*. New York: Crown Publishers; Scott Mainwaring and Timothy Scully (eds). 1995. "Party Systems in Latin America." In *Building Democratic Institutions: Party Systems in Latin America*, 1–34. Cambridge: Cambridge University Press; Nancy Bermeo and Deborah J. Yashar. 2017. *Parties, Movements, and Democracy in the Developing World*. New York: Cambridge University Press; Fernando Bizzarro, John Gerring, Carl Henrik Knutsen, Allen Hicken, Michael Bernhard, Svend-Erik Skaaning, Michael Coppedge, and Staffan I. Lindberg. 2018. "Party Strength and Economic Growth." *World Politics* 70(2): 275–320.
6. Barrington Moore. 1966. *Social Origins of Dictatorship and Democracy*. Boston: Beacon Press.
7. Goran Therborn. 1977. "The Rule of Capital and the Rise of Democracy." *New Left Review* 103(May), p. 7.
8. Larry Diamond. 2019. *Ill Winds: Saving Democracy from Russian Rage, Chinese Ambition, and American Complacency*. New York: Penguin Random House; Moises Naim. 2022. *The Revenge of Power: How Autocrats Are Reinventing Politics for the 21st Century*. New York: St. Martin's Press; Yascha Mounk. 2018. *The People vs. Democracy: Why Our Freedom Is in Danger and How to Save It*. Cambridge, MA: Harvard University Press; Timothy Snyder. 2017. *On Tyranny: Twenty Lessons from the Twentieth Century*. New

York: Crown; Jan-Werner Muller. 2014. "The Party's Over." *London Review of Books* 36, no. 10 (May); Anne Applebaum. 2021. *Twilight of Democracy.* New York: Anchor.

9. Yochai Benkler, Robert Faris, and Hal Roberts. 2018. *Network Propaganda: Manipulation, Disinformation, and Radicalization in American Politics.* Oxford: Oxford University Press; Shoshana Zuboff. 2019. *The Age of Surveillance Capitalism: The Fight for a Human Future at the New Frontier of Power.* New York: PublicAffairs; Joshua A. Tucker and Nathaniel Persily. 2020. *Social Media and Democracy: The State of the Field and Prospects for Reform.* Cambridge: Cambridge University Press.

10. Robert Kuttner. 2018. *Can Democracy Survive Global Capitalism?* New York: W. W. Norton.

11. Anne Case and Angus Deaton. 2020. *Deaths of Despair and the Future of Capitalism.* Princeton, NJ: Princeton University Press.

12. Matthew Smith, Owen Zidar, and Eric Zwick. 2023. "Top Wealth in America: New Estimates Under Heterogeneous Returns," *The Quarterly Journal of Economics* 138(1): 515–573.

13. Seymour M. Lipset and Stein Rokkan. 1967. *Party Systems and Voter Alignments: Cross-national Perspectives.* New York: Free Press.

14. Maurice Duverger. 1951. *Political Parties: Their Organization and Activity in the Modern State.* London: Methuen; Moisei Ostrogorski. 1903. *Democracy and the Organization of Political Parties.* Garden City, NY: Anchor Books.

15. Susan Strange. 1995. "The Limits of Politics." *Government and Opposition* 30, no. 5 (Summer): 291–311; Peter Mair. 2013. *Ruling the Void: The Hollowing of Western Democracy.* London: Verso.

16. Peter A. Hall. 2019. "The Electoral Politics of Growth Regimes." *Perspectives on Politics* 18, no. 1 (March): 185–199.

17. Richard Youngs. 2019. *Civic Activism Unleashed: New Hope or False Dawn for Democracy?* Oxford: Oxford University Press; Erica Chenoweth. 2021. *Civil Resistance: What Everyone Needs to Know.* Oxford: Oxford University Press

18. Robert Mickey. 2015. *Paths Out of Dixie: The Democratization of Authoritarian Enclaves in America's Deep South, 1944–1972.* Princeton, NJ: Princeton University Press; Edward Gibson. 2012. *Boundary Control: Subnational Authoritarianism in Federal Democracies.* New York: Cambridge University Press

19. Wolfgang Streeck. 2014. *Buying Time: The Delayed Crisis of Democratic Capitalism.* London: Verso; Wendy Brown. 2017. *Undoing the Demos: Neoliberalism's Stealth Revolution.* Cambridge, MA: Zone Books/MIT Press.

20. Theda Skocpol. 1999. "Advocates without Members: The Recent Transformation of American Civic Life." In *Civic Engagement in American Democracy,* edited by Theda Skocpol and Morris P. Fiorina. Washington, DC: Brookings Institution Press: 506.

CHAPTER 2

1. William L. Riordon. 1995. *Plunkitt of Tammany Hall.* New York: Signet Classics.

2. Harold D. Moser, David R. Hoth, and George H. Hoemann eds. *The Papers of Andrew Jackson,* vol. 4: 1816–1820. Knoxville: University of Tennessee Press, 75.

3. Martin Van Buren to Thomas Ritchie, January 13, 1827. Letters of Martin Van Buren, Library of Congress.

4. Peter A. Hall. 2019. "The Electoral Politics of Growth Regimes." *Perspectives on Politics* 18, no. 1 (March): 185–199.

5. Maurice Duverger. 1951. *Political Parties: Their Organization and Activity in the Modern State*. London: Methuen, quoted in Otto Kirchheimer. 1966. "The Transformation of the Western European Party Systems." In *Political Parties and Political Development*, edited by Joseph LaPalombara and Myron Weiner. Princeton, NJ: Princeton University Press, 178.

6. See David Alexander Bateman. 2018. *Disenfranchising Democracy: Constructing the Electorate in the United States, the United Kingdom, and France*. New York: Cambridge University Press. Democratization was not linear, and periods of democratic expansion were accompanied by backlash; see Didi Kuo. 2020. "Democratization and the Francise." *Comparative Politics* 52(3): 515–532. There were episodes of authoritarian retrenchment or the outright overthrowing of democracy, particularly in the American South (before and after the Civil War) and in interwar Germany and France. See Robert Mickey. 2015. *Paths Out of Dixie: The Democratization of Authoritarian Enclaves in America's Deep South, 1944–1972*. Princeton, NJ: Princeton University Press; Sheri Berman. 2019. *Democracy and Dictatorship in Europe*. New York: Oxford University Press; Barrington Moore. 1966. *Social Origins of Dictatorship and Democracy*. Boston: Beacon Press.

7. Alexis de Tocqueville. 1840. *Democracy in America*. Translated by Henry Reeve and John C. Spencer. New York: J. & H. G. Langley.

8. Friendly societies took different forms, but they included mutual-aid or benefit groups, as well as fraternal organizations.

9. Robert Wiebe. 1967. *The Search for Order*. Westport, CT: Greenwood Press; Elisabeth Clemens. 1997. *The People's Lobby: Organizational Innovation and the Rise of Interest Group Politics in the United States, 1890–1925*. Chicago: University of Chicago Press.

10. Moisei Ostrogorski. 1902. *Democracy and the Organization of Political Parties*. New York: Macmillan.

11. Jan-Werner Muller. 2014. "The Party's Over." *London Review of Books* 36, no. 10 (May).

12. Karl Polanyi. 1944; 2001. *The Great Transformation*. 2nd ed. Boston: Beacon Press.

13. Dawn Langan Teele. 2018. *Forging the Franchise: The Political Origins of the Women's Vote*. Princeton, NJ: Princeton University Press.

14. A long literature argues that democracies have less inequality than authoritarian regimes; see Allan H. Meltzer and Scott F. Richard. 1981. "A Rational Theory of the Size of Government." *Journal of Political Economy* 89(5): 914–927; Daron Acemoglu and James A. Robinson. 2006. *Economic Origins of Dictatorship and Democracy*. Cambridge: Cambridge University Press; Peter H. Lindert. 2004. *Growing Public: Social Spending and Economic Growth since the Eighteenth Century*. Cambridge: Cambridge University Press; Torsten Persson and Guido Tabellini. 2003. *The Economic Effects of Constitutions*. Cambridge, MA: MIT Press. This is an active scholarly debate; for a more recent analysis and summary of the literature, see Daron Acemoglu, Suresh Naidu, Pascual Restrepo, and James A. Robinson. 2015. "Democracy, Redistribution, and Inequality." In *The Handbook of Income Distribution*, edited by Anthony B. Atkinson and François Bourguignon. Elsevier, 1885–1966.

15. Alessandro Lizzeri and Nicola Persico. 2001. "The Provision of Public Goods under Alternative Electoral Incentives." *American Economic Review* 91, no. 1 (March): 225–239; Alessandro Lizzeri and Nicola Persico. 2004. "Why Did the Elites Extend the

Suffrage? Democracy and the Scope of Government, with an Application to Britain's 'Age of Reform.'" *The Quarterly Journal of Economics* 119, no. 2 (May): 707–765;

16. Esra Kose, Elira Kuka, and Na'ama Shenhav. 2021. "Women's Suffrage and Children's Education." *American Economic Journal: Economic Policy* 13, no. 3 (August): 374–405. I thank Abhay Aneja for a discussion about franchise expansion and inequality and for pointing me in the direction of much of this excellent work.

17. Grant Miller. 2008. "Women's Suffrage, Political Responsiveness, and Child Survival in American History," *The Quarterly Journal of Economics* 123, no. 3 (August): 1287–1327.

18. Gerald Gamm and Thad Kousser. 2021. "Life, Literacy, and the Pursuit of Prosperity: Party Competition and Policy Outcomes in 50 States." *American Political Science Review* 115(4): 1442–1463; Daron Acemoglu, Suresh Naidu, Pascual Restrepo, and James A. Robinson. 2019. "Democracy Does Cause Growth." *Journal of Political Economy* 127(1): 47–100.

19. Elizabeth U. Cascio and Ebonya Washington. 2013. "Valuing the Vote: The Redistribution of Voting Rights and State Funds following the Voting Rights Act of 1965." *The Quarterly Journal of Economics* 129, no. 1 (October): 379–433; Gavin Wright. 2018. *Sharing the Prize: The Economics of the Civil Rights Revolution in the American South.* Cambridge, MA: Harvard University Press.

20. Anthony Downs. 1957. *An Economic Theory of Democracy.* New York: Harper.

21. Kirchheimer 1966.

22. Ibid.

23. Richard Katz and Peter Mair. 1995. "Changing Models of Party Organization and Party Democracy: The Emergence of the Cartel Party." *Party Politics* 1(1): 5–28.

24. Angelo Panebianco. 1988. *Political Parties: Organization and Power.* New York: Cambridge University Press.

25. Katz and Mair 1995, 17.

26. Daniel M. Shea. 1999. "The Passing of Realignment and the Advent of the 'BaseLess' Party System." *American Politics Quarterly* 27, no. 1 (January): 51.

27. Panebianco 1988, 274.

28. Russell J. Dalton and Martin Wattenberg. 2000. *Parties without Partisans: Political Change in Advanced Industrial Democracies.* New York: Oxford University Press; Martin P. Wattenberg. 1991. *The Rise of Candidate-Centered Politics: Presidential Elections of the 1980s.* Cambridge, MA: Harvard University Press.

29. Mark Blyth and Richard Katz. 2005. "From Catch-all Politics to Cartelisation: The Political Economy of the Cartel Party." *West European Politics* 28(1): 33–60; Richard Katz and Peter Mair. 2009. "The Cartel Party Thesis: A Restatement." *Perspectives on Politics* 7(4): 753–766.

30. Bernard Manin. 1997. *The Principles of Representative Government.* Cambridge: Cambridge University Press.

31. Joseph Schumpeter. 1942. *Capitalism, Socialism, and Democracy.* New York: Harper and Brothers.

32. Nolan McCarty and Eric Schickler. 2018. "On the Theory of Parties." *Annual Review of Political Science* 21: 184.

33. Russell Muirhead and Nancy L. Rosenblum. 2020. "The Political Theory of Parties and Partisanship: Catching Up." *Annual Review of Political Science* 23: 18.

34. Julia Azari. 2016. "Weak Parties and Strong Partisanship Are a Bad Combination." Vox, November 3.

35. See also Daniel Schlozman and Sam Rosenfeld. 2024. *The Hollow Parties: The Many Pasts and Disordered Present of American Party Politics*. Princeton, NJ: Princeton University Press; Samuel Issacharoff. 2017. "Outsourcing Politics: The Hostile Takeover of Our Hollowed-Out Political Parties." *Houston Law Review Frankel Lecture Series* 54, no. 4 (April): 845–880; Richard H. Pildes. 2014. "Romanticizing Democracy, Political Fragmentation, and the Decline of American Government." *Yale Law Journal*, 124, no. 3 (December): 806–852; Bruce E. Cain and Cody Gray. 2018. "Parties by Design: Pluralist Party Reform in a Polarized Era." *New York University Law Review* 93(October): 621–646.

36. There is a large literature on political polarization that measures party-line roll-call votes in Congress showing that polarization began in the late 1970s and accelerated after the 1990s.

37. Susan Stokes, Thad Dunning, Marcelo Nazareno, and Valeria Brusco. 2013. *Brokers, Voters, and Clientelism: The Puzzle of Distributive Politics*. New York: Cambridge University Press; Rebecca Weitz-Shapiro. 2014. *Curbing Clientelism in Argentina: Politics, Poverty, and Social Policy*. Cambridge: Cambridge University Press.

38. Judith Chubb. 1982. *Patronage, Power, and Poverty in Southern Italy: A Tale of Two Cities*. Cambridge: Cambridge University Press; Sidney Tarrow. 1977. "The Italian Party System between Crisis and Transition." *American Journal of Political Science* 21, no. 2 (May): 193–224.

39. Steven I. Wilkinson. 2007. "Explaining Changing Patterns of Party-Voter Linkages in India." In *Patrons, Clients, and Policies*, edited by Herbert Kitschelt and Steven Wilkinson, 110–140. Cambridge: Cambridge University Press.

40. Tabatha Abu El-Haj. 2018. "Networking the Party: First Amendment Rights and the Pursuit of Responsive Party Government." *Columbia Law Review* 118(1): 1–76.

41. Panebianco 1998, 265; see also Giovanni Sartori. 1976. *Parties and Party Systems: A Framework for Analysis*. Cambridge: Cambridge University Press.

42. Charles Anderson. 1978. "The Political Economy of Charles Lindblom." *The American Political Science Review* 72(3): 1012.

43. There is a more recent definition of political economy that has to do with methodology, particularly the use of quantitative methods to examine politics. A recent article describes political economy with "a methodological definition . . . mean[ing] work that either uses formal theory or empirically tests falsifiable arguments using quantitative methods." This encapsulates the economics-ization of political science as "political economy." I prefer to use the term to describe the interface of politics and economics, but given that the discipline has taken a sharp turn toward methodology, it is not surprising that the terminology of political economy has also narrowed. See Volha Charnysh, Eugene Finkel, and Scott Gehlbach. 2023. "Historical Political Economy: Past, Present, and Future." *Annual Review of Political Science* 26: 175–191.

44. Seymour M. Lipset and Stein Rokkan. 1967. *Party Systems and Voter Alignments: Cross-National Perspectives*. New York: Free Press.

45. Scott Mainwaring, ed. 2018. *Party Systems in Latin America: Institutionalization, Decay, and Collapse*. New York: Cambridge University Press; Scott Mainwaring and Timothy Scully (eds). 1995. "Party Systems in Latin America." In *Building Democratic Institutions: Party Systems in Latin America*, 1–34. Cambridge: Cambridge University Press; Nancy Bermeo and Deborah J. Yashar. 2017. *Parties, Movements, and Democracy in the Developing World*. New York: Cambridge University Press; Daniel Ziblatt. 2018.

Conservative Political Parties and the Birth of Modern Democracy. New York: Cambridge University Press; Fernando Bizzarro et al. 2018. "Party Strength and Economic Growth." *World Politics* 70(2): 275–320; Nancy Rosenblum. 2010. *On the Side of Angels: An Appreciation of Parties and Partisanship.* Princeton, NJ: Princeton University Press.

46. Bizzarro et al. 2018, 278.
47. Margit Tavits. 2013. *Post-Communist Democracies and Party Organization.* New York: Cambridge University Press, 83.
48. Joseph LaPalombara and Myron Weiner, eds. 1966. *Political Parties and Political Development.* Princeton, NJ: Princeton University Press.
49. Allen Hicken and Rachel Beatty Riedl. 2018. "From the Outside Looking In: Latin American Parties in Comparative Perspective." In *Party Systems in Latin America*, edited by Scott Mainwaring. Cambridge: Cambridge University Press, 426–440.
50. Noam Lupu. 2011. *Party Brands in Crisis: Partisanship, Brand Dilution, and the Breakdown of Political Parties in Latin America.* New York: Cambridge University Press; Jana Morgan. 2011. *Bankrupt Representation and Party System Collapse.* University Park: Pennsylvania State University Press; Jason Seawright. 2012. *Party System Collapse: The Roots of Crisis in Peru and Venezuela.* Stanford: Stanford University Press.
51. Bermeo and Yashar 2017; Hesham Sallam. 2022. *Classless Politics: Islamist Movements, the Left, and Authoritarian Legacies in Egypt.* New York: Columbia University Press.
52. Hicken and Riedl 2018, 431.
53. Pablo Beramendi, Silja Häusermann, Herbert Kitschelt, and Hanspeter Kriesi. 2015. *The Politics of Advanced Capitalism.* New York: Cambridge University Press; Jacob S. Hacker, Alexander Hertel-Fernandez, Paul Pierson, and Kathleen Thelen. 2021. *The American Political Economy: Politics, Markets, and Power.* Cambridge: Cambridge University Press; Peter Hall, Georgina Evans, and Sung In Kim. 2023. *Political Change and Electoral Coalitions in Western Democracies.* New York: Cambridge University Press
54. Charles E. Lindblom. 1977. *Politics and Markets.* New York: Basic Books, 172; Adam Przeworski and Michael Wallerstein. 1988. "Structural Dependence of the State on Capital." *American Political Science Review* 82(1): 11–29.
55. Kay Lawson and Peter H. Merkl. 1988. *When Parties Fail: Emerging Alternative Organizations.* Princeton, NJ: Princeton University Press, 3.

CHAPTER 3

1. Quoting Katharine Lusk, co-director of the Boston University Initiative on Cities, in Joanna Slater. 2021. "Two Women of Color Will Compete to Become Boston's Next Mayor." *Washington Post*, September 15.
2. Ellen Barry.2021. "Michelle Wu Makes Her Play for Power in Boston." *New York Times*, November 3.
3. The first usage of "retail politics," according to the Oxford English Dictionary, was in 1901, when the *Chicago Tribune* wrote, "He has only commercial instinct to see that while his own vote is worth only $5, a 'block' of ten votes is worth not $50, but a 'job' which will pay him, say $1,000 a year. This is retail politics." See https://www.cjr.org/languagecorner/politics_for_sale.php.

4. Isaac Arnsdorf, Doug Bock Clark, Alexandra Berzon and Anjeanette Damon. 2021. "Heeding Steve Bannon's Call, Election Deniers Organize to Seize Control of the GOP—and Reshape America's Elections." *ProPublica*, September 2.

5. Alexandra Berzon. 2022. "Lawyer Who Plotted to Overturn Trump Loss Recruits Election Deniers to Watch Over the Vote." *New York Times*, May 30.

6. Nancy Rosenblum. 2010. *On the Side of Angels: An Appreciation of Parties and Partisanship*. Princeton, NJ: Princeton University Press.

7. Daniel Schulman. 2014. *Sons of Wichita: How the Koch Brothers Became America's Most Powerful and Private Dynasty*. New York: Grand Central Publishing.

8. Jeffrey Toobin. 2014. "The Absolutist." *The New Yorker*, June 23.

9. Ingrid Van Biezen, Peter Mair, and Thomas Poguntke. 2012. "Going, Going. . . Gone? The Decline of Party Membership in Contemporary Europe." *European Journal of Political Research*, 51: 24–56; Ingrid van Biezen and Thomas Poguntke. 2014. "The Decline of Membership-Based Politics." *Party Politics* 20(2): 205–216
Peter Mair and Ingrid van Biezen. 2001. "Party Membership in Twenty European Democracies, 1980–2000." *Party Politics* 7(1): 5–21; Nancy Bermeo and Philip Nord. 2000. *Civil Society before Democracy: Lessons from Nineteenth-Century Europe*. Lanham, MD: Rowman and Littlefield.

10. Herbert Kitschelt. 1989. *The Logics of Party Formation*. Ithaca, NY: Cornell University Press.

11. Bermeo and Nord 2000.

12. Susan E. Scarrow. 2015. *Beyond Party Members: Changing Approaches to Partisan Mobilization*. New York: Oxford University Press; see also Geoff Eley, *Forging Democracy: The History of the Left in Europe, 1850–2000*. Oxford: Oxford University Press.

13. Robert Wiebe. 1967. *The Search for Order*. Westport, CT: Greenwood Press.

14. Daniel Ziblatt. 2018. *Conservative Political Parties and the Birth of Modern Democracy*. New York: Cambridge University Press.

15. Ibid., citing Moisei Ostrogorski. 1903. *Democracy and the Organization of Political Parties*. Garden City, New York: Anchor Books, 85.

16. Ostrogorski 1903, 85–95.

17. Scarrow 2015.

18. Ostrogorski 1903; Ivor Bulmer-Thomas. 1965. *The Growth of the British Party System*, vol. 1, *1640–1923*. London: John Baker.

19. The changes at this time became the backbone of modernization theory, which posited that as societies shift from agrarian to industrial economies, they also become more urban, more educated, and more literate. A rigid class structure defined by a very small aristocratic elite and large peasantry gives way to a fluid class structure defined by a large middle class. Modernization theory is one of the foremost theories of political development in political science, with a literature far too expansive to enumerate here. The canon includes Seymour M. Lipset. 1959. "Some Social Requisites of Democracy: Economic Development and Political Legitimacy." *American Political Science Review* 53, no. 1 (March): 69–105; Barrington Moore. 1966. *Social Origins of Dictatorship and Democracy*. Boston: Beacon Press; Dankwart A. Rustow. 1970. "Transitions to Democracy: Toward a Dynamic Model." *Comparative Politics* 2, no. 3 (April): 337–363. For a deep exploration of political development, see Francis Fukuyama. 2014. *Political Order: From the Industrial Revolution to the Globalization of Democracy*. New York: Farrar, Straus and Giroux. On the relationship of inequality and democracy, see Daron Acemoglu

and James Robinson. 2006. *The Economic Origins of Dictatorship and Democracy*. Cambridge: Cambridge University Press; Carles Boix. 2003. *Democracy and Redistribution*. New York: Cambridge University Press

20. Rosa Mulé. 1998. "Financial Uncertainties of Party Formation and Consolidation in Britain, Germany and Italy." In *Funding Democratization*, ed. Peter J. Burnell and Alan Ware. Manchester: Manchester University Press, 47–72.

21. Ibid.

22. Didi Kuo. 2018. *Clientelism, Capitalism, and Democracy: The Rise of Programmatic Politics in the United States and Britain*. New York: Cambridge University Press.

23. Jesse Macy. 1904. *Party Organization and Machinery*. New York: Century Co.

24. Frank J. Sorauf. 1980. *Party Politics in America*. Boston: Little, Brown; James L. Gibson, Cornelius Cotter, John Bibby and Robert Huckshorn. 1983. "Assessing Party Organizational Strength." *American Journal of Political Science* 27 (2): 193–222.

25. Macy 1904.

26. Ibid.

27. Cornelius P. Cotter and John F. Bibby. 1980. "Institutional Development of Parties and the Thesis of Party Decline." *Political Science Quarterly* 95, no. 1 (Spring): 1–27.

28. Ibid., 4.

29. Hugh A. Bone. 1958. *Party Committees and National Politics*. Seattle: University of Washington Press

30. The RNC dispatched members to congressional districts when they thought there might be a risk of party breakdown, for example; ibid.

31. Ibid.

32. Cotter and Bibby 1980.

33. Daniel J. Galvin. 2010. *Presidential Party Building: Dwight D. Eisenhower to George W. Bush*. Princeton, NJ: Princeton University Press.

34. Ibid.; Daniel J. Galvin. 2012. "The Transformation of Political Institutions: Investments in Institutional Resources and Gradual Change in the National Party Committees." *Studies in American Political Development* 26(April): 50–70.

35. Galvin 2012.

36. Cotter and Bibby 1980.

37. Bone 1958.

38. Cornelius P. Cotter, James L. Gibson, John F. Bibby, and Robert J. Huckshorn. 1984. *Party Organizations in American Politics*. New York: Praeger.

39. Douglas D. Roscoe and Shannon Jenkins. 2014. "Changes in Local Party Structure and Activity, 1980–2008." In *The State of the Parties: The Changing Role of Contemporary American Parties*, 7th ed., edited by John C. Green, Daniel J. Coffey, and David Cohen. Lanham, MD: Rowman and Littlefield.

40. Douglas D. Roscoe and Shannon Jenkins. 2015. *Local Party Organizations in the Twenty-First Century*. Albany, NY: SUNY Press.

41. James Q. Wilson. 1966. *The Amateur Democrat*. Chicago, IL: University of Chicago Press.

42. Francis Carney. 1963. "The Rise of the Democratic Clubs in California." In *Cases on Party Organization*, edited by Paul Tillett, 32–63. New Brunswick, NJ: Rutgers University Press.

43. Ibid., 45.

44. Sorauf 1980.

45. Martin P. Wattenberg. 1991. *The Rise of Candidate-Centered Politics: Presidential Elections of the 1980s*. Cambridge, MA: Harvard University Press; Daniel M. Shea. 1999. "The Passing of Realignment and the Advent of the 'Base-Less' Party System." *American Politics Quarterly* 27, no. 1 (January): 33–57.

46. Wattenberg 1991; Shea 1999; Cotter et al. 1984;Paul S. Herrnson. 2002. "National Party Organizations at the Dawn of the Twenty-First Century." In *The Parties Respond: Changes in American Parties and Campaigns*, ed. L. Sandy Maisel. Boulder, CO: Westview Press: 47–78.

47. Cotter and Bibby 1980.

48. Ibid.

49. Galvin 2012.

50. R. Kenneth Godwin. 1988. "The Structure, Content, and Use of Political Direct Mail." *Polity* 20, no. 3 (Spring): 527–538.

51. Paul S. Herrnson. 1988. *Party Campaigning in the 1980s*. Cambridge, MA: Harvard University Press.

52. Some literature on American parties describes the role of local- and county-level party committees as adaptive, or as engaging in "adaptive brokerage" to help campaigns and candidates. See, for example, James L. Gibson, John P. Frendreis, and Laura L. Vertz. 1989. "Party Dynamics in the 1980s: Change in County Party Organizational Strength, 1980–1984." *American Journal of Political Science* 33(1): 67–90; John P. Frendreis, James L. Gibson, and Laura L. Vertz. 1990. "The Electoral Relevance of Local Party Organizations." *The American Political Science Review* 84(1): 225–235; John Frendreis and Alan R. Gitelson. 1999. "Local Parties in the 1990s: Spokes in a Candidate-Centered Wheel." In *The State of the Parties: The Changing Role of Contemporary American Parties*, edited by John C. Green and Daniel Shea. Lanham, MD: Rowman & Littlefield, 135-153; Daniel M. Shea, J. Cherie Strachan, and Michael Wolf. 2013. "Local Party Viability, Goals, and Objectives in the Information Age." In *The Parties Respond* edited by Mark Brewer, 5th ed. London: Routledge, 103–132.

53. Robert Michels. 1915 [1911]. *Political Parties: A Sociological Study of the Oligarchic Tendency of Modern Democracy*. New York: Hearst's International Library.

54. Jamie Sanchez Jr. 2020. "Revisiting McGovern-Fraser: Party Nationalization and the Rhetoric of Reform." *Journal of Policy History* 32, no. 1 (January): 1–24; Schlozman and Rosenfeld 2024; Levitsky and Ziblatt 2018.

55. Cotter and Bibby 1980, 17.

56. Clarence A. Berdahl. 1942. "Party Membership in the United States, I." *American Political Science Review* 36, no. 1 (February): 16–50.

57. Levitsky and Ziblatt 2018; Frances Rosenbluth and Ian Shapiro. 2018. *Responsible Parties*. New Haven, CT: Yale University Press.

58. See Joshua Ferrer and Michael Thorning. 2023. "2022 Primary Turnout: Trends and Lessons for Boosting Participation." Washington, DC: Bipartisan Policy Center.

59. Lee Drutman. 2021. "What We Know about Congressional Primaries and Congressional Primary Reform." Washington, DC: New America.

60. Yamiche Alcindor. 2016. "Party Leader's Resignation a Sign of Bernie Sanders's Influence, His Backers Say." *The New York Times*, July 24. The trove of leaked emails was later discovered to be the work of Russian hackers interfering in the American election.

61. Ben Schreckinger. 2016. "RNC Lawyers Look at Options for Replacing Trump." *Politico*, October 8.

62. David W. Brady, Hahrie Han, and Jeremy C. Pope. 2007. "Primary Elections and Candidate Ideology: Out of Step with the Primary Electorate?" *Legislative Studies Quarterly* 32(1): 79–105; see also the Brookings Institution Primaries Project https://www.brookings.edu/projects/the-primaries-project/.

63. Peter Mair. 2013. *Ruling the Void: The Hollowing of Western Democracy.* London: Verso.

64. Theda Skocpol. 2004. "Voice and Inequality: The Transformation of American Civic Democracy." *Perspectives on Politics* 2, no. 1 (March): 3–20.

65. There is an incredibly rich literature on Progressive-era organizing in the United States. For some examples, see Elisabeth Clemens. 1997. *The People's Lobby: Organizational Innovation and the Rise of Interest Group Politics in the United States, 1890–1925.* Chicago: University of Chicago Press; Wiebe 1967; Louis Galambos. 1970. "The Emerging Organizational Synthesis in Modern American History." *The Business History Review* 44(3): 279–290.

66. Jeffrey M. Berry. 1977. *Lobbying for the People: The Political Behavior of Public Interest Groups.* Princeton, NJ: Princeton University Press.

67. Julian E. Zelizer. 2002. "Seeds of Cynicism: The Struggle over Campaign Finance, 1956–1974." *Journal of Policy History* 14(1): 73–111.

68. Ibid., 91.

69. Kate Andrias. 2014. "Hollowed-Out Democracy." *New York University Law Review* 89:48–51.

70. Stefano Bartolini. 2000. *The Political Mobilization of the European Left, 1860–1980: The Class Cleavage.* Cambridge: Cambridge University Press; Taylor E. Dark. 1999. *The Unions and the Democrats: An Enduring Alliance.* Ithaca, NY: Cornell University Press.

71. Henry S. Farber, Daniel Herbst, Ilyana Kuziemko, and Suresh Naidu. 2021. "Unions and Inequality over the Twentieth Century: New Evidence from Survey Data." *The Quarterly Journal of Economics* 136(3): 1325–1385; J. David Greenstone. 1969. *Labor in American Politics.* New York: Knopf; Jake Rosenfeld. 2014. *What Unions No Longer Do.* Cambridge, MA: Harvard University Press; Kathleen Thelen. 2019. "The American Precariat: U.S. Capitalism in Comparative Perspective." *Perspectives on Politics* 17, no. 1 (March): 5–27; Steven Greenhouse. 2020. *Beaten Down, Worked Up: The Past, Present, and Future of American Labor.* New York: Knopf Doubleday.

72. Thomas B. Edsall. 1993. "Are Labor Tactics on NAFTA Real Threats or Tough Love?" *Washington Post*, November 16.

73. James Piazza. 2001. "De-linking Labor: Labor Unions and Social Democratic Parties under Globalization." *Party Politics* 7(4): 413–435; Sheri Berman. 2016. "The Specter Haunting Europe: The Lost Left." *Journal of Democracy* 27(4): 69–76.

74. Kai Arzheimer. 2006. "'Dead Men Walking?' Party Identification in Germany, 1977–2002." *Electoral Studies* 25(4): 791–807.

75. Giacomo Benedetto, Simon Hix, and Nicola Mastrorocco. 2020. "The Rise and Fall of Social Democracy, 1918–2017." *American Political Science Review* 114(3): 928–939.

76. Emilie van Haute and Anika Gauja. 2015. *Party Members and Activists.* London: Routledge.

77. Thomas Poguntke, Susan E. Scarrow, and Paul D. Webb. 2016. "Party Rules, Party Resources and the Politics of Parliamentary Democracies: How Parties Organize in the 21st Century." *Party Politics* 22(6): 661–678.

78. Richard Katz and Peter Mair. 1995. "Changing Models of Party Organization and Party Democracy: The Emergence of the Cartel Party." *Party Politics* 1(1): 5–28.
79. Jon Pierre, Lars Svåsand, and Anders Widfeldt. 2000. "State Subsidies to Political Parties: Confronting Rhetoric with Reality." *West European Politics* 23(3): 1–24; Paul F. Whiteley. 2011. "Is the Party Over? The Decline of Party Activism and Membership across the Democratic World." *Party Politics* 17(1): 21–44.
80. Russell J. Dalton. 2000. "The Decline of Party Identifications." In *Parties without Partisans*, ed. Russell J. Dalton and Martin P. Wattenberg. Oxford: Oxford University Press: 19–36; Ronald Inglehart. 1997. *Modernization and Postmodernization: Cultural, Economic and Political Change in 43 Nations*. Princeton, NJ: Princeton University Press.
81. David E. Price. 1984. *Bringing Back the Parties*. Washington, DC: CQ Press.
82. Ibid.
83. Ibid.
84. Susan E. Scarrow, Paul D. Webb, and Thomas Poguntke, eds. 2017. *Organizing Political Parties: Representation, Participation, and Power*. Oxford: Oxford University Press.
85. Galvin 2012.

CHAPTER 4

1. *Time*. 1998. "The Third Way Wonkfest." May 18.
2. Tony Blair and Gerhard Schröder. 1998. "Europe: The Third Way/Die Neue Mitte." Available at https://library.fes.de/pdf-files/bueros/suedafrika/02828.pdf
3. Herbert Kitschelt. 1994. *The Transformation of European Social Democracy*. New York: Cambridge University Press.
4. Sheri Berman. 2019. *Democracy and Dictatorship in Europe*. New York: Oxford University Press.
5. Michael Crozier, Samuel Huntington, and Juji Watanabe. 1975. *The Crisis of Democracy*. New York: New York University Press.
6. Kim Phillips-Fein. 2010. *Invisible Hands: The Businessmen's Crusade against the New Deal*. New York: W. W. Norton.
7. Alice O'Connor. 2008. "Financing the Counterrevolution." In *Rightward Bound: Making America Conservative in the 1970s*, edited by Bruce J. Schulman and Julian E. Zelizer. Cambridge, MA: Harvard University Press: 148–168.
8. Paul Pierson and Theda Skocpol, eds. 2007. *The Transformation of American Politics: Activist Government and the Rise of Conservatism*. Princeton, NJ: Princeton University Press.
9. David E. Rosenbaum. 1981. "Reagan's Thesis: Issue Is Entitlements." *New York Times*, March 24.
10. Examples include the House Democratic Caucus's Committee on Party Effectiveness and the National House Democratic Caucus. Policy reports include "Rebuilding the Road to Opportunity" (1982) and "Renewing America's Promise" (1984); see Kenneth S. Baer. 2000. *Reinventing Democrats: The Politics of Liberalism from Reagan to Clinton*. University of Kansas Press.
11. The DLC included ten governors, fourteen senators, and eighteen members of the House of Representatives; the *New York Times* announced the council with the headline "Dissidents Defy Top Democrats" (reported by Phil Gailey, March 1, 1985).
12. Baer 2000.

13. Al From. 2013. *The New Democrats and the Return to Power*. New York: St. Martin's Press, 70.

14. Ibid.

15. In 1983, the *Washington Monthly*, a publication that prided itself on its heterodox approach and focus on policy, convened a conference in Reston, Virginia, that drew some 350 participants. The editor, Charles Peters, later published "A New Road for America: The Neoliberal Movement" with Phillip Keisling, laying out the potential for a neoliberal politics divorced from traditional party positions. At the conference, the goals of neoliberalism included "freeing [liberalism] from its old automatic responses in favor of unions and big government and against business and the military." Quoted in William E. Farrell. 1983. "'Neoliberals' in Need of Constituents." *New York Times*, October 24.

16. Victor Ferkiss. 1986. "'Neoliberalism: How New? How Liberal? How Significant?': A Review Essay." *The Western Political Quarterly* 39(1): 165–179; see also Randall Rothenberg, who described the neoliberals as "insurgents" who cared little about the "established constituencies" of the party. Randall Rothenberg. 1984. *The Neoliberals: Creating the New American Politics*. New York: Simon & Schuster. The neoliberals were compared to the Atari Democrats, Democratic politicians like Paul Tsongas and Gary Hart, who emphasized renewing the party's commitments to business, particularly technology. For an excellent history of the neoliberals and the Democratic agenda in the 1990s, see Geismer 2022.

17. The DLC's first policy paper, released in 1985, was titled "Winning in the World Economy." It emphasized changing the party's orientation from a focus on domestic constituencies of the left to the constituencies of skeptical voters. The paper advocated reducing barriers to trade—a position very unpopular with unions—and positioning America's economy for global competition. Al From (2013) proudly described the way the paper broke ranks with the rest of the Democratic Party around trade and economic policy. From worked with the Wharton School to show that trade deficits and uncompetitive policies were harming the U.S. economy.

18. From 2013, 113.

19. William Galston and Elaine Kamarck. 1989. "The Politics of Evasion: Democrats and the Presidency." Washington, DC: Progressive Policy Institute, September.

20. Mark Schmitt. 2011. "When the Democratic Leadership Council Mattered." *The American Prospect*, February 10.

21. Robin Toner. 1990. "Eyes to Left, Democrats Edge toward Center." *New York Times*, March 25.

22. Dennis W. Johnson. 2016. *Democracy for Hire: A History of American Political Consulting*. Oxford: Oxford University Press: 320.

23. Jeffrey Frankel and Peter Orszag, eds. 2002. *American Economic Policy in the 1990s*.Cambridge, MA: MIT Press.

24. Ibid., p. 5-6.

25. Peter Kilborn. 1993. "Unions Gird for War over Trade Pact." *New York Times*, October 4.

26. Reich is now Carmel P. Friesen Professor of Public Policy at the University of California, Berkeley, and a prominent critic of contemporary capitalism. He was known for being more progressive than other economic advisers in the Clinton administration. On NAFTA, see William Neikirk. 1993. "Reich: Labor 'Plain Wrong' on NAFTA." *Chicago Tribune*, July 14.

27. Timothy P. R. Weaver. 2021. "Market Privilege: The Place of Neoliberalism in American Political Development." *Studies in American Political Development* 35(1): 104–126.
28. Frankel and Orszag 2002.
29. Lawrence Jacobs and Desmond King. 2017. *Fed Power: How Finance Wins*. New York: Oxford University Press.
30. Sheri Berman and Kathleen R. McNamara. 1999. "Bank on Democracy: Why Central Banks Need Public Oversight." *Foreign Affairs* 78(2): 2–8; Jacobs and King 2017.
31. Curtis Atkins. 2016. "The Third Way International." *Jacobin*, February 11.
32. Anthony Giddens. 1998. *The Third Way: The Renewal of Social Democracy*. Cambridge: Polity Press.
33. Geoffrey Evans and James Tilley. 2017. *The New Politics of Class: The Political Exclusion of the British Working Class*. Oxford: Oxford University Press; Andrew Glyn. 2001. *Social Democracy in Neoliberal Times: The Left and Economic Policy since 1980*. Oxford: Oxford University Press; Julia Lynch. 2020. *Regimes of Inequality: The Political Economy of Health and Wealth*. Cambridge: Cambridge University Press; Jonathan Hopkin and Kate Alexander Shaw. 2016. "Organized Combat or Structural Advantage? The Politics of Inequality and the Winner-Take-All Economy in the United Kingdom." *Politics and Society* 44(3): 345–371.
34. Andrew Glyn and Stewart Wood. 2001. "Economic Policy under New Labour: How Social Democratic Is the Blair Government?" *The Political Quarterly* 72(1): 50–66.
35. Ibid.
36. Atkins-2016.
37. Lucio Baccaro and Chris Howell. 2017. *Trajectories of Neoliberal Transformation: European Industrial Relations since the 1970s*. Cambridge: Cambridge University Press.
38. Paul Webb. 2000. *The Modern British Party System*. London: Sage.
39. Mark A. Pollack. 2000. "Blairism in Brussels: The Third Way in Europe since Amsterdam." In *The State of the European Union: Risks, Reform, Resistance, and Revival*, edited by Maria Green Cowles and Michael Smith. Oxford: Oxford University Press: 266–291.
40. William Boston. 1999. "A Decade of Change: The Battle for Berlin." *Wall Street Journal*, September 27.
41. Ibid.
42. Niklas Engbom, Enrica Detragiache, and Faezeh Raei. "The German Labor Market Reforms and Post-unemployment Earnings." *IMF Working Papers* 15, no. 162(2015): 1, https://doi.org/10.5089/9781513531250.001.
43. Atkins 2016.
44. Blair and Schroeder 1998.
45. Cecilie Rohwedder. 2020. "Third Way Is Passe for the Center-Left." *Wall Street Journal*, June 5.
46. Robert Taylor. 1999. "Some Comments on the Blair/Schroeder 'Third Way/Neue Mitte' Manifesto." *Transfer: European Review of Labour and Research* 5(3): 411–414.
47. Ralf Dahrendorf. 1999. "The Third Way and Liberty: An Authoritarian Streak in Europe's New Center." *Foreign Affairs* 78(5): 13–17.
48. Peter A. Hall. 2019. "The Electoral Politics of Growth Regimes." *Perspectives on Politics* 18, no. 1 (March): 185–199; Mark Blyth. 2012. *Great Transformations: Economic Ideas and Institutional Change in the Twentieth Century*. Cambridge: Cambridge University Press.
49. Timothy Hellwig. 2014. *Globalization and Mass Politics: Retaining the Room to Maneuver*. Cambridge: Cambridge University Press.

50. Stephanie L. Mudge. 2018. *Leftism Reinvented: Western Parties from Socialism to Neoliberalism*. Cambridge, MA: Harvard University Press; see also Wolfgang Streeck and Kathleen Thelen, eds. 2005. *Beyond Continuity: Institutional Change in Advanced Political Economies*. Oxford: Oxford University Press; Baccaro and Howell 2017.

51. Nils D. Steiner and Christian W. Martin. 2012. "Economic Integration, Party Polarisation and Electoral Turnout." *West European Politics* 35(2): 238–265; Helen V. Milner and Benjamin Judkins. 2004. "Partisanship, Trade Policy, and Globalization: Is There a Left-Right Divide on Trade Policy?" *International Studies Quarterly* 48, no. 1 (January): 95–119; Hugh Ward, Lawrence Ezrow, and Han Dorussen. 2011. "Globalization, Party Positions, and the Median Voter." *World Politics* 63(3): 509–547.

52. Jae-Jae Spoon and Heike Kluver. 2019. "Party Convergence and Vote Switching: Explaining Mainstream Party Decline across Europe." *European Journal of Political Research* 58: 1021–1042; Dalston Ward, Jeong Hyun Kim, Matthew Graham, and Margit Margit. 2015. "How Economic Integration Affects Party Issue Emphases." *Comparative Political Studies* 48(10): 1227–1259.

53. Jonathan Hopkin. 2020. *Anti-system Politics: The Crisis of Market Liberalism in Rich Democracies*. Oxford: Oxford University Press.

54. Spoon and Kluver 2019.

55. Noam Lupu. 2011. *Party Brands in Crisis: Partisanship, Brand Dilution, and the Breakdown of Political Parties in Latin America*. New York: Cambridge University Press.

56. John Williamson (ed). 1990. "What Washington Means by Policy Reform." In *Latin American Adjustment: How Much Has Happened?* Washington, DC: Institute for International Economics.

57. Kenneth M. Roberts. 2015. *Changing Course in Latin America: Party Systems in the Neoliberal Era*. New York: Cambridge University Press.

58. Susan Stokes. 2001. *Mandates and Democracy: Neoliberalism by Surprise in Latin America*. Cambridge: Cambridge University Press.

59. Kenneth M. Roberts. 2013. "Market Reform, Programmatic (De)alignment, and Party System Stability in Latin America." *Comparative Political Studies* 46(11): 1422–1452.

60. Stokes 2001.

61. Roberts 2015.

62. Lupu 2011; Steven Levitsky. 2003. *Transforming Labor-Based Parties in Latin America: Argentine Peronism in Comparative Perspective*. New York: Cambridge University Press.

63. Maria Victoria Murillo. 2000. "From Populism to Neoliberalism: Labor Unions and Market Reforms in Latin America." *World Politics* 52, no. 2 (January): 135–174.

64. Spoon and Kluver 2019; Niklas Potrafke. 2012. "Political Cycles and Economic Performance in OECD Countries: Empirical Evidence from 1951–2006." *Public Choice* 150(1): 155–179; Mudge 2018.

65. Kitschelt 1994; Thomas Piketty. 2020. *Capital and Ideology*. Cambridge, MA: Harvard University Press; Tarik Abou-Chadi and Simon Hix. 2021. "Brahmin Left versus Merchant Right? Education, Class, Multiparty Competition, and Redistribution in Western Europe." *The British Journal of Sociology* 72(1): 79–92; Amory Gethin, Clara Martinez-Toledano, and Thomas Piketty. 2021. "Brahmin Left versus Merchant Right: Changing Political Cleavages in 21 Western Democracies, 1948–2020." *The Quarterly Journal of Economics* 137, no. 1 (October): 1–48.

66. Kitschelt 1994, 26.

67. Jane Gingrich and Silja Häusermann. 2015. "The Decline of the Working-Class Vote, the Reconfiguration of the Welfare Support Coalition and Consequences for the Welfare State." *Journal of European Social Policy* 25(1): 50–75.
68. Ibid.
69. Dalton and Wattenberg 2000; Ronald Inglehart. 1997. *Modernization and Postmodernization: Cultural, Economic and Political Change in 43 Nations*. Princeton, NJ: Princeton University Press.
70. Dalton 2000.
71. Adam Bonica and Maya Sen. 2020. *The Judicial Tug of War: How Lawyers, Politicians, and Ideological Incentives Shape the American Judiciary*. Cambridge: Cambridge University Press; Evans and Tilley 2017; Jonathan Klick. 2017. "The Wealth of Congress." *Harvard Journal of Law & Public Policy* 40(3): 603–637.
72. See https://www.pewresearch.org/fact-tank/2021/03/10/the-changing-face-of-congress/.
73. Evans and Tilley 2017, 128.
74. Ibid., 119.
75. Hall 2019.
76. Lynch 2020; Evans and Tilley 2017.
77. Silja Hausermann and Hanspeter Kriesi. 2015. "What Do Voters Want? Dimensions and Configurations in Individual-Level Preferences and Party Choice." In *The Politics of Advanced Capitalism*, edited by Pablo Beramendi, Silja Häusermann, Herbert Kitschelt, and Hanspeter Kriesi(eds), Cambridge: Cambridge University Press, 202–230.; Hanspeter Kriesi, Edgar Grande, Romain Lachat, Martin Dolezal, Simon Bornschier, and Timotheos Frey. 2008. *West European Politics in the Age of Globalization*. Cambridge: Cambridge University Press.
78. Peter Mair. 2013. *Ruling the Void: The Hollowing of Western Democracy*. London: Verso.

CHAPTER 5

1. Al Gore is often considered one of the "Atari Democrats" who championed the technology industry. As a senator, he voted to pass legislation expanding ARPANET.
2. Adam Sheingate. 2016. *Building a Business of Politics: The Rise of Political Consulting and the Transformation of American Democracy*. New York: Oxford University Press. See also: Rachel K. Gibson and Andrea Römmele. 2009. "Measuring the Professionalization of Political Campaigning." *Party Politics* 15(3): 265-293.
3. Ibid.
4. See https://www.opensecrets.org/elections-overview/cost-of-election.
5. Daniel J. Galvin. 2010. *Presidential Party Building: Dwight D. Eisenhower to George W. Bush*. Princeton, NJ: Princeton University Press; Cornelius P. Cotter and John F. Bibby. 1980. "Institutional Development of Parties and the Thesis of Party Decline." *Political Science Quarterly* 95, no. 1 (Spring): 1–27.
6. Quoted in Elizabeth Kolbert. 1992. "Selling Themselves: Candidates on TV." *New York Times*, July 17.
7. Kevin M. Kruse. 2015. "America at the Ballot Box: Elections and Political History." In *"Why Don't You Just Get an Actor?" The Advent of Television in the 1952 Campaign*, edited by Gareth Davies and Julian E. Zelizer, 167–183. Philadelphia: University of Pennsylvania Press.

8. Ibid.; David Greenberg. 2016. *Republic of Spin: An Inside History of the American Presidency*. New York: W. W. Norton; Kathryn Cramer Brownell. 2014. *Showbiz Politics: Hollywood in American Political Life*. Chapel Hill: University of North Carolina Press.

9. Sheingate 2016.

10. Dennis W. Johnson. 2016. *Democracy for Hire: A History of American Political Consulting*. Oxford: Oxford University Press; see also Sasha Issenberg. 2013. *Victory Lab: The Secret Science of Winning Campaigns*. New York: Crown; Eitan D. Hersh. 2015. *Hacking the Electorate: How Campaigns Perceive Voters*. New York: Cambridge University Press; Daniel Kreiss. 2016. *Prototype Politics: Technology-Intensive Campaigning and the Data of Democracy*. Oxford: Oxford University Press.

11. David A. Dulio. 2004. *For Better or Worse? How Political Consultants Are Changing Elections in the United States*. Albany: State University of New York Press; Stephen Medvic. 2001. *Political Consultants in the U.S. Congressional Elections*. Columbus: Ohio State University Press.

12. Paul S. Herrnson. 2002. "National Party Organizations at the Dawn of the Twenty-First Century." In *The Parties Respond: Changes in American Parties and Campaigns*, ed. L. Sandy Maisel. Boulder, CO: Westview Press, 47–78.

13. Douglas D. Roscoe and Shannon Jenkins. 2014. "Changes in Local Party Structure and Activity, 1980–2008." In *The State of the Parties: The Changing Role of Contemporary American Parties*, 7th ed., edited by John C. Green, Daniel J. Coffey, and David Cohen. Lanham, MD: Rowman and Littlefield.

14. Ibid.

15. Johnson 2016.

16. Paul A. Beck and Erik D. Heidemann. 2014. "Changing Strategies in Grassroots Canvassing: 1956–2012." *Party Politics* 20(2): 261–274; Betsy Sinclair, Margaret McConnell, and Melissa R. Michelson. 2013. "Local Canvassing: The Efficacy of Grassroots Voter Mobilization." *Political Communication* 30(1): 42–57; Lisa Garcia Bedolla and Melissa R. Michelson. 2012. *Mobilizing Inclusion: Transforming the Electorate through Get-Out-the-Vote Campaigns*. New Haven, CT: Yale University Press; Donald P. Green and Alan S. Gerber. 2004. *Get Out the Vote! How to Increase Voter Turnout*. Washington, DC: Brookings Institution Press; Daniel Bischof and Thomas Kurer. 2023. "Place-Based Campaigning: The Political Impact of Real Grassroots Mobilization." *The Journal of Politics* 85(3): 984–1002.

17. Ryan D. Enos and Eitan Hersh. 2015. "Party Activists as Campaign Advertisers: The Ground Campaign as a Principal-Agent Problem." *American Political Science Review* 109(2): 252–278.

18. Matt Grossman. 2009. "Campaigning as an Industry: Consulting Business Models and Intra-Party Competition." *Business and Politics* 11(1): 1–19; Gregory J. Martin and Zachary Peskowitz. 2015. "Parties and Electoral Performance in the Market for Political Consultants." *Legislative Studies Quarterly* 40(3): 441–470; Robin Kolodny and Angela Logan. 1998. "Political Consultants and the Extension of Party Goals." *PS: Political Science and Politics* 31(2): 155–159.

19. Johnson 2016.

20. Quoted in *Business Wire*. 2004. "24.8 Million Email Addresses Now Available for Political Communications from the Voter Emailing Company." August 6.

21. Jon Gertner. 2004. "The Very, Very Personal Is the Political." *New York Times Magazine*, February 15.

22. Johnson 2016, 330.
23. Jeremy W. Peters. 2012. "As Viewing Habits Change, Political Ads Switch Screens." *New York Times*, April.
24. Sheingate 2016.
25. Lois Beckett. 2012. "How Companies Have Assembled Political Profiles for Millions of Internet Users." *ProPublica*, October 22.
26. Terrence McCoy. 2012. "The Creepiness Factor: How Obama and Romney Are Getting to Know You." *The Atlantic*, April 10; Reid Wilson. 2013. "What Your Favorite Drink Says about Your politics, in One Chart." *Washington Post*, December 31; Suzanne Kapner and Dante Chinni. 2019. "Are Your Jeans Red or Blue? Shopping America's Partisan Divide." *Wall Street Journal*, November 19.
27. Nicholas Confessore. 2018. "Cambridge Analytica and Facebook: The Scandal and the Fallout So Far." *New York Times*, April 4.
28. Sue Halpern. 2018. "Cambridge Analytica and the Perils of Psychographics." *The New Yorker*, March 30.
29. Elizabeth Gibney. 2018. "The Scant Science behind Cambridge Analytica's Controversial Marketing Techniques." *Nature*, March 29.
30. Jamie Bartnett, Josh Smith, and Rose Acton. 2018. "The Future of Political Campaigning." Washington, DC: Demos, July.
31. Jeff Chester and Kathryn C. Montgomery. 2017. "The Role of Digital Marketing in Political Campaigns." *Internet Policy Review* 6(4): https://doi.org/10.14763/2017.4.773.
32. Sheingate 2016.
33. Johnson 2016.
34. Edward T. Walker. 2014. *Grassroots for Hire: Public Affairs Consultants in American Democracy*. New York: Cambridge University Press.
35. Ibid., 43.
36. E. E. Schattschneider. 1960. *The Semi-Sovereign People: A Realist's View of Democracy in America*. Holt, Rinhart and Winston, 35.
37. Nathaniel Persily, Robert F. Bauer, and Benjamin L. Ginsberg. 2018. "Campaign Finance in the United States: Assessing an Era of Fundamental Change". Washington, DC: Bipartisan Policy Center.
38. Rebecca Ballhaus. 2016. "Billionaires' Spending on 2016 Election Reaches $88 Million." *Wall Street Journal*, October 23.
39. Ibid.
40. Ibid.
41. See opensecrets.org, "Who Are the Biggest Donors?"
42. Michela Tindera. 2021. "These Billionaire Donors Spent the Most Money on the 2020 Election." *Forbes.com*, February 25.
43. Raymond J. La Raja and Brian F. Schaffner. 2015. *Campaign Finance and Political Polarization: When Purists Prevail*. Ann Arbor: University of Michigan Press; Richard H. Pildes. 2019–2020. "Small-Donor Based Campaign Finance Reform and Political Polarization." *Yale Law Journal Forum* 129: 149-170.
44. Hans J. G. Hassell. 2016. "Party Control of Party Primaries: Party Influence in Nominations for the US Senate." *The Journal of Politics* 78(1): 75–87; Paul S. Herrnson. 2009. "The Roles of Party Organizations, Party-Connected Committees, and Party Allies in Elections." *The Journal of Politics* 71(4): 1207–1224.

45. Daniel J. Hopkins. 2018. *The Increasingly United States: How and Why American Political Behavior Nationalized.* Chicago: University of Chicago Press.

46. Brandice Canes-Wrone and Kenneth M. Miller. 2022. "Out-of-District Donors and Representation in the US House." *Legislative Studies Quarterly* 47(2): 361–395.

47. Michael Barber. 2016. "Donation Motivations: Testing Theories of Access and Ideology." *Political Research Quarterly* 69(1): 148–159.

48. See Rachel A. Porter and Sarah A. Treul. 2024. "Evaluating (In)experience in Congressional Elections," *American Journal of Political Science*, forthcoming.

49. Ibid. for races without an incumbent. See also Joseph Bafumi and Michael C. Herron. 2010. "Leapfrog Representation and Extremism: A Study of American Voters and Their Members in Congress." *American Political Science Review* 104(3): 519–542.

50. Lynda W. Powell. 2012. *The Influence of Campaign Contributions in State Legislatures: The Effects of Institutions and Politics.* Ann Arbor: University of Michigan Press.

51. Examples of corporations that asked executives to donate included Gulf Oil, Union Carbide, McDonnell Douglas, General Electric, and Ford, according to Julian E. Zelizer. 2002. "Seeds of Cynicism: The Struggle over Campaign Finance, 1956–1974." *Journal of Policy History* 14(1): 73–111.

52. Ibid.

53. Ibid.

54. Michael B. Malbin, Aaron Dusso, Gregory Fortelny, and Brendan Glavin. 2010. "The Need for an Integrated Vision of Parties and Candidates: National Political Party Finances, 1999–2008." In *The State of the Parties*, 6th ed., edited by John Green and Daniel J. Coffey. Lanham, MD: Rowman and Littlefield: 185–204.

55. Daniel M. Shea. 1999. "The Passing of Realignment and the Advent of the 'BaseLess' Party System." *American Politics Quarterly* 27, no. 1 (January): 33–57.

56. Samuel Issacharoff and Pamela S. Karlan. 1999. "The Hydraulics of Campaign Finance Reform." *Texas Law Review* 77: 1705–1738.

57. Samuel Issacharoff. 2017. "Outsourcing Politics: The Hostile Takeover of Our Hollowed Out Political Parties." *Houston Law Review Frankel Lecture Series* 54, no. 4 (April): 845–880.

58. Nathaniel Persily. 2004. "Soft Parties and Strong Money." *Election Law Journal* 3(2): 315–323.

59. Bruce A. Desmarais, Raymond J. La Raja, and Michael S. Kowal. 2015. "The Fates of Challengers in U.S. House Elections: The Role of Extended Party Networks in Supporting Candidates and Shaping Electoral Outcomes." *American Journal of Political Science* 59(1): 194–211; Gregory Koger, Seth Masket, and Hans Noel. 2009. "Partisan Webs: Information Exchange and Party Networks." *British Journal of Political Science* 39(3): 633–653.

60. Martin Gilens, Shawn Patterson, and Pavielle Haines. 2021. "Campaign Finance Regulations and Public Policy." *American Political Science Review* 115(3): 1074–1081; William W. Franko, Nathan J. Kelly, and Christopher Witko. 2016. "Class Bias in Voter Turnout, Representation, and Income Inequality." *Perspectives on Politics* 14(2): 351–368.

61. La Raja and Schaffner 2015.

62. Cain and Gray 2018; Issacharoff 2017

63. Micah Sifry. 2017. "Obama's Lost Army," *The New Republic* (February 9).

64. Ibid.

65. Desmarais et al. 2015.

66. Kim Barker. 2012. "Karl Rove's Dark Money Group Promised IRS It Would Spend 'Limited' Money on Elections." *ProPublica*, December 14.
67. Fredreka Schouten. 2013. "10 People Heavily Fund Conservative Antitax Super PAC." *USA Today*, September 25.
68. Bruce E. Cain and Cody Gray. 2018. "Parties by Design: Pluralist Party Reform in a Polarized Era." *New York University Law Review* 93(October): 621–646.
69. Ibid.; Tabatha Abu El-Haj. 2018. "Networking the Party: First Amendment Rights and the Pursuit of Responsive Party Government." *Columbia Law Review* 118(1): 1–76.
70. For scholarly books, see Nolan McCarty, Keith T. Poole, and Howard Rosenthal. 2016. *Polarized America: The Dance of Ideology and Unequal Riches*. 2nd ed. Cambridge, MA: MIT Press; Nathaniel Persily, ed. 2015. *Solutions to Political Polarization in America*. Cambridge: Cambridge University Press; Matthew Levendusky. 2009. *The Partisan Sort: How Liberals Became Democrats and Conservatives Became Republicans*. Chicago: University of Chicago Press. Popular treatments include Ezra Klein. 2021. *Why We're Polarized*. New York: Simon & Schuster; Amy Chua. 2019. *Political Tribes*. New York: Penguin Random House.
71. Liliana Mason. 2018. *Uncivil Agreement: How Politics Became Our Identity*. Chicago: University of Chicago Press; Shanto Iyengar, Yphtach Lelkes, Matthew Levendusky, Neil Malhotra, and Sean J. Westwood. 2019. "The Origins and Consequences of Affective Polarization in the United States." *Annual Review of Political Science* 22(1): 129–146.
72. American Political Science Association. 1950. "Toward a More Responsible Two Party System." *American Political Science Review* 44(3): Supplement.
73. Ibid., p. 1.
74. The report itself became the subject of controversy. As Mark Wickham-Jones details, the leadership of the American Political Science Association distanced itself from the committee's recommendations, and academics criticized many of its claims as unfounded and problematic. In 1971, an article in *The American Political Science Review* called the report a "failure . . . of policy science." The report became a microcosm of bigger questions evaluating the role of political scientists in policy matters. See Mark Wickham-Jones. 2018. *Whatever Happened to Party Government? Controversies in American Political Science*. Ann Arbor: University of Michigan Press.
75. Morris P. Fiorina. 1980. "The Decline of Collective Responsibility in American Politics." *Daedalus* 109(3): 25–45.
76. Ibid., 27.
77. David S. Broder. 1972. *The Party's Over: The Failure of Politics in America*. New York: Harper & Row.
78. Associated Press. 1985. "President Beats Drum for Tax Reforms." September 13.
79. Dominic Tierney. 2012. "Grover Norquist and the Unbreakable Vow." *The Atlantic*, December 21.
80. Sean M. Theriault. 2013. *The Gingrich Senators: The Roots of Partisan Warfare in Congress*. Oxford: Oxford University Press; Matthew Gentzkow, Jesse M. Shapiro, and Matt Taddy. 2019. "Measuring Group Differences in High-Dimensional Choices: Method and Application to Congressional Speech." *Econometrica* 87(4): 1307–1340.
81. Frances E. Lee. 2016. *Insecure Majorities: Congress and the Perpetual Campaign*. Chicago: University of Chicago Press.

82. Thomas E. Mann and Norman Ornstein. 2012. *It's Even Worse Than It Looks: How the American Constitutional System Collided with the New Politics of Extremism.* New York: Basic Books; Jacob Hacker and Paul Pierson. 2015. "Confronting Asymmetric Polarization." In *Solutions to Political Polarization in America*, edited by Nathaniel Persily, 59–70. Cambridge: Cambridge University Press; Joseph Fishkin and David E. Pozen. 2018. "Asymmetric Constitutional Hardball." *Columbia Law Review* 118(3): 915–982.

83. Tilman Klumpp, Hugo M. Mialon, and Michael A. Williams. 2016. "The Business of American Democracy: Citizens United, Independent Spending, and Elections." *The Journal of Law and Economics* 59(1): 1–43; Anna Harvey and Taylor Mattia. 2022. "Does Money Have a Conservative Bias? Estimating the Causal Impact of *Citizens United* on State Legislative Preferences." *Public Choice* 191: 417–441.

84. Martin Gilens, Shawn Patterson, and Pavielle Haines. 2021. "Campaign Finace Regulations and Public Policy." *American Political Science Review* 115(3): 1074–1081; Nour Abdul-Razzak, Carlo Prato, and Stephane Wolton. 2020. "After *Citizens United*: How Outside Spending Shapes American Democracy." *Electoral Studies* 67: 1–14.

85. Jacob M. Grumbach. 2022. *Laboratories against Democracy: How National Parties Transformed State Politics.* Princeton, NJ: Princeton University Press. On the way far more corporate money goes toward Republicans within the states—including Republican governors and attorneys general—see Jacob S. Hacker and Paul Pierson. 2021. "Conflicted Consequences." Washington, DC: Center for Political Accountability; Alexander Hertel-Fernandez. 2016. "Explaining Liberal Policy Woes in the States: The Role of Donors." *PS: Political Science and Politics* 49(3): 461–465.

86. Daniel J. Hopkins, Eric Schickler, and David L. Azizi. "From Many Divides, One? The Polarization and Nationalization of American State Party Platforms, 1918–2017." *Studies in American Political Development* 36, no. 1 (2022): 1–20.

87. Shea 1999.

88. Paul A. Beck and Erik D. Heidemann. 2014. "Changing Strategies in Grassroots Canvassing: 1956–2012." *Party Politics* 20(2): 261–227; Abu El-Haj 2018.

89. Joseph Gershtenson. 2003. "Mobilization Strategies of the Democrats and Republicans." *Political Research Quarterly* 56(3): 293–308.

90. Brian S. Kreuger. 2006. "A Comparison of Conventional and Internet Political Mobilization." *American Politics Research* 34, no. 6 (November): 759–776.

91. Roscoe and Jenkins 2015.

92. Raymond J. La Raja and Jonathan Rauch. 2016. "The State of State Parties—And How Strengthening Them Can Improve Our Politics." *Brookings Institution: Center for Effective Public Management* March: 1–25.

93. John C. Ranney. 1946. "Do the Polls Serve Democracy?" *Public Opinion Quarterly* 10, no. 3 (Fall): 349–360.

94. Eitan Hersh. 2020. *Politics Is for Power: How to Move beyond Political Hobbyism, Take Action, and Make Real Change.* New York: Simon & Schuster.

95. Pew Research Center. 2022. "As Partisan Hostility Grows, Signs of Frustration with the Two-Party System." August. https://www.pewresearch.org/wp-content/uploads/sites/20/2022/08/PP_2022.09.08_partisan-hostility_REPORT.pdf

96. Samara Klar, Yanna Krupnikov, and John Barry Ryan. 2018. "Affective Polarization or Partisan Disdain? Untangling a Dislike for the Opposing Party from a Dislike of Partisanship." *Public Opinion Quarterly* 82(2): 379–390.

97. Samara Klar and Yanna Krupnikov. 2016. *Independent Politics: How American Disdain for Parties Leads to Political Inaction*. Cambridge: Cambridge University Press.
98. La Raja and Rauch 2016.

CHAPTER 6

1. Allan H. Meltzer and Scott F. Richard. 1981. "A Rational Theory of the Size of Government." *Journal of Political Economy* 89(5): 914–927; Jonas Pontusson and David Rueda. 2010. "The Politics of Inequality: Voter Mobilization and Left Parties in Advanced Industrial States." *Comparative Political Studies* 43(6): 675–705.
2. See, e.g., Joseph E. Stiglitz. 2003. *Globalization and Its Discontents*. New York: W. W. Norton; Dani Rodrik. 2012. *The Globalization Paradox: Why Global Markets, States, and Democracy Can't Coexist*. Oxford: Oxford University Press.
3. The intellectual roots of neoliberalism are far beyond the scope of this project, but see Angus Burgin. 2015. *The Great Persuasion: Reinventing Free Markets since the Depression*. Cambridge, MA: Harvard University Press; Quinn Slobodian. 2018. *Globalists: The End of Empire and the Birth of Neoliberalism*. Cambridge, MA: Harvard University Press. Daniel Stedman Jones. 2012. *Masters of the Universe: Hayek, Friedman, and the Birth of Neoliberal Politics*. Princeton, NJ: Princeton University Press.
4. Gary Gerstle. 2022. *The Rise and Fall of the Neoliberal Order: America and the World in the Free Market Era*. Oxford: Oxford University Press, 2; see also Mark Blyth. 2013. *Austerity: The History of a Dangerous Idea*. Oxford: Oxford University Press.
5. Gerstle 2022, 2.
6. Samuel J. Palmisano. 2006. "The Globally Integrated Enterprise." *Foreign Affairs* 85, no. 3 (May): 127–136.
7. Robert Kuttner. 2018. *Can Democracy Survive Global Capitalism?* New York: W. W. Norton.
8. Elizabeth Popp Berman. 2022. *Thinking Like an Economist: How Efficiency Replaced Equality in U.S. Public Policy*. Princeton, NJ: Princeton University Press; Lily Geismer. 2022. *Left Behind: The Democrats' Failed Attempt to Solve Inequality*. New York: Public Affairs; Stephanie L. Mudge. 2018. *Leftism Reinvented: Western Parties from Socialism to Neoliberalism*. Cambridge, MA: Harvard University Press; Binyamin Appelbaum. 2019. *The Economists' Hour: False Prophets, Free Markets, and the Fracture of Society*. Boston: Little, Brown.
9. Luciano Bardi, Stefano Bartolini, and Alexander Trechsel. 2014. "Responsive and Responsible? The Role of Parties in 21st Century Politics." *West European Politics* 37(2): 235–252; Luciano Bardi, Stefano Bartolini, and Alexander Trechsel. 2014. "Party Adaptation and Change and the Crisis of Democracy." *Party Politics* 20(2): 151–159; Peter Mair. 2013. *Ruling the Void: The Hollowing of Western Democracy*. London: Verso.
10. Adam Przeworski. 1992. "The Neoliberal Fallacy." *Journal of Democracy* 3(3): 45–59.
11. Mark Andreas Kayser. 2007. "How Domestic Is Domestic Politics? Globalization and Elections." *Annual Review of Political Science* 10(1): 341–362; Brian Burgoon. 2009. "Globalization and Backlash: Polayni's Revenge?" *Review of International Political Economy* 16(2): 145–177; Henry Farrell and Abraham Newman. 2017. "BREXIT, Voice and

Loyalty: Rethinking Electoral Politics in an Age of Interdependence." *Review of International Political Economy* 24(2): 232–247; Dalston Ward, Jeong Hyun Kim, Matthew Graham, and Margit Tavits. . 2015. "How Economic Integration Affects Party Issue Emphases." *Comparative Political Studies* 48(10): 1227–1259; Hugh Ward, Lawrence Ezrow, and Han Dorussen. 2011. "Globalization, Party Positions, and the Median Voter." *World Politics* 63(3): 509–547; Stefanie Walter. 2021. "The Backlash against Globalization." *Annual Review of Political Science* 24: 421–442; Hanspeter Kriesi, Edgar Grande, Romain Lachat, Martin Dolezal, Simon Bornschier, and Timotheos Frey. 2008. *West European Politics in the Age of Globalization.* Cambridge: Cambridge University Press; Timothy Hellwig. 2008. "Globalization, Policy Constraints, and Vote Choice." *The Journal of Politics* 70(4): 1128–1141; Timothy Hellwig. 2014. *Globalization and Mass Politics: Retaining the Room to Maneuver.* Cambridge: Cambridge University Press.

12. Christopher H. Achen and Larry M. Bartels. 2016. *Democracy for Realists: Why Elections Do Not Produce Responsive Government.* Princeton, NJ: Princeton University Press.

13. Martin Gilens and Benjamin Page. 2014. "Testing Theories of American Politics: Elites, Interest Groups, and Average Citizens." *Perspectives on Politics* 12(3): 564–581; Martin Gilens. 2012. *Affluence and Influence: Economic Inequality and Political Power in America.* Princeton, NJ: Princeton University Press; Martin Gilens. 2005. "Inequality and Democratic Responsiveness." *Public Opinion Quarterly* 69, no. 5 (January): 778–796; Benjamin Page and Martin Gilens. 2017. *Democracy in America? What Has Gone Wrong and What We Can Do about It.* Chicago: University of Chicago Press.

14. Jacob Hacker and Paul Pierson. 2011. *Winner-Take-All Politics: How Washington Made the Rich Richer—and Turned Its Back on the Middle Class.* New York: Simon & Schuster; Jacob Hacker and Paul Pierson. 2020. *Let Them Eat Tweets: How the Right Rules in an Age of Extreme Inequality.* New York: Liveright; Frederick Solt. 2008. "Economic Inequality and Democratic Political Engagement." *American Journal of Political Science* 52, no. 1 (January): 48–60; Christian Houle. 2018. "Does Economic Inequality Breed Political Inequality?" *Democratization* 25(8): 1500–1518.

15. Ibid.

16. Noam Lupu and Jonas Pontusson. 2024. *Unequal Democracies: Public Policy, Responsiveness, and Redistribution in an Era of Rising Economic Inequality.* Cambridge: Cambridge University Press; Pablo Beramend, Silja Häusermann, Herbert Kitschelt, and Hanspeter Kriesi.. 2015. *The Politics of Advanced Capitalism.* Cambridge: Cambridge University Press; Lea Elsässer and Armin Schäfer. 2023. "Political Inequality in Rich Democracies." *Annual Review of Political Science* 26(1): 469–487.

17. Mikael Persson. 2021. "From Opinions to Policies: Examining the Links between Citizens, Representatives, and Policy Change." *Electoral Studies* 74:102413.

18. Noam Lupu and Alejandro Tirado Castro. 2022. "Unequal Policy Responsiveness in Spain." *Socio-Economic Review* 21, no. 3 (July): 1697–1720.

19. Lea Elsässer, Svenja Hense, and Armin Schäfer. 2021. "Not Just Money: Unequal Responsiveness in Egalitarian Democracies." *Journal of European Public Policy* 28(12): 1890–1908.

20. Wouter Schakel. 2019. "Unequal Policy Responsiveness in the Netherlands." *Socioeconomic Review* 19, no. 1 (April): 37–57.

21. Mads Andreas Elkjaer. 2020. "What Drives Unequal Policy Responsiveness? Assessing the Role of Informational Asymmetries in Economic Policy-Making." *Comparative Political Studies* 53(14): 2213–2245.

22. Daniel Ziblatt. 2018. *Conservative Political Parties and the Birth of Modern Democracy*. Cambridge: Cambridge University Press.

23. Noam Gidron and Daniel Ziblatt. 2019. "Center-Right Political Parties in Advanced Democracies." *Annual Review of Political Science* 22(1): 17–35.

24. Kim Phillips-Fein. 2010. *Invisible Hands: The Businessmen's Crusade against the New Deal*. New York: W. W. Norton.

25. Alexander Hertel-Fernandez. 2019. *State Capture: How Conservative Activists, Big Businesses, and Wealthy Donors Reshaped the American States—and the Nation*. Oxford: Oxford University Press; Jane Mayer. 2016. *Dark Money: The Hidden History of the Billionaires Behind the Rise of the Radical Right*. New York: Doubleday.

26. Theda Skocpol and Vanessa Williamson. 2011. *The Tea Party and the Remaking of Republican Conservatism*. Oxford: Oxford University Press. On the Tea Party as backlash politics, see Christopher S. Parker and Matt A. Barreto. 2013. *Change They Can't Believe In: The Tea Party and Reactionary Politics in America*. Princeton, NJ: Princeton University Press.

27. Katherine J. Cramer. 2016. *The Politics of Resentment: Rural Consciousness in Wisconsin and the Rise of Scott Walker*. Chicago: University of Chicago Press; Arlie Russell Hochschild. 2018. *Strangers in Their Own Land: Anger and Mourning on the American Right*. New York: New Press.

28. Eric Cantor, Paul Ryan, and Kevin McCarthy. 2010. *Young Guns: A New Generation of Conservative Leaders*. New York: Threshold Editions.

29. The report nonetheless framed these third-party groups as "friends and allies," noting that they supported Republican candidates. See the Growth and Opportunity Project Report, available at https://www.wsj.com/public/resources/documents/RNCreport03182013.pdf; see also Thomas B. Edsall. 2013. "The Republican Autopsy Report." *New York Times*, March 20.

30. On the Republican Party, see Heather Cox Richardson. 2014. *To Make Men Free: A History of the Republican Party*. New York: Basic Books; Geoffrey Kabaservice. 2011. *Rule and Ruin: The Downfall of Moderation and the Destruction of the Republican Party, from Eisenhower to the Tea Party*. Oxford: Oxford University Press.

31. Herbert Kitschelt. 1995. *The Radical Right in Western Europe: A Comparative Analysis*. Ann Arbor: University of Michigan Press; Kai Arzheimer and Elisabeth Carter. 2006. "Political Opportunity Structures and Right-Wing Extremist Party Success." *European Journal of Political Research* 45(3): 419–443; Sara B. Hobolt and James Tilley. 2016. "Fleeing the Centre: The Rise of Challenger Parties in the Aftermath of the Euro Crisis." *West European Politics* 39(5): 971–991; Matt Golder. 2016. "Far Right Parties in Europe." *Annual Review of Political Science* 19(1):477–497; Catherine de Vries and Sara Hobolt. 2020. *Political Entrepreneurs: The Rise of Challenger Parties in Europe*. Princeton, NJ: Princeton University Press.

32. Cas Mudde and Cristobal Rovira Kaltwasser. 2017. *Populism: A Very Short Introduction*. Oxford: Oxford University Press; Jan-Werner Muller. 2016. *What Is Populism?* Philadelphia: University of Pennsylvania Press; Anna Grzymala-Busse, Didi Kuo, Michael McFaul, and Francis Fukuyama. 2020. "Global Populisms and Their

Challenges." *White Paper*. Stanford: Freeman-Spogli Institute for International Studies.

33. Simon Bornschier. 2010. "The New Cultural Divide and the Two-Dimensional Political Space in Western Europe." *West European Politics* 33(3): 419–444; Hanspeter Kriesi and Julia Schulte-Cloos. 2020. "Support for Radical Parties in Western Europe: Structural Conflicts and Political Dynamics." *Electoral Studies* 65: 102138; Zach P. Grant and James Tilley. 2023. "Why the Left Has More to Lose from Ideological Convergence Than the Right." *Party Politics* 29(5): 803–816.

34. Helen V. Milner. 2018. "Globalization and Its Political Consequences: The Effects on Party Politics in the West." Working Paper. Princeton University. On the China shock, see David H. Autor, David Dorn, and Gordon H. Hanson. 2013. "The China Syndrome: Local Labor Market Effects of Import Competition in the United States." *American Economic Review* 103(6): 2121–2168.

35. Herbert Kitschelt. 1994. *The Transformation of European Social Democracy*. New York: Cambridge University Press; Giacomo Benedetto, Simon Hix, and Nicola Mastrorocco. 2020. "The Rise and Fall of Social Democracy, 1918–2017." *American Political Science Review* 114(3): 928–939.

36. Dennis Spies. 2013. "Explaining Working-Class Support for Extreme Right Parties: A Party Competition Approach." *Acta Politica* 48(3): 296–325.

37. Jonathan Hopkin and Caterina Paolucci. 1999. "The Business Firm Model of Party Organisation: Cases from Spain and Italy." *European Journal of Political Research* 35: 307–339.

38. Oscar Mazzoleni and Gerrit Voerman. 2017. "Memberless Parties: Beyond the Business Firm Party Model?' *Party Politics* 23(6): 783–792.

39. The party and the Rousseau platform are separate as of 2021.

40. For a selection, see Robert B. Reich. 2008. *Supercapitalism: The Transformation of Business, Democracy, and Everyday Life*. New York: Vintage; Fred Block. 2018. *Capitalism: The Future of an Illusion*. Berkeley: University of California Press; Paul Collier. 2018. *The Future of Capitalism: Facing the New Anxieties*. New York: Harper Collins; Wolfgang Streeck. 2014. *Buying Time: The Delayed Crisis of Democratic Capitalism*. London: Verso; Branko Milanovic. 2019. *Capitalism, Alone: The Future of the System That Rules the World*. Cambridge, MA: Belknap Press; Thomas Piketty. 2014. *Capital in the Twenty-First Century*. Cambridge, MA: Harvard University Press; Thomas Piketty. 2020. *Capital and Ideology*. Cambridge, MA: Harvard University Press; David Harvey. 2005. *A Brief History of Neoliberalism*. Oxford: Oxford University Press; Wendy Brown. 2017. *Undoing the Demos: Neoliberalism's Stealth Revolution*. Cambridge, MA: Zone Books.

41. Wolfgang Streeck. 2014. "How Will Capitalism End?" *New Left Review* 87(May–June): 35–64; Dani Rodrik and Stefanie Stantcheva. 2021. "Fixing Capitalism's Good Jobs Problem." *Oxford Review of Economic Policy* 37(4): 824–837.

42. Ralph Gomory and Richard Sylla. 2013. "The American Corporation." *Daedalus* 142(2): 102–118; Kathleen Thelen. 2019. "The American Precariat: U.S. Capitalism in Comparative Perspective." *Perspectives on Politics* 17, no. 1 (March): 5–27.

43. Eileen Appelbaum and Rosemary Batt. 2014. *Private Equity at Work: When Wall Street Manages Main Street*. New York: Russell Sage; David Weil. 2017. *The Fissured Workplace: Why Work Became So Bad for So Many and What Can Be Done to Improve It*. Cambridge, MA: Harvard University Press.

44. Greta R. Krippner. 2011. *Capitalizing on Crisis: The Political Origins of the Rise of Finance*. Cambridge, MA: Harvard University Press.

45. Colin Crouch. 2013. *Making Capitalism Fit for Society*. Cambridge, UK: Polity Press.

46. Lawrence Jacobs and Desmond King. 2017. *Fed Power: How Finance Wins*. New York: Oxford University Press; Karthik Ramanna. 2015. *Political Standards: Corporate Interest, Ideology, and Leadership in the Shaping of Accounting Rules for the Market Economy*. Chicago: University of Chicago Press; Brink Lindsey and Steven Teles. 2017. *The Captured Economy: How the Powerful Enrich Themselves, Slow Down Growth, and Increase Inequality*. Oxford: Oxford University Press.

47. On the impact of finance capitalism, see Piketty 2014.

48. Suzanne Mettler. 2018. *The Government-Citizen Disconnect*. New York: Russell Sage.

49. Marc Benioff. 2019. "We Need a New Capitalism." *New York Times*, October 14.

50. Aaron K. Chatterji and Michael W. Toffel. 2018. "The New CEO Activists." *Harvard Business Review* Jan-Feb: 78-89.

51. For a summary, see Andrea Louise Campbell. 2012. "Policy Makes Mass Politics." *Annual Review of Political Science* 15(1): 333–351.

52. Jane Gingrich and Sara Watson. 2016. "Privatizing Participation? The Impact of Private Welfare Provision on Democratic Accountability." *Politics & Society* 44(4): 573–613.

53. Suzanne Mettler. 2018. *The Government-Citizen Disconnect*. New York: Russell Sage; Suzanne Mettler. 2011. *The Submerged State: How Invisible Government Policies Undermine American Democracy*. Chicago: University of Chicago Press; Christopher Howard. 2007. *The Welfare State Nobody Knows: Debunking Myths about U.S. Social Policy*. Princeton, NJ: Princeton University Press; Andrea Campbell and Kimberley J. Morgan. 2011. *The Delegated Welfare State?* New York: Oxford University Press.

54. Lee Drutman. 2015. *The Business of America Is Lobbying: How Corporations Became Politicized and Politics Became More Corporate*. Oxford: Oxford University Press; John J. Dilulio. 2014. *Bring Back the Bureaucrats: Why More Federal Workers Will Lead to Better (and Smaller!) Government*. West Conshohocken, PA: Templeton Press.

55. Amy E. Lerman. 2019. *Good Enough for Government Work: The Public Reputation Crisis in America (And What We Can Do to Fix It)*. Chicago: University of Chicago Press; Eric M. Patashnik and Julian E. Zelizer. 2013. "The Struggle to Remake Politics: Liberal Reform and the Limits of Policy Feedback in the Contemporary American State." *Perspectives on Politics* 11(4): 1071–1087.

56. Marius R. Busemeyer and Kathleen Thelen. 2020. "Institutional Sources of Business Power." *World Politics* 72, no. 3 (July): 448–480.

57. Samuel J. Palmisano. 2006. "The Globally Integrated Enterprise." *Foreign Affairs* 85, no. 3 (May): 127–136.

58. Emma Saunders-Hastings. 2018. "Plutocratic Philanthropy." *Journal of Politics* 80(1): 149–161; Kristin A. Goss. 2016. "Policy Plutocrats: How America's Wealthy Seek to Influence Governance." *PS: Political Science and Politics* July: 442–448; Rob Reich. 2018. *Just Giving: Why Philanthropy Is Failing Democracy and How It Can Do Better*. Princeton, NJ: Princeton University Press.

59. James B. Stewart and Nicholas Kulish. 2020. "Leading Foundations Pledge to Give More, Hoping to Upend Philanthropy." *New York Times*, June 16.

60. Goss 2016; Matthew Bishop and Michael Green. 2015. "Philanthrocapitalism Rising." *Society* 52(6): 541–548.

61. Bill Gates. 2014. "Catalytic Philanthropy: Innovating Where Markets Won't and Governments Can't." *GatesNotes* [Blog], March 27.

62. Kirstin R. W. Matthews and Vivian Ho. 2008. "The Grand Impact of the Gates Foundation: Sixty Billion Dollars and One Famous Person Can Affect the Spending and Research Focus of Public Agencies." *EMBO Reports* 9, no. 5 (May): 409–412.

63. Joan Roelofs. 2003. *Foundations and Public Policy: The Mask of Pluralism*. Albany: State University of New York Press.

64. Business Roundtable. 2019. Statement on the Purpose of a Corporation. https://www.businessroundtable.org/ourcommitment#

CHAPTER 7

1. See Tabatha Abu El-Haj and Didi Kuo. 2022. "Associational Party-Building: A Path to Rebuilding Democracy." *Columbia Law Review Forum* 122(7): 127–176.

2. Lerman 2019; Donald F. Kettl. 2017. *Can Governments Earn Our Trust?* Cambridge, UK: Polity Press; Amy Fried and Douglas B. Harris. 2021. *At War with Government: How Conservatives Weaponized Distrust from Goldwater to Trump.* New York: Columbia University Press.

3. Susan Scarrow. 2005. "Political Parties and Democracy in Theoretical and Practical Perspectives: Implementing Intra-Party Democracy." Washington, DC: National Democratic Institute for International Affairs.

4. International Institute for Democracy and Electoral Assistance. 2020. "New Forms of Political Party Membership: Political Party Innovation Primer." 15–16. https://doi.org/10.31752/idea.2020.25

5. Susan Achury, Susan E. Scarrow, Karina Kosiara-Pedersen, and Emilie van Haute. 2020. "The Consequences of Membership Incentives: Do Greater Political Benefits Attract Different Kinds of Members?" *Party Politics* 26(1): 56–68.

6. Susan E. Scarrow, Paul D. Webb, and Thomas Poguntke, eds. 2017. *Organizing Political Parties: Representation, Participation, and Power*. Oxford: Oxford University Press.

7. The Economist Intelligence Unit. 2020. "Democracy Index 2020: In Sickness and in Health?" https://www.eiu.com/n/campaigns/democracy-index-2020/.

8. Sarah Repucci and Amy Slipowitz. 2021. "Freedom in the World 2021: Democracy under Siege." Freedom House. https://freedomhouse.org/report/freedom-world/2021/democracy-under-siege.

9. See, e.g., Larry Diamond. 2019. *Ill Winds: Saving Democracy from Russian Rage, Chinese Ambition, and American Complacency*. New York: Penguin Random House.

10. International Institute for Democracy and Electoral Assistance. 2019. "The Global State of Democracy 2019: Addressing the Ills, Reviving the Promise." https://www.idea.int/sites/default/files/publications/the-global-state-of-democracy-2019-summary.pdf.

11. Rachel Beatty Riedl, Dan Slater, Joseph Wong, and Daniel Ziblatt. 2020. "Authoritarian-Led Democratization." *Annual Review of Political Science* 23: 315–332, James

Loxton. 2015. "Authoritarian Successor Parties." *Journal of Democracy* 26(3): 157–170.

12. Francis Fukuyama. 1992. *The End of History and the Last Man.* New York: Free Press.

13. Richard Wike and Janell Fetterolf. 2018. "Liberal Democracy's Crisis of Confidence." *Journal of Democracy* 29(4): 136–150.

14. International Institute for Democracy and Electoral Assistance 2020; see also Patrick Liddiard. 2018. "Are Political Parties in Trouble?" Occasional Paper. Washington, DC: Wilson Center for History and Public Policy; Daniel I. Weiner and Ian Vandewalker. 2015. "Stronger Parties, Stronger Democracy: Rethinking Reform." New York: Brennan Center for Justice.

15. Erica Chenoweth and Maria J. Stephan. 2011. *Why Civil Resistance Works: The Strategic Logic of Nonviolent Conflict.* New York: Columbia University Press; Richard Youngs. 2019. *Civic Activism Unleashed: New Hope or False Dawn for Democracy?* Oxford: Oxford University Press.

16. See the Scholars Strategy Network Working Group on Local Political Parties, chaired by Lara Putnam and Daniel Schlozman, May 2020, https://scholars.org/contribution/local-political-parties-guide.

17. Tabatha Abu El-Haj. 2018. "Networking the Party: First Amendment Rights and the Pursuit of Responsive Party Government." *Columbia Law Review* 118(1): 1–76

18. Danielle Allen, Stephen B. Heintz, and Eric P. Liu. 2020. "Our Common Purpose: Reinventing American Democracy for the 21st Century." Report of the Commission, American Academy of Arts and Sciences.

19. Erica Chenoweth and Zoe Marks. 2022. "Pro-democracy Organizing against Autocracy in the United States." Working Paper Series RWP22-017. Cambridge, MA: Harvard Kennedy School Faculty Research.

20. Admittedly, this was also part of a Republican backlash to technology firms and Amazon in particular.

21. For more examples of how contemporary parties might engage in party-building, see Abu El-Haj and Kuo 2022.

22. Suresh Naidu, Dani Rodrik, and Gabriel Zucman. 2019. "Economics for Inclusive Prosperity: An Introduction." Research Brief. January, 1–9. https://econfip.org/wp-content/uploads/2019/02/1.Economics-for-Inclusive-Prosperity-An-Introduction.pdf

23. Larry Kramer. 2018. "Beyond Neoliberalism: Rethinking Political Economy." Menlo Park: Hewlett Foundation.

24. See, e.g., Gordon Hanson and Dani Rodrik. 2021. "Reimagining the Economy." Proposal to the Hewlett Foundation, available at https://scholar.harvard.edu/files/gordonhanson/files/reimagining_the_economy_program.pdf;

25. Bjorn Bremer. 2023. *Austerity from the Left: Social Democratic Parties in the Shadow of the Great Recession.* Oxford: Oxford University Press; Abel Bojar, Björn Bremer, Hanspeter Kriesi, and Chendi Wang. 2022. "The Effect of Austerity Packages on Government Popularity during the Great Recession." *British Journal of Political Science* 52(1): 181–199.

26. Margaret Levi. 2021. "Capitalism: What Has Gone Wrong? How Can It Be Fixed?" *Oxford Review of Economic Policy* 37, no. 4 (November): 773–782

27. See Jacob S. Hacker, Alexander Hertel-Fernandez, Paul Pierson, and Kathleen Thelen, eds. 2021. *The American Political Economy: Politics, Markets, and Power.* Cambridge: Cambridge University Press.

28. See, e.g., Michael Porter and Katherine Gehl. 2017. " Why Competition in the US Politics Industry Is Failing America." Report. Cambridge, MA: Harvard Business School.

29. See the National Association of Nonpartisan Reformers' description at https://nonpartisanreformers.org.

30. Steven M. Teles and Robert P. Saldin. 2020. "The Future Is Faction." *National Affairs* 60 (Fall): 181–196.

Index

For the benefit of digital users, indexed terms that span two pages (e.g., 52–53) may, on occasion, appear on only one of those pages.